P. S. I Love You

P. S. I Love You

Peter Sellers 1925 – 1980

MICHAEL SELLERS

with Sarah and Victoria Sellers

COLLINS

St. James's Place, London

1981

William Collins Sons and Co Ltd
London . Glasgow . Sydney . Auckland
Toronto . Johannesburg

Sellers, Michael
P.S. I Love You
1. Sellers, Peter – Biography
I. Title
791.43'092'4   PN1998.A3S
ISBN 0-00-216649-6

In association with Solo, London. Edited by Don Short.
First published 1981

Photoset in Baskerville
Made and Printed in Great Britain by
William Collins Sons & Co Ltd Glasgow

We dedicate this book to
the memory of our father

Michael, Sarah and Victoria Sellers

ACKNOWLEDGEMENTS

Sarah and I would like to thank Mother for all her kind assistance in the preparation of this book, and Victoria similarly expresses her thanks to her mother, Britt Ekland.

CONTENTS

ILLUSTRATIONS

Illustrations continued

Between pages 168 and 169

Peter with Miranda Quarry (*Syndication International*)
Peter at Elstead
Ringo Starr with Michael and Sarah
Nicky Henson with Michael
Peter in Los Angeles
An unusual array of vehicles at Elstead
Peter with Spike Milligan at the Round House
Peter at Michael's wedding
Ted Levy, daughter Katie, Anne Howe, Michael and Sarah
Theo Cowan, Peter, Anne Howe and Michael
Peter in St Moritz
The house at Gstaad
Lynne Frederick (*Photographers International*)

Foreword

My father had some funny ways of showing that he loved us.

His behaviour towards us was always unpredictable but that did not mean that he loved us any the less.

The tragedy was that he did not know how to communicate with us, or how to express his love.

That is why this book is necessary. Our inheritance is our memory of him – the memory of a man and a genius who happened to be our father.

Loved by millions.

But loved more by us, his three children.

We miss him greatly and still mourn him. We always will.

His influence on our lives, in spite of all, will remain with us for ever.

Michael Sellers
April 1981

I

The Last Hours

The confusion and conflict that was my father's life was with us all to the end.

I kept vigil with Sarah and Victoria at his bedside, praying he might wake from his coma and that he would live to build a peaceful future with us. We wanted to pledge our love and loyalty, so that family feuds of the past could be healed forever.

What did Dad want us to do? We waited desperately for words from his lips that would be so precious to us: like pawns stranded on a chessboard, we were all in an unfinished state of play.

What of our own lives? What was to become of Sarah, disowned by Dad at the height of their last bitter row, and of Victoria, still nursing sad memories of the abrasive events of her last meeting with Dad three months before. My relationship with Dad over the years didn't bear scrutiny either. But in recent times we had made amends and laid the foundations for re-establishing family ties.

It didn't need anyone to remind us that Dad was a genius; a man whose brilliant wit and extraordinary talent would always hold a unique place in cinematographic history. But there was a penalty incurred for his genius and we, as a family, duly paid it, absorbing like a buffer the whims and insanities of his incredibly complex character which could change faster than the colours of the chameleon, and with lethal effect.

When the elements were correctly balanced, Dad could inspire and motivate others, engendering new opportunities and inspiring ideas beyond the realms of normal limitations. In periods like this Dad could be kind, gentle, caring and considerate. He could fill us with joy and laughter, as he might an audience.

But when the horizons clouded, and the horrific black depressive moods descended abruptly upon him, he could snarl like a tortured animal, haunted by suspicion and trapped by a persecution mania, convinced that the world, and his family, were set against him. Every member of the household, at one stage or another, experienced the bitter-sweet extremes of Dad's psychotic nature.

But now in London, as doctors battled to save his life in the Middlesex Hospital, we had forgiven him for everything. We longed only to show him that we loved him, that we didn't want him to die. If he survived we would try to begin again, to reach fresh understanding and maybe bring happiness into his life once more.

Dad's heart condition went back to a series of attacks he sustained and miraculously survived in California in 1964. Since then his life had been precariously balanced by a daily intake of fifty or sixty pills and with the assistance of a pacemaker fitted some years later.

Having cheated death so many times, Dad clung frantically to the belief that he was a survivor and relied on the word of a clairvoyant that he would live until he was seventy-five. That prediction might not have been impossible if Dad had not wasted an opportunity that came in 1976 when his good friend, the famous South African heart surgeon Dr Christiaan Barnard, assured him that his condition could easily be remedied.

Barnard wanted Dad to undergo open heart surgery – an operation that would have meant using an artery from the leg to by-pass the troubled blood channels to his heart. He flew to Johannesburg to have the operation but he was never able to conceal his anxieties. Dr Barnard sensed his worries and suggested that he should first observe a similar operation in action so that his fears would be dispelled.

Dad marvelled at the technical brilliance of the operation, which he actually recorded with his camera, being an avid photographer. But on the very morning that he himself was due to go into hospital, he lost his nerve and locked himself away in his hotel suite. Then he booked the next plane home.

It was a sad mistake. Since then he had always tried to justify his error of judgement. Would he have now been lying stricken in a coma at the age of fifty-four if he had heeded Dr Barnard's advice?

I was the first to get to the hospital, after Dad's secretary Sue Evans rang and told me Dad had collapsed at the Dorchester Hotel. Sarah was contacted on holiday in Portugal and Victoria in Sweden where she was with her mother, Britt Ekland. They were in London within hours.

We were not surprised, but rather embarrassed when we heard that Dad's wife Lynne Frederick was also flying in from Los Angeles. Only days before, he had told me that their marriage was over and that he was proceeding with a divorce at the earliest opportunity. A reconciliation attempt had been abortive.

All his life Dad had taken pleasure in being surrounded by young, beautiful women, and if that is one of the perks of being a star – and a millionaire – then I think he was entitled to it.

But I was against him marrying Lynne. She was my age, twenty-two, and it didn't seem to make sense. How could they bridge the twenty-eight years between them? She was also Dad's fourth wife. How could she hope to succeed when his three earlier marriages had failed? Lynne was an aspiring actress and there was much to be gained by marrying Dad. But whatever her motives, Dad must have become aware of them in the days when the marriage turned sour and finally brought him to the decision to divorce her. But now Lynne was on her way to London too; I felt that the hospital vigil was stress enough without any other domestic strain weighing down on us.

I had trouble in getting into the hospital. It was already under siege from reporters and photographers. Someone had leaked news of Dad's illness to the press.

'Please let me through,' I said to a commissionaire at the front gate, 'I've come to see my father. He's had a heart attack ...'

'You're Peter Sellers' son?' asked a policeman disbelievingly, no doubt suspecting that I was a reporter trying to bluff my way through.

'Yes,' I nodded.

'Just a minute,' he said, 'I'll go and check.'

The commissionaire blocked my way and I waited for several minutes until the constable reappeared with Dad's personal assistant Michael Jeffery, who came to identify me.

I hurried inside, following Michael as he threaded his way along the antiseptic corridors. We went to the matron's office where Sue and Dad's chauffeur were waiting.

'Is Dad alive? Is he going to be all right?' I asked. She nodded tearfully, 'He's alive, but we don't know what is going to happen, Mike. It's going to need a miracle ...'

Sobbing, Sue recounted the drama at the Dorchester.

Dad had complained of feeling faint and short of breath just after 2 p.m. He lay back in an armchair and asked for a tissue. Just as he was being handed one, he seemed to have a spasm and one side of his face sagged as he passed out in the chair. The Dorchester's resident doctor and nursing staff were called at once. Two nurses gave him artificial respiration. When there was no response the doctor began heart massage.

Dad's pacemaker had failed.

For two whole minutes the doctor strived to resuscitate him and was on the point of giving up hope when the heart suddenly began beating again. He was still alive. By then ambulance-men were shuttling into the suite with a stretcher and oxygen mask to rush him to the Middlesex Hospital.

We waited in the matron's office until 5 p.m. before a sister beckoned me out to say that I would be able to go up to the intensive care unit to see my father.

'If you haven't been in an intensive care unit before then I must warn you it can be very upsetting,' she said. She explained the heart pump machine, the oxygen equipment, the visual monitors tracking my father's condition second by second, and the mesh of wires necessary to make that equipment function.

She said, 'Your father is not conscious, but please speak to him. He may be able to recognize your voice and understand everything you are saying. Try, if you can, to conduct a normal conversation with him.'

Before I entered the unit I was handed a white medical smock. It was as well I had not deceived myself into believing I could absorb the shock of seeing him. The unit was like a scientific laboratory, the walls banked with all kinds of intricate equipment. My father's heart bleep was running across the monitoring screens like a tennis ball in a video game which has gone on the blink.

My eyes settled on Dad, his motionless body shrouded in white and harnessed to the life support systems around him. He breathed through an oxygen mask but there was also a tube, inserted in his throat. The heart pump at his side vibrated like a Salvation Army musician's squeeze-box. His chest and wrists were taped with endless wires, and a drip feed was suspended above one of his arms. Another monitor kept check on his blood pressure. Protective gauze squares covered his eyes.

He was borrowing life.

I sat down next to him on a metal chair that had been placed at his bedside and clasped his hand. It was cold and clammy. I suppose the last time I had held my father's hand was when I was a boy and we had gone out on long walks over Hampstead Heath to see the kites flying on the hillside. Now, at twenty-six, I was holding his hand once more, trying to squeeze life back into him. I loved my father. Like Sarah and Victoria, I had so much wanted to be closer to him. Now that I had at last found some affinity with him, was it going to be too late? I prayed that God might spare him once more.

A nurse interrupted my thoughts. She motioned to me, urging me to speak to him. 'Dad,' I said nervously once she had disappeared, 'this is Michael. Can you hear me?'

There was silence. Silence apart from the gentle humming of the machinery. My father's hand did not tighten or relax. Neither was there any change in his expression.

The nurse came back into view, as if prompting me. I stumbled on ... It seemed very strange, like talking to a blank wall. Or a ghost.

'You're going to be all right, Dad,' I scrambled words together. 'You won't be here very long. We'll soon have you home.'

I nearly said – Dad you've been like this before and you've got through. You can do it again. But he might have heard me and my words would only have underlined just how serious his condition was. It was better left unsaid.

Telegrams were arriving at the hospital by the hour. Television and radio stations were now headlining their bulletins with news of Dad's ordeal. I opened a message from Prince Charles. The Prince, a long-time fan of the Goons who had become a close friend of my father when he was doing the weekly BBC show, said, 'All our thoughts are with you. Get well soonest.'

Another telegram arrived from David Bowie and one also from fellow-Goon Harry Secombe, as a flood of other messages continued to arrive. One by one I read them out to my father, trying to put an edge of excitement into my voice. Emotion choked my words, for in that hour I realized just how much my father's life mattered to so many other people. Members of the public too were swamping the hospital with calls and messages. I told him, 'Dad, they all really care about you.'

I stayed with him for twenty minutes before the nurses indicated that the various routine checks had to be conducted, and that I might get in the way. I went down to the matron's office; the small cream-washed room with its metal desk and filing cabinets was now full of people and cigarette smoke.

Sue and Michael leaned forward. 'How is he?' asked Sue, her eyes searching mine for an answer.

'He is still alive, but the doctors can't tell us what his chances are,' I said.

There was news of Lynne. Sue said she would be arriving on the early morning plane from Los Angeles.

'She's taken it badly,' said Sue.

'Yes,' I said, resignedly, 'I imagine she has.'

We needed to freshen up and returned to the Dorchester for an hour or two, taking over Dad's suite. From the hotel's room service we ordered some sandwiches and drinks and then got the chef to make up a hamper to carry us through the night. I asked for a bottle of brandy to be packed in with it. We were going to need it.

I switched on the television set. The main BBC news led its bulletin with a report about Dad's condition, with film of scenes outside the hospital. Michael Jeffery sorted through some legal papers, and in the bedroom his eye caught a framed wallet photo album that my father always travelled with. When unfolded it displayed a well-preserved picture of his parents, Bill and Peg and was of much sentimental value to him. The other frames in the wallet were noticeably vacant. Lynne's picture had once occupied the other section, but presumably Dad had discarded her photograph in the same way that he had tossed aside the portraits of his three previous wives. Pictures of the three of us as children had also long been removed. Michael picked it up and suggested we take it back to the hospital with us. I thought it was a good idea, and slipped it into my pocket.

It was now 9.30 and we drove back to the hospital feeling refreshed, but still harbouring deep anxieties.

Dad's condition remained unchanged and the night sister said I could visit him once more. On the sixth floor corridor I saw a familiar figure slumped in a chair. It was Spike Milligan, his face grey and haunted. 'Am I too late, Mike?' he stuttered, 'I was told he was dead.' Spike the Confederate, Spike the Confessor, Spike the Conspirator ... a founder Goon and the loyalest of Dad's friends. He could not have rested in mind or soul without coming to the hospital.

'No, Dad is still alive, Spike,' I said, 'but he is unconscious. The doctors can't say what his chances are.' He grasped my arm to comfort me. Tears streamed from his eyes.

'I guess he knows how we feel about him,' he said, and then disappeared through the swing doors. I walked on into the room, wishing I could have taken Spike in with me. But only members of the family were being admitted.

My eyes took time to focus in the dim light but the signal lights of the life-support systems were burning brightly, and the heart bleep was mercifully still crossing the monitor screens. I pinned Peg and Bill's picture on the wall facing my father's bed. It would be the first thing he would see when he became conscious.

I sat down beside him once more and a nurse handed me another pile of telegrams. One from Lord Snowdon. He had once given me a camera as a kid, and had sent a long letter of encouragement to Sarah when she thought about becoming a photographer. Although long divorced from Princess Margaret, Tony stayed a close friend to Dad and his telegram wished him a speedy recovery. One fan had also sent a telegram wishing Dad well and asking him for his autograph. I wished I could show it to him; it would have made him laugh.

Again I started to talk to Dad, conducting a one-way conversation. I didn't feel quite so self-conscious this time. It was like speaking into a tape recorder or an ansaphone. I only hoped that he could hear but I could not detect any indication that he was even aware of my presence. His hand felt clammy, and I shivered.

But Dad survived that night.

Setting out for the hospital next morning I was stopped by a young reporter in the foyer. It was his first day with one of the London evening papers. 'Can you give me just a few words?' he pleaded, 'I need the break ... I've been waiting here since 5 a.m. for you to come down.' I gave him the quotes he asked for and wished him luck.

But at the hospital, bedlam raged. Photographers, reporters and television crews were posted all over the precincts. They needed organizing and I knew there was only one man who could undertake the task and issue the bulletins they demanded. Dad had sacked his press agent, Theo Cowan, only a few weeks ago, but that was a routine procedure which occurred whenever Dad felt neglected. Sue called Theo and put him back on the payroll straight away. He would protect us from being hounded, while supervising any statements we felt able to make.

Once in the hospital I went up to see Dad. Overnight he had been wrapped in thermo-foil to retain his body temperature. I could not hold his hand until a nurse unwrapped the foil which covered his arms. When it was removed and I slid my hand into his I found that his palm was wringing with cold sweat.

One of the doctors thought there had been a discernible improvement overnight in my father's condition, but any hope I felt gave way to fresh anxiety. Supposing he did pull through, would he have suffered brain damage during the two minutes his heart had stopped after his collapse?

'If my father regains consciousness, will he be all right?' I asked the doctor nervously. 'Will he have all his faculties?' I knew that lack of oxygen to the brain could reduce a human being to a cabbage. I searched for some sign of reassurance in the doctor's eyes, but found none.

'We won't know that until we see signs of consciousness,' he replied. 'Only then will we be able to form any kind of assessment. I wish I could tell you more, but I can't be that specific.' The thought of my father being reduced to a state of vegetation, was beyond comprehension.

An hour later Victoria, having arrived from Stockholm, joined me at Dad's bedside, donning a white smock at the door. I imagined it must have been a really terrible ordeal for her. She was only fifteen, and when she realized that he wasn't conscious a rush of tears welled in her eyes. She was beckoned by a nurse to another chair on the opposite side of the bed; she sat down and took his right hand in hers. I encouraged her to talk to Dad, explaining that the doctors thought that at some stage he might come to recognize our voices.

With her dark eyes and slightly sultry features Victoria was more like my father than either Sarah or myself. She was also inclined to seek refuge in her own quiet moods – again something reminiscent of my father's character. She adored and idolized him, despite the hostility and insensitivity he sometimes displayed towards her, which sprang from the hate he felt for her mother, whom he always referred to as 'Ekland'.

Sarah, too, was deeply distressed when she arrived from Portugal. Coming straight to the hospital from the airport she did not stop to go home and change. She was still in tee-shirt and jeans and must have got past the posse of photographers at Heathrow as a returning tourist.

Sue had taken another car to meet Lynne at the airport; she now stepped from the plane in a suede jacket, blouse and black skirt. She also wore tinted glasses and a sombre expression. She did not escape the attention of the photographers.

Her appearance at the hospital was unsettling to us all as she immediately began to assert her authority as Mrs Sellers, while adopting a somewhat condescending attitude towards us as though we were children in need of shepherding. The result was incongruous. Lynne refused to recognize the fact that she was part of our generation.

'Tell me, how is he?' Lynne asked.

I looked at her and thought 'Why are you really here?' I wanted to tell her that Dad, if he pulled through, did not want to see her again. But this was not the time, nor the place, to cause further disharmony. Only Dad's survival mattered.

I conveyed all I could to Lynne of his plight. 'I'm afraid he is still in a coma,' I said.

'Then I had better go up and see him now,' she replied. As a nurse had kindly prepared me before facing the ordeal of the intensive care unit, I thought I should give similar warning to Lynne. I need not have bothered. I started to say something, but she brusquely cut me short. 'Michael,' she said, 'I know precisely what to expect. This situation isn't new to me. I've been in an intensive care unit before.'

She turned on her heel and took the lift to the sixth floor. In the matron's office where we were gathered, Sarah barely exchanged a word with Lynne, other than the first greeting. She suspected, justifiably or otherwise, that Lynne had turned Father against her.

Lynne stayed at my father's bedside for an hour while Sarah fumed. She had not yet seen Dad, but she did not want to go up to the sixth floor while Lynne was still there. 'I know I shall cry when I see Dad, and I don't want Lynne to start patting me on the head to console me – and knowing Lynne that's what she is likely to do.'

Eventually, I went up to the unit to tell Lynne that Sarah and Victoria would like to see their father. She stared back at me in surprise. 'Well, let them come in!' she exclaimed.

'They would prefer to be on their own with him, if you don't mind,' I said.

Lynne, who was showing no visible signs of emotion about Dad's condition, suddenly looked flustered.

'All right,' she said, 'I understand. I'll go. Bring them in.' She got up and left without glancing at Sarah or Victoria as I showed them in. Sarah reacted as I did. She kept staring at the monitor as my father's heart bleep raced across the screens, as petrified as Victoria and I had been.

We stayed at the hospital throughout the day and tried to be optimistic about Dad's chances. Several of his friends dropped by: among them David Lodge and Jim Maloney. They both said that he had survived before, and he would survive again. Our spirits rose.

But those hopes did not last for long. They were shattered by Lynne, when she reappeared after spending another period on her own with my father. 'I don't like telling you this,' she said, 'but the doctors say there isn't much chance. Not much chance at all.' Both Sarah and Victoria started weeping again, and the room fell silent.

Later I saw Dr Swainson, one of the consultants on Dad's case. He told me they had acquired the expert opinions of five top specialists. 'But if there is someone else you want to bring in, someone you trust who has tended your father before then don't hesitate to say so,' he said.

The strain of our vigil was beginning to tell. Victoria and Sarah left the hospital in the early evening to get something to eat at Sarah's flat in Primrose Hill, before Victoria returned to the Montcalm Hotel to join Britt who was keeping a low profile. I felt grateful and relieved at this since the situation with Lynne was already delicate.

Sarah returned and we checked again on Dad's condition.
A nurse was changing the gauze on his eyes and she explained
that they were also going to turn Dad on to his side a little so
that he wouldn't get too stiff from lying in one position. His
breathing seemed steady and the heart bleep on the monitor
looked stable enough. There was hope that he might make
progress through the night.

Since the ordeal began I had had less than two hours' sleep
and was utterly exhausted. We left for the Dorchester Hotel just
before midnight. Lynne, suffering from jet lag, was now looking
drawn. She too needed to sleep and moved into Dad's suite. I
took another room, and also one for Sarah who badly needed
some rest as well.

I lay back on my bed still dressed and had only just slithered
off the mattress to untie my shoes when there was an urgent rap
at the door. I recognized Lynne's panic-stricken voice.

'Michael!' she gasped when I opened the door, 'come quickly.
It's your father. The hospital have been on. He's taken a turn
for the worse. We've got to get there ...'

We made the hospital within minutes and using the side
entrance, we ran through basement corridors to avoid the main
hall where press men would still be entrenched. We swept out
of the elevator on to the sixth floor, Lynne a stride or two ahead
of us, but as we entered the intensive care unit she stopped in
her tracks.

Her frozen expression broke as she turned and burst into
tears. 'Michael – he's dead!' she wailed. 'Oh my God, he's
dead!'

We entered Dad's room. He was lying unobscured now by
either oxygen mask or breathing tubes. All the life support
systems had been disconnected; even the wires to his chest and
wrists had been removed. His eyelids were closed like large
shells, his dry lips were slightly parted: but in death, Dad looked
peaceful. He had taken his leave with dignity.

Lynne moved across to his bedside and cradled him in her
arms. She was kissing him, first one cheek then the other,
refusing even now to believe that he was dead. 'Oh, my darling

husband,' she wept, her tears tumbling over Dad's pale, motionless face, 'I love you. I love you. I know you're not dead. You can't die.'

She stood up and turned towards me, laying her head on my shoulder. 'Isn't there anything we can do, Michael? There must be something. We've got to save him ...' Standing discreetly in the background behind us were two nurses and a doctor, offering to console us. I exchanged an uneasy glance with the doctor, but he shook his head. 'I'm sorry,' he said, 'we did all that it was possible to do.'

It was 12.30. Dad had been dead for several minutes; in an office below someone was already writing his death certificate, dated 24 July 1980.

Lynne clung to Dad once more, still crying bitterly. Sarah stood weeping quietly in the corner of the room ... and Victoria, too, started sobbing.

I tried to contain my own grief, feeling perplexed and embarrassed by the strength of Lynne's emotions.

2

Early Days

My father was only a few months old when the General Strike paralysed Britain. Depression descended on the cities, towns and villages with the encompassing density of an impenetrable fog. The great trade unions had brought the country to a halt in backing the persecuted miners, who were faced with pay cuts against a call for longer working hours.

Riots, demonstrations and chaos erupted. The scenes were bitter and ugly. Families, stricken with despair, had little money to get by on. Food became scarce as shops put up their shutters. Without transport, the people were lost and survival became their only cause. They could not look farther than the next morning.

To a devastated nation, perspectives became confused and unclear. It might have followed that those whose work was not essential to others would have been the first to perish. Nothing could have been regarded as more superficial, or as expendable in this grim, bleak period than the entertainment profession.

But, as in times of war, the need for people to escape from strife and conflict was more necessary than ever. If anything the crisis paradoxically brought a boom to the theatre, not only in London, but in the provinces too.

My father's parents, Peg and Bill Sellers, were seasoned vaudeville troupers, themselves descendants of Victorian music hall artistes. They performed in revue shows that toured the length and breadth of the country.

Peg, whose vibrant personality concealed her lack of beauty, would sing and entertain with all the skill of the professional artiste, her *pièce de resistance* being a series of projected images from behind a lantern-lit screen of Queen Victoria, Boadicea, Joan of Arc and other great women of history.

She had seriously studied the rudiments of the art from her mother, the fabled Ma Ray, who was toasted throughout the land as the 'Queen of Spectacle'. The high point of her reign was a daring aqua-act in which she would swim with other nymphets in a glass tank. Once, it shattered from pressure beyond its capacity, and the nymphets were cascaded on to the laps of a delighted, if soaked audience.

Her ancestry could be traced back to the eighteenth century. The Portuguese–Jewish Daniel Mendoza was a famous bare-fisted prizefighter who became champion of England, and who later trained the young Prince of Wales before the latter's enthronement as King George IV. Yellow-tinged drawings of Mendoza, passed down through the generations, bore an uncanny resemblance to my father, who basked in the complimentary comparisons often made between their profiles. Dad jealously guarded this unique slice of heritage, feeling it compensated for our omission from the ruling classes.

Bill Sellers' background was far less glamorous, although my father tried to rectify this in later years by saying he was a former county cricket captain of Yorkshire. It was just one of Dad's harmless fantasies, accepted in most circles with wry amusement. That Bill originated from Yorkshire was beyond argument. He came from a working-class home in which family discipline was strong. From childhood he had taken piano lessons and music became his life's passion. He was still a young man when he was appointed organist at Bradford Cathedral. The rewards were not great and Bill realized he would have to adopt a much more commercial attitude if music was going to be his career. He was drawn into the theatrical world as a pianist, playing for singers and artistes who performed with the revue companies. Later, Bill was to master the ukelele and play in a duo.

Unlike the more dominant and animated Peg, he was modest, quiet and shy, prepared to play a supporting role which he uncomplainingly fulfilled throughout his lifetime.

Peg and Bill were married in London in 1923, having met two summers before when they appeared in a show at the King's Theatre in Portsmouth. There, in between long spells of touring, they made their first home, moving into a small apartment above a shop known in the neighbourhood as 'Postcard Corner'. Views of the harbour and the local seafront were sold there.

My father was born in the apartment on 8 September 1925, being delivered into the world by a Dr Little. Two weeks later he made his theatrical debut, being proudly held aloft by Bill on the King's Theatre stage for the approval of the audience, who sang 'For He's a Jolly Good Fellow'.

When he was three years old, and before he had even started school, Dad was already performing. Peg had togged him out in white topper and tails, along with a silver-knobbed cane, and she taught him to sing the familiar Albert Chevalier song 'My Old Dutch'.

Inevitably, the stage was much more acceptable to him than school. Dancing lessons were infinitely less demanding than arithmetic. His first school, St Mark's, a fee-paying kindergarten, was not far from a little house that Peg and Bill rented in Regent's Park when they eventually moved to London. Later he was enrolled into St Aloysius College in Hornsey Lane, a Catholic school run by the Brothers of Our Lady of Mercy.

Dad was always puzzled by his parents' reasoning in sending him there. His mother was Jewish and his father a Protestant: it seemed illogical that he should be dispatched to a Catholic school. My father once expressed the notion that his parents were trying to turn him into a 'religious hybrid'. If this was the case, they sadly failed.

Dad was an only child. The theatre flowed too deeply in his parents' bloodstream for them to want to enlarge the family. They moved nearby to Highgate and opened a small antique shop as a means of supplementing their income. It was soon to curtail the amount of time that Peg would spend touring. She and Bill, reinforced by the presence of 'Uncle Bert', would try to persuade the affluent occupants of country mansions and wealthy town houses to part with antique furniture, as well as unwanted gold and silver trinkets, with which to stock the shop. Often, to lend an air of respectability to their trade, they would say they were from the 'London Gold Refining Company'. During school holidays my father was allowed to tag along with them as long as he kept out of sight behind garden fences and bushes while their doorstep business was conducted.

Dad always said that the first seeds of his emergent talent as an impersonator were sown during this period. He would put on imaginary faces to match the voices that would drift to him over the garden walls: he would envisage lace-frilled frosty ladies from Cheltenham, pompous, retired Colonels, self-effacing white-collared vicars, dotty, absent-minded professors and many others.

His childhood, at that stage, was clouded by the shadow of World War II. On its outbreak my father was sent to the comparative safety of the seaside resort at Ilfracombe in Devon, where one of Peg's brothers ran a theatre.

Needless to say, my father did not return to school. Instead, he was put to work in the theatre, with its aspidistra-adorned foyer and Victorian decor. Cleaning and sweeping the theatre stage, as well as the carpets in the auditorium, were among his daily chores. He would also be seconded to sell programmes and occasionally to man the box office, before being given the opportunity to operate the limes – swivelling spotlights – in the wings.

Not many acts got as far as Ilfracombe. Not in wartime at least. But the sleepy resort and its younger generation were dramatically awoken by the spectacular drumming of a musician known as Joe Daniels who performed with 'The Hotshots'.

Dad didn't need further inspiration. He determined to become a drummer, pursuing the ambition with enthusiasm. His parents, now bombed out of their home by the German raiders at the time of the Blitz, were receptive to his needs, and bought him a second-hand drum kit on which to take lessons.

If life in Ilfracombe lacked excitement, Dad usually managed to manufacture some. At fifteen years of age, inspired by tales of Dashiell Hammett, he formed a detective agency with a friend. They called it 'Selman Investigations' and had business cards printed which they pushed through letterboxes all over the neighbourhood.

Convinced that they were now a couple of super sleuths, they waited for the calls to pour in, ready to undertake any assignment. Someone, surely, needed them to trace a missing diamond necklace or keep watch on an errant husband. 'But no one phoned us,' Dad would recall in later years, 'not even to catch their missing tom cat.' So Dad got back to playing his drums, entering talent shows and queueing for auditions. Eventually he was engaged for seasonal gigs by three celebrated bandleaders of the day: Oscar Rabin, Henry Hall and Waldini and his Gypsy Orchestra.

The war was almost over but my father, approaching the military call-up age of eighteen, volunteered for the RAF hoping to become a Spitfire pilot, but poor eyesight meant that he could never qualify.

His profession, on entering the service, was listed as an 'entertainer', a tag which led to his posting to India. There, a variety company known as the RAF Gang Show, was entertaining the homesick troops. In charge of the company was Squadron Leader Ralph Reader, who was to earn fame later for his Gang Shows with the Boy Scouts. Dad soon established himself as a Gang Show star of many talents, but the praise he earned did little to relieve the boredom that crept in on the free days between rehearsals and performance.

Mischief was soon afoot as Dad's inventive mind was applied to lighten these more tedious periods in His Majesty's Service. Being an ordinary airman without rank or title, provided him with sufficient temptation to promote himself as a Senior Officer. Suitable uniforms were purloined from the Gang Show's extensive costume department and various disguises were worked out.

At first Dad tested changes of identity on guard-house doors. Satisfied these masquerades worked perfectly, he gambled on a master ruse to impersonate an Air Commodore on an 'informal' visit to an isolated RAF camp not too familiar with VIP's.

The sheer grandeur of the rank he had chosen to play was far too impressive for junior officers to begin to question. Salutes were smartly returned, handshakes exchanged and words of praise and encouragement offered. The 'Air Commodore' dined well in the officers' mess, regaled his newly-found contemporaries with tales of his frontline expeditions in Burma and then made a diplomatic exit.

Deceptions like these gave Dad a great kick.

Even the boys in the barrack room next to his own, fell victims to another of his masquerades. They jumped promptly to attention when a moustachioed Flight Lieutenant walked in unannounced.

'Stand at ease,' said the Flight Lieutenant, 'this is not an inspection. But as I am visiting the base today I thought I would drop by to see whether any of you had any complaints about your accommodation, your duty rosta or perhaps your canteen food?' An hour later, bereft of moustache and changed back into his normal airman's uniform, Dad queued up in the canteen among the chums he'd just duped. The results impressed even him. Lunchtime conversation was only about the considerate Flight Lieutenant who was now investigating the barrack room grumbles.

These sorties took great nerve on Dad's part. One mistake and he would have been court martialled. Only one friend was in on the deception. In civilian life David Lodge was an actor, but now he was also an airman like Dad and occupied a neighbouring bunk. When he saw Dad embark on a similar subterfuge in another camp in Germany where the Gang Show was to tour, he was filled with trepidation. On this occasion Dad was playing Squadron Leader to a bunch of three-stripers in the Sergeants' Mess. David Lodge, who became a life-long friend, was certain that one day Dad would get rumbled, but when the military police finally got on his tail it was too late.

Dad was back in civilian life. The games continued. To obtain a room in an overcrowded hotel in Norwich, where he had gone to work as a fairground barker, he posed as 'Lord Beaconsfield'. Two military policemen arrived at the hotel suspecting he was a deserter, but Dad was able to show them his papers proving he had been legally demobilized from the service.

Civilian life was pretty austere in those early post-war days and Dad found it difficult to re-adjust. But his fairground stint in Norwich gave him time to work things out, as well as providing him with running cash. He moved on to Jersey, in the Channel Islands, taking a job as entertainments manager of a holiday camp for a while, but the yearning to perform was still very strong.

His dreams of becoming a star band drummer had somewhat dimmed: there was too much professional competition around. Instead, he devised an act as a mimic and comedian, practising for hours in front of a mirror to perfect the correct expressions.

Peg was still ambitious for him. She persuaded a Soho agent, Dennis Selinger, to see her son.

'Sign him, Mr Selinger,' she urged, 'and you will be doing your best day's work. Listen to an old woman who knows.'

Dad stayed with Dennis for almost twenty years, after surviving early catastrophes. An unresponsive Monday night audience nearly led to Father's sacking from an early booking in Peterborough, but top-of-the-bill singer Dorothy Squires persuaded the management to allow him to finish his week's engagement.

Dad travelled all over the country, staying in damp-walled, mouse-infested doss houses which he loathed, but which provided shelter for struggling artists who could afford little more. He was earning only £15 a week.

His fortunes changed in the spring of 1948.

Vivian Van Damm, the entrepreneur who launched London's sauciest non-stop striptease theatre, The Windmill, was conducting auditions for comedians.

Dad was urged to go along by a friend and try his luck, even though the role of the comedian at The Windmill required the courage of a soldier at Dunkirk.

Survival was the crux of the operation, for the wretched

comedian was Van Damm's stopgap to fill the intervals needed by his strippers to change costume. The comic would have to weather the impatience of the feverish front rows of the audience demanding the urgent return to the footlights of the strip girls.

Dad came through his 'Dunkirk' scarred and battered but he hung on for six weeks, which was enough for the magnanimous Van Damm to inscribe his name on the theatre's roll of honour, a bronze wall plaque which bore the immortal words 'Stars of Today Who Started Their Careers in this Theatre'. Dad's name fell beneath that of Harry Secombe, a fellow artist he had not yet met but one who was to form a vital part in his future.

Dad's talents were now widely recognized. His humour was sparkling but subtle, his impersonations sharp and convincing. The voices of Winston Churchill, Jimmy Durante, Humphrey Bogart and others came easily to him. So too did the antics of Groucho Marx.

His first broadcast on the BBC programme 'Show Time' led to an acceleration of bookings and a spate of appearances on 'Variety Bandbox'. Suddenly Dad was a success. He was to become a resident artist on the top-rated radio show 'Ray's a Laugh' hosted by Ted Ray, who was distantly related to us through the vivacious Ma Ray's kinsfolk.

In October 1949 it might have been assumed that he had reached the zenith of his career when playing the London Palladium in support of the charismatic Gracie Fields. A London Palladium booking is regarded as something of an accolade in the entertainment profession.

What more could my father produce than this, the London evening newspapers were asking. His act, 'Speaking for the Stars' which was predominantly his series of impersonations, was thought to be his definitive work.

But in a tavern in London's bustling Victoria a radio show was in embryonic stage. Dad had fallen among friends: three conspiratorial comedy forces whose theatrical insanities were almost parallel to his own. Spike Milligan, Harry Secombe and Michael Bentine joined league with him to devise a devastatingly new brand of humour which was to enliven the air waves. The format was outrageous, anarchic, anti-establishment and bizarre. It changed the whole basis of traditional English humour, still dominated by the music hall tradition. But the Goons would never have become the cult they did if they had bowed to convention.

Stardom was just around the corner, but at the age of twenty-four his interests were elsewhere.

3

Marriage and Stardom

In his early twenties my father might have more easily passed as an East End spiv in the dole queue who was about to sign on rather than an entertainer on the verge of stardom.

His unseemly appearance certainly threw my mother.

He wore flashy drape suits with padded shoulders and his dark hair was slickly greased down. He was oblivious, at that stage, to his weight problem. He then weighed fourteen and a half stone and at 5 ft 9 in. he didn't have the build to carry it. His raw, ungroomed manners didn't strike the right note with Mother either.

'No one could have described him as elegant,' my mother was to say, 'and I don't think he knew the meaning of etiquette. He never knew which knife and fork to use and he was the kind of boy who would immediately grab the first cake off the plate without considering others present.'

She remembers him, on one of their early encounters, sitting in front of a mirror and saying to himself, 'There's no doubt about it. I'm just a big, fat jolly boy.'

He was, incongruous as it seems, more conscious of the fact that he was short-sighted, a disability discovered in his early youth. But he kept his prescription spectacles in their leather case, stored in his top pocket.

The mirror didn't reflect the invisible facets of Dad's complex character, otherwise Mum might have thought twice about marrying him. Eventually she came to regard him as two separate – and entirely different – people. 'There was Peter the actor,' she says, 'and Peter the person. On one hand he was one of the most seductive people I'd ever met, while on the other hand the most terrifying. He was amoral, dangerous, vindictive, totally selfish – and yet had the charm of the devil.'

Mum's life with him was to become a mixture of fear, tears and laughter. At nineteen years of age she was already an aspiring actress who had come back from Australia after the war to train at the Royal Academy of Dramatic Art where she studied with Dorothy Tutin, Lionel Jeffries, Warren Mitchell and Dolores Gray.

Her family background was essentially middle class. Her father was an English tea planter and in the mid-thirties he had brought his family back to England where they settled in Hendon.

My mother had changed her professional name to Anne Hayes to avoid the obvious connotations implied by her real name of Anne Howe. Even through college she had been taunted, 'And how?'

Since arriving in London she had done well for herself. She was already playing in repertory and had landed a juvenile lead in a West End play by Alan Melville. One of her friends was Dennis Selinger, the agent who was now organizing Father's affairs with some panache. By coincidence, they all happened to be in the BBC Studios in Great Portland Place one afternoon and Dennis arranged a dinner party that night, inviting both my parents along.

The telephone rang at eight the next morning at Mother's Hendon home and Dad was telling her, 'I love you . . . when can I see you again?'

When he fell in love, he wasn't able to contain his feelings for a second longer than was absolutely necessary.

My mother was very amused. Although slightly put off by his appearance, she was captivated by his outrageous humour. As far as Dad was concerned he was gazing into the bluest eyes of the most beautiful girl on earth. She was blonde – the first of a whole succession of blondes who would come to figure in his life. But she also possessed a sense of humour and a certain style and elegance that Father had not seen in any other girl he'd met before. She was organized and well disciplined.

From their very first date, at a country club on the fringes of London where young people danced and congregated, Dad was completely besotted with her. At first he felt guilty, thinking he was stealing her away from Dennis. But Dennis assured him that they were not romantically involved and encouraged him to pursue her. This he proceeded to do, with phone calls, letters, telegrams, flowers and nightly excursions to Hendon in the hope of seeing her.

My mother was astounded by his persistence.

Meanwhile, my father was still living with his parents in a tiny, cluttered three-roomed flat at 211b High Road, East Finchley. It was filled with ramshackle furniture, antiques and obscure bric-a-brac that might have been surplus stock from their shop. Two temperamental Siamese cats viciously defended any available room space and clawed visitors who dared occupy their favourite chairs. Peg, always the dominating influence over her husband, openly conspired to sabotage her son's new friendship when she realized it was something more serious than a casual affair.

When she suspected that they were talking of marriage, she telephoned Dad's prospective mother-in-law and pleaded with her: 'Anne is going to ruin his life. His whole career. Surely you can recognize this? He is going to be a star. Keep your daughter away from my son.'

Dad, infuriated by his mother's attitude, left home and moved into his own flat off Baker Street. Having been so strongly influenced by his mother this was a traumatic step for him to take. But he no longer wanted his mother to threaten his romance.

Undeterred, Peg continued to try to prise them apart during the eighteen months they were engaged; whenever they had a tiff they were at their most vulnerable to her scheming. In a moment of anger, my mother once hurled her triple-diamond engagement ring back at my father saying, 'That's it. It's over.'

Dad, who had paid £400 for the ring, promptly gave it to Peg for safe keeping. Peg must have drooled. She didn't lose a minute in selling the ring to a local jewellery shop, sure now that the engagement was effectively broken. Three or four days later Mum and Dad were reconciled, but an embarrassed husband-to-be couldn't return the ring to his prospective bride. Dad promised my mother he would replace it, but of course never did. However, he next invested £70 in a gold watch for her. It was very prettily designed and my mother wore it every day until Dad demanded its return when he was broke.

'Look, I've got to have some money,' he pleaded with my mother, as though his life depended on it. My mother dutifully gave him back the watch and Dad pawned it. When she asked with some curiosity what he had done with the money, she was fascinated to learn that he had bought a watch for himself!

There were consolations – at least in Dad's mind.

'Have you ever been up in a plane?' he asked my mother one day.

'No, I haven't,' she said, believing he was going to suggest a romantic weekend in Paris.

'Okay,' he said, 'I've hired a plane. Just wait until you see *London* from the air.'

They drove to Croydon Airport where Dad had booked a 30-minute flight in a monoplane, run by a small private charter company. The pilot wanted to cancel the trip because heavy fog was descending. But Dad, having paid his £10 fee, insisted on taking off.

They circled at 500 feet and had to come down. My mother recounts that the fog was so thick they couldn't see a thing on the ground.

She was always tolerant and patient of my father's impetuous nature, and without these qualities it is doubtful if the engagement would have been sustained.

Countless hours were spent accompanying him to motor car sales and auctions. He was, she discovered, a man of passionate obsessions. Cars, cameras, watches and gadgetry figured hugely in his life. When they first went out together, he was the proud owner of a second-hand grey Rover which he traded against a similar model in green, a colour he was later to detest.

Next, he bought a Jaguar. One day he put Graham Stark the actor and his friend in the boot to trace an annoying rattle. They had gone four miles down the road when Dad was stopped for speeding by the police.

Graham, sensing something was wrong and already gasping for air, started banging the top of the boot to be released. The astonished policeman, suspicion creeping into his eyes, gazed at Dad thinking he was attempting a kidnap. Moving quickly round to the boot the officer lifted it open to discover Graham slumped on the floor.

'Hello, hello, hello,' said the policeman, straight from the manual, 'who have we got here then?'

Most of Dad's second-hand bargains came from a garage then conducting mass sales on the North Circular Road outside London.

It was from there that he bought his first Rolls-Royce. For some weeks he had been earning £150 a week from his shows and he was gullible enough to believe that his luck would continue.

The Rolls was second-hand, of course, but it had all the refinements of its vintage, including – to my father's delight – a cocktail bar. It was finished in black coachwork and the model was one of the larger versions, consuming a gallon of petrol for every eight miles it travelled. When Mum was appearing in repertory at Bedford she could easily have gone by train from London on a return fare of 50 pence, but Dad would insist on taking her in the Rolls even though the petrol bill was £5 for each journey he made.

When finally they were married at Caxton Hall on 15 September 1951, there was no suggestion of a reprieve from the unforgiving Peg. She and Bill refused to attend the wedding and she devised all sorts of devious schemes to wreck the marriage. She wanted her son back at all costs.

They had only been married six months when Mum had a miscarriage. She was in hospital for quite a spell, allowing Peg to entice Dad home for evening meals at her home to which she invited a conspicuous number of his past girl-friends.

One of them was his former childhood sweetheart who only two years earlier had given birth to a baby daughter.

Dad, still an airman in the RAF at the time of conception, proudly claimed to be the father. However, the infant was adopted when the girl refused to marry Dad, a decision which must have filled Peg with relief at the time. Very late in his life Dad made an impassioned plea in a bid to trace his 'lost daughter' but no possible candidates stepped forward.

It is possible that Mum, who knew of friends associated with Dad's wild youth, might have been able to trace the girl. But her clear-eyed view of life helped her to resist the temptation.

'Why subject this poor girl, whoever she may be, to such a dreadful bombshell? She is now in her thirties and let's assume she's had a very happy life with folks she respects and loves. Look at the way Peter has treated Michael, Sarah and Victoria. That's bad enough. To find this girl and then dump her – as he well might – would be horrendous. Why should I help him ruin someone else's life?'

Coming from Mum these were harsh words but she was only trying to protect the unknown girl from a fate that might well have disturbed her whole life, if not her way of thinking. On what grounds could my mother expose the girl's identity simply to inflate Dad's vanity? Somewhere in the world we have a half-sister. I sincerely trust that her life has been less dramatic than ours.

Once Mum was out of hospital, having recovered from her miscarriage, she was determined to prevent the destruction of her marriage at the hands of her mother-in-law. In polite terms she told Peg to go to hell, and the medicine seemed to have its effect.

In the early part of their marriage, my parents occupied a penthouse with lovely views over Hyde Park to be seen from the large and airy living rooms. It was all very smart and luxurious. Many show people lived in the block – theatre critic Ken Tynan was one.

My parents' earnings fluctuated precariously and they were always stretched to make ends meet. They were able to afford their £13 a week rent without too much trouble, but Dad was paying for his latest car on credit terms, as well as buying furniture on hire purchase from Heal's.

Finally they realized they would have to find something more reasonable and a year later moved into a smaller flat they found in Highgate, where the rent was only £6.

They also found they had a lodger: none other than Spike Milligan, who had temporarily attached himself to my parents. When my mother had been living at home with her parents before the marriage, Spike and Dad had driven them all nuts with their crazy antics. It was too much even for her grandfather to absorb and he would disappear to bed at the first sight of their coming.

Mum introduced him to her best friend June Marlowe, who was dark, very striking and often mistaken for an Italian.

Over dinner at the Edgware Bury Country Club, Spike masqueraded as an Italian at Dad's connivance, and June innocently persevered in trying to teach English to Spike.

Eventually they became engaged and Spike spent his last days as a bachelor with my parents.

'The only reason he came to us,' explained Mum, 'was because we had a spare bed. He was tired of sleeping under people's carpets.'

Mum was very fond of Spike who became like a brother to her. He went shopping with her, putting Dad to shame. At that time both Spike and Dad discovered the poems of William McGonagall. They would put a Penguin paperback edition of his poems on a velvet cushion and recite his poetry with mock reverence. Every night would end in hysterical laughter, with Spike and Dad giving their own imitations of the poet.

My parents bought their first house in Muswell Hill. It was a very modest affair with three bedrooms and a living room below. Dad requisitioned my mother's kitchen as a dark room, for he was now buying and exchanging cameras with the same lunacy he displayed over cars. Mum could rarely cook any meals because her sink would invariably be full of processing chemicals containing Dad's latest rolls of film.

He would take pictures everywhere, of all subjects, without

specific purpose, although he was always sentimental about his past and often photographed the houses he lived in as a boy, his old school and the theatre he first played in as an entertainer. This feeling of nostalgia dominated him in later life, when friends and family would be given tours of the landmarks of his early life.

Dad was still spending money ridiculously and was making no provision for income tax or any other emergency, and his accountant Bill Wills had to lecture him firmly and restrict him to a £12 a week allowance, which of course was constantly overspent.

There was hardly a period in his life when my father was rational in his thinking. One might have imagined that he would have been pleased that Mum was still working and contributing to the home, in view of their financial position. But his primary objective at this time was to persuade my mother to abandon her career. His reasons were totally selfish. He could not bear to think of my mother being involved in any other way of life that did not include him.

Mum was doing well in the theatre, but if she signed up to tour with a play he would become insanely jealous and accuse her of conducting clandestine affairs. Once, she was appearing at Coventry and Dad arrived at the stage door to inform her that he had swallowed a hundred aspirins because she refused to give up work. Mum still remembers that night: 'I went out on stage knowing that Peter was slumped at the steering wheel of his car, and not knowing whether he actually had taken an overdose or not ...'

There was another occasion when Dad locked Mum in their bedroom when she was due to appear on stage at Hammersmith. He was well acquainted with the first sin of the theatre: unpunctuality. Despite that he was now consciously placing Mother in threat of dismissal, which could have jeopardized her whole future. Only when her screams to be released threatened to disturb neighbours was the door grudgingly unlocked. Somehow, she managed to get to the theatre with five minutes to spare to the relief of the stand-in who was already rehearsing her lines.

Eventually my mother acceded to Dad's wishes. She quit. But it wasn't too great a sacrifice since she considered the prospect of having a family a greater cause than her own career. Most of all she felt that having children – and the doctors said her earlier miscarriage wouldn't affect her chances – would bring a degree of stability to her marriage.

I came to the aid of Mum's mission on 2 April 1954, weighing in at 7 lbs 11 ozs at the London Clinic and was christened Michael Peter Anthony Sellers.

The first visitor to the maternity ward was Peg. Since the last confrontation she had barely spoken to my mother, but now she wanted to let bygones be bygones, overwhelmed with the thought of becoming a doting grandmother. Dad, who had bought a £300 train set during the first month of my mother's pregnancy, was elated to think that his hopes of having a son had been fulfilled.

Despite Dad's reluctance to increase the family Mum desperately wanted another baby so that I would not be an only child like my father. Sarah Jane was logged into the London Clinic three and a half years later. It was the night of 16 October 1957, and Dad rather left Mum to accomplish things herself, because he had been invited to attend the opening performance of Judy Garland's season at the London Palladium.

We were given pet names. I was Pooh from *Winnie the Pooh* and Sarah was just simply 'SJ'.

We were now living in a pseudo-Tudor house in the village of Whetstone, a few miles north of London. The pebble-dashed house, built in the thirties, was in an area favoured by artists such as Ian Carmichael and Winifred Attwell who lived close by. So too, did John and Roy Boulting the film producers who were to hold the key to Dad's future career.

During our infancy, Dad smothered us with cuddly toys and presents; buying them in bulk from Harrods or Hamleys and spreading them all over the house. Dad felt that this was the surest method of conveying his love to us. Every fluffy bear or doll he bought, every tin soldier or new game, signified to him the action of a loving father. Santa Claus would have seemed a scrooge alongside Dad. Being a boy, I did rather better than Sarah. The first train set, which Dad had been practising with months before my birth, had grown into a vast network, the layout of tracks, engines, rolling stock, station and accessories filling the whole of the loft.

My nursery floor provided space for the electric car racing track and of course I had radios, walkie-talkies and other gadgetry which Dad liked to demonstrate in person to my god-father David Lodge. When I grew to a toddler and began to appreciate my toys, I found that Dad retained first option. Only when he grew tired of playing with them himself was I permitted to touch them. But even then things could be awkward.

One afternoon I played with some soldiers and cannons that Dad had assembled overnight from a plastic kit. Staging a mock war game, I wiped out the blue regiment with plastic bullets from the enemy's barrage of cannons. Dad, cheated out of the battle because he was at work, was livid when he saw the havoc on the carpet.

'Look at what you have done!' he despaired. 'I spent hours putting that kit together. The soldiers ... they're all broken. Well, you can stick them back together again.' Later I accident-ally clipped off the wings of a model aeroplane he had built; once more he lost his temper with me as he tossed the broken pieces into the dustbin.

However, I would not have dared to touch the miniature stagecoach that he and Graham Stark had taken months to assemble in their spare time. It was so delicate that they had used a magnifying glass to piece it together. When it was com-pleted it was promptly put on a shelf out of reach of my fingers.

I could not help but feel that the toys were bought more for Dad's own pleasure than mine, but whenever my mother had the opportunity she would remind him: 'Well who did you buy them for? You or Michael?' Sometimes shamed, Dad would sheepishly disappear until the air had cleared.

When I was four years old I really ran into trouble – by touching a toy that was truly Dad's. Since marrying my mother he had already bought and sold forty cars. But now he acquired his first status symbol: a red Bentley Continental that cost £9000. It had special coachwork and hand-finished interior fittings. Naturally, after a succession of second-hand cars, Dad was immensely proud of it, carefully putting it through its paces on family drives around the neighbourhood. The day came when a hail of flying grit badly chipped the coachwork, and Dad was very upset. Feeling sorry for him, I set out to repair the car with a tin of touch-up paint I knew to be in his garage toolbox.

Unfortunately, I couldn't actually see the chip marks, so to make sure every one of them was covered, I ran a stripe right around the car. Getting home from school that day I expected to find Dad glowing with gratitude. Instead, he was waiting for me at the garden gate, his face crimson with rage.

'Do you know what you have done?' he yelled, grabbing me from the doorstep by the scruff of the neck. 'You've ruined my car. What the hell made you do such a thing?'

'Daddy, I was only trying to make it look beautiful for you again,' I sobbed.

But Dad wasn't listening to my protests. Hauling me up to my bedroom he yanked down my trousers and whipped me with his leather belt. Mum attempted to intervene as I screamed with pain, but she was thrown aside, my father's temper, once lost, being utterly uncontrollable.

My handiwork on the Bentley had made a terrible mess of the coachwork, but Dad gave no thought to my good intentions, being too blind with rage even to consider them. I was refused supper, ordered to stay in bed and as a final punishment every single toy in my bedroom was removed and confiscated. I did not retrieve them all until several months later.

Soothing ointment, applied by my mother, eased my discomfort. She was appalled by the whole episode and at the first opportunity, questioned Dad.

'It's only a car,' she reminded him.

'Only a car?' he screamed back at her. 'It cost the earth. It's a Bentley Continental or hadn't you bloody well noticed?'

His pique over the Bentley was carried through to its bitter conclusion. The car had to be sold, irrespective of financial loss, when it could have easily been resprayed.

On his next car, Dad had an 'airwave' telephone installed. Mum would get a message via the operator saying: 'Would you please put the kettle on for tea? Mr Sellers says he's on his way home.'

When car telephones became more sophisticated, and one could dial straight through to a number, Dad tried his new instrument out on Graham Stark. Parking on Graham's drive he telephoned him and said: 'I'm phoning from my car.' Graham asked: 'Where are you, Pete?' Dad replied, 'If you look out through your front window you'll see.'

But domestic crises always seemed to hound Dad, mostly because his temperament was not tailored to deal with domestic responsibilities.

Our first nanny was called Frieda Heinlein and she came from Germany. She was very kind and sweet to us and tried to bring us up in the way to which she was accustomed, having once been a Lutheran nun. She would take us to Sunday School and while neither of our parents was particularly 'religious, they encouraged her to do it as they felt it was a good experience for their children.

Frieda stayed some time with the family, and today she lives as a companion in my mother's home, but in those early years, daily exposed to Dad's critical gaze she was constantly being taken to task over our upbringing. In his fits of anger he would call poor Frieda a 'German swine' and upset her greatly. Twice he sacked her for no reason and one of Sarah's earliest memories was on the second occasion this occurred. As she was about to leave for school Dad told her she needn't say goodbye to Frieda.

'Why, Daddy?' asked Sarah innocently.

'Because Frieda won't be here when you get back,' he replied.

Frieda was heartbroken, packed her things and left. She was replaced by Nanny Clarke who was very proper and the epitome of a trained nanny in her neat, white uniform. Unfortunately for Dad she was not afraid to express her wishes, along with her opinions. It was soon to rub against the grain. We didn't help matters ·either, challenging everything Nanny

Clarke told us to do and calling her a witch behind her back. Angry words about our welfare soon filled the air between them, with Mum trying to keep the peace on the sidelines.

One night, after a particularly heated affray, Dad stormed out of the house and drove to London to check into the Royal Automobile Club. From his room he immediately called Mum and said: 'What the bloody hell am I doing here? I'm coming home. It's my house. If anyone is going to leave, it's that bloody nanny.'

Dad drove home and stormed into the house shouting for Nanny Clarke who had gone to bed. 'I'll kill you, you cow,' he yelled. He grabbed a large carving knife and stormed upstairs where he embedded it in her door, splitting one of the panels. Nanny Clarke was so terrified that she leaped out of her window still in her night clothes to escape, landing ten feet below in a rose bush and spraining an ankle in the process. Somehow she managed to crawl to the next door neighbour's. She was taken to hospital for treatment and Dad sought to infer to the police that she had gone off her head. Though they did not believe such nonsense, they decided not to take the matter further.

Dad was only too pleased to see the return of Frieda – whose most endearing characteristic was that despite the indifferent way Dad treated her, she never bore him any lasting grudge. She felt that he really tried to be a good father. Sarah remembers how he earned Frieda's praise when he read us nightly passages from *Chitty Chitty Bang Bang* and dubbed in all the voices of the characters.

Yes, he did try. Every morning at breakfast he would kiss us both on the cheek as we juggled with our cornflakes and I can remember him laughing at Mum when she poured a bowl of cereal over my head for not dressing in time for school. We also spent good times with Dad at the London Zoo where he liked to take us on odd Sunday mornings during the summer holidays, which would mean having lunch in some smart restaurant afterwards. Some times we would go to the Savoy or the Ritz.

When filled with high spirits he would involve the whole family and often start a musical session, playing drums on the plates and glasses in the kitchen or on the dinner table. He would also pretend to be a circus clown, perching one of us on each shoulder while riding his bicycle round the garden.

Unfortunately, the good times were quickly clouded over by the bad, and catastrophe was never far away.

For instance, our departure from the village of Whetstone went with something of a bang. Dad, in one of his expansive moods, decided to throw a Guy Fawkes party, inviting along many friends and stars to celebrate the occasion.

Dad had stored a massive bundle of fireworks in a tea chest in the lounge; suddenly a stray rocket flew into the room through an open window.

Within seconds, pandemonium broke loose.

Whining, shrieking rockets screamed round the lounge, giving off a profusion of brilliant colours as they exploded against the ceiling and walls. The television set received a direct hit and blew up. Curtains and furniture were set ablaze.

Guests scuttled on to the terrace and Dad, intent on making a fast getaway from the disaster, yelled at Mum: 'Grab the kids!' We were bundled through to the garage – only to find that Dad had left the car battery on charge.

He untangled the wires and, slamming down the bonnet, lunged towards the driver's seat. Then came an awful ripping noise. Goon-like, he'd managed to get his coat caught under the bonnet and it was torn from his shoulders. In the distance we could hear the urgent clanging of engine bells. At this point, knowing that safety was on its way, Mother burst into a fit of hysterical laughter, not shared by her panic-stricken husband.

A large part of the house was gutted, but we were only able to assess the full extent of the damage the next morning when daylight came. To make matters worse Dad had only just sold the house. He telephoned the unfortunate purchaser, the British comic actor Alfred Marks, and said: 'Do you want to choose your own decorations? I'm afraid we've just burnt the house down.'

Alfred, dismissing this as a typical piece of Goonery that he wasn't going to fall victim to, duly arrived on the scene. Only two words were distinguishable on his lips. 'Oh lor . . .' he said, sighting the smitten house.

As a family, we didn't stay in any one place too long: rarely more than two years. That was about the limit for Dad's restless, impatient nature. Next we moved into an Elizabethan mansion, a magnificent twenty-roomed manor house at Chipperfield, close to Kings Langley, in the heart of the English countryside. It was set amid seven acres of glorious grounds, which had been beautifully landscaped and cultivated. We had our own tennis court and swimming pool while two Tudor tithe barns stood in the paddocks.

Parts of the house were thought to have once been part of a hunting lodge, and an extension had been built during the Queen Anne period. Some of the oak panelling in the lounge dated back to the reign of Richard II: the whole house breathed with history.

All of Dad's cronies were brought to the house to give it their approval. Graham Stark, stopping short of the imposing wrought iron entrance gates to the drive, blinked at Dad. 'You've bought bleedin' Buckingham Palace. What the hell do you think you're doing?'

My mother certainly faced problems of that dimension when she came to consider the furnishing and staffing of the house. Dad had already acquired a chauffeur. He had also appointed a secretary, Hattie Stevenson. Now we were to have a butler, a maid, a valet for Dad, two part-time housekeepers and three gardeners. Our nanny Frieda also came with us.

My mother wanted to keep the house in traditional style, but she worried about Dad's insensitivity towards the preservation of the past. Without her knowledge, he persuaded the gardeners to chop down a row of beautiful old apple trees that ran to the end of the sweeping lawns. Their blossom had greeted each spring for fifty years and the trees, standing proud in their foliage, can be seen in drawings passed on to us. Now felled on the lawns, their trunks ready to be hewn for firewood, Dad didn't think he had done anything wrong.

He couldn't understand why the apple trees had been planted

there in the first place. 'Why weren't they with the rest of the fruit trees in the orchard?' he asked.

Mum bought some lovely original furniture, creating a Georgian atmosphere in the lounge. She insisted that the dining room should continue to be lit by candlelight as it had been through the centuries and she bought a resplendent set of Georgian silver to grace the massive oak refectory table.

Our butler, Bruno, would forever hit his head on the wrought iron chandelier when serving meals. Every time Bruno appeared we waited in suspense and Dad would say, 'Here we go . . . any minute now.'

Everyone's eyes would be glued to the lights until Bruno clanged his head on the chandelier; as he invariably dropped the plates we would all lurch back from the table to avoid having the food plopped in our laps.

Soon the house was alive with parties, especially during the summer months when the swimming pool and tennis court were put to full use. Some of Dad's pals were cricket fans. So he had part of the grounds rolled out in the paddock area for a pitch and practice nets to be put in.

We loved it there. We spent our days exploring the sprawling grounds, seeking out every nook and cranny. Frieda tried to exercise some discipline over us, but we would play hide and seek on her. Our lives were comparatively happy at this time. I think Sarah and I had both learned how to fade into the landscape. If Dad came home in a bad mood we would scatter fast and there were plenty of places on the estate where we could lie low.

I once got caught, slithering down, Tarzan-style, from the house vine, but luckily Dad didn't carry out his threat to beat me with his leather belt once more.

We were filled with awe, if not trepidation, by Dad's inconsistent moods. Yet when he felt he had been harsh with us he would express his remorse by giving us more presents.

Only a week or two after the vinery incident he bought me a twelve-volt battery Mercedes racer which I could climb into and drive around the estate. Dad actually got the gardeners to lay down ramps over the tricky areas between paths.

Seeing the enjoyment I got from it he said, 'It's a pity it's too small for me to drive.' Standing on the forecourt was his new Rolls-Royce.

Our move to Chipperfield underlined Dad's newly acquired affluence, which was a reflection of his mounting professional success, although as youngsters we were still unaware of the meaning of fame. When first seeing Dad on television, it didn't strike us as strange or unique in any way. Maybe it was because the drift of conversation in the household was invariably directed towards the media. We were more or less weaned on it.

I remember wanting to talk back to Dad when he said 'hello' to me from the screen of Cliff Michelmore's television news programme 'Tonight' on the BBC. Sitting in my highchair at home I leaned forward ready to respond, but my mother bewildered me by saying that Dad couldn't see me, nor would he be able to hear me.

It was eventually through friends at school, persistently asking, 'Is it true your father is Peter Sellers?' that both Sarah and I started thinking that Dad must be important in some way.

We didn't attach any particular significance to the Goons, because they had become an almost normal part of our everyday lives. When guests came, or good moods prevailed, then we would be treated to yet more of the Goons' favourite characterizations.

By now millions were familiar with the Goons. Dad's creations included the raving simpleton Henry Crun, the villainous Grytpype Thynne, the pompous Major Bloodnok of the Indian Army and the erudite Bluebottle, inspired by a bearded Scoutmaster that Dad had known in real life.

Spike was rampant as the toothless dimwit Eccles, the decaying Moriarty doomed to be one of life's eternal failures, the bantering Indian servant Abdul and the vague, hen-like Minnie Bannister.

Harry Secombe took the stalwart role of Neddy Seagoon, pioneer of the British Empire whose expeditions always ended in disaster.

The Goons revelled in the bizarre. Their crazy escapades involved the conquest of Everest from the inside, the implantation of London's Albert Memorial on the Moon, the search for an author by the six Charlies and the last leather-omnibus ride of the phantom batter-pudding hurler.

The dialogue often alarmed the BBC censors and behind the scenes a constant battle ensued over the material.

One of the irresistible Goon ploys at this time was to refer to one of their more respectable creations 'Hugh Hampton' as 'Huge Hampton', 'Hampton' being a slang term for a vital part of the male anatomy. In his innocence the BBC censor allowed 'Huge Hampton' to slip through his net, quite unaware of the connotation, much to the jubilation of the Goons.

Dad also loved to play a character known to them as 'Old Mate', a down and out stage doorman who could not perform any responsible duty without having a chit. 'You can't do that, mate,' he would warn, 'not unless you've got a chit.'

Goon humour rapidly spread into real life. Dad, whenever confronted by bureaucratic red tape, would mutter in a self-deprecating way: 'No, you can't do that, mate. Not without a chit ...' Into the exercise were brought junior 'Old Mates' who worked for the BBC. They were ex-Army diehards who didn't know anything, say anything or do anything. Their only defence in not answering a question would be, 'Sorry, it's more than my job's worth.' So to Dad and the Goons such characters were known as 'Jobsworth'. 'Well, sir, it's more than my job's worth to tell you that, sir ...' they would jibe.

Goon characters also had an uncanny way of becoming flesh and blood. Whenever Dad recognized one of life's losers then he would immediately cast him as Moriarty. If he bumped into a nincompoop then it would be: 'Do you see Henry Crun over there?' Others would be categorized as Mins, Abduls and Bloodnoks.

Dad, together with Spike, the real eccentric of the quartet, often pursued the craziest adventures. They would drive out into the West End in a 1929 Austin Twelve 'Tin Lizzie' they affectionately called 'Min', dressed in crash helmets, goggles and leather jackets like pioneer pilots.

'Min' was held in great affection by both Spike and Dad. I think Dad actually found her first in one of his garages and then sold her to Spike's wife. Suspecting that 'Min' was being left to rust on the Milligans' drive, he took her back one dark night and put her into dock for a complete renovation. 'Min' came out of the overhaul looking very fine and spruce and Dad gave her an outing into the countryside but blew a piston ring when unkindly pushing the pedal down to 50 m.p.h. She didn't normally like to go more than 12 m.p.h.

Goon capers often brightened dull days.

They once rode a steam roller into the West End for a gala premiere, arriving as other guests were sedately climbing out of Rolls-Royces, Bentleys and Mercedes. Dad, in a pair of woollen long johns, posed as Bluebottle and Spike went clad as Eccles, wearing only a white sheet and wielding a lethal-looking Stone Age club.

The Goons loved a challenge and nothing appealed to Dad and Spike's humour more than to play a Cambridge University team of undergraduates at a game of tiddly-winks in one of the college halls.

When Spike was ill – and he once had a nervous breakdown – Dad played all the Goon parts, but it was impossible for the public to distinguish any difference between their voices.

Much easier to identify were Mum and Graham Stark laughing on the Goons' recorded shows in the studios. Spike said about mother's laugh: 'I don't know anyone who looks so angelic and has such a filthy laugh.'

The Goons also practised yoga – and once Michael Bentine was carried off a train sitting cross-legged in the Lotus position, unable to extricate himself because of cramp. He looked like an Egyptian statue, according to Spike.

Michael was educated at Eton. His father was a Peruvian scientist. Few entertainers could claim to have had that kind of pedigree. His creative ability greatly inspired the Goons, but a point was reached when he and Spike no longer saw eye to eye. Dad said the crunch really came when they began accusing one another of filching the other's material.

Ultimately Michael quit, though from time to time he would make token re-appearances.

It was the kind of jealousy that can often occur between two creative people. Fortunately, in the case of Spike and Dad, the combination of talents only led to inspiration. They would goad each other into deeper regions of absurd and nonsensical thinking. They would send one another ridiculous telegrams; and write notes in legal jargon on specially headed Goon stationery. Through manic depressive periods, which would descend on them equally, Spike and Dad would pour out their troubles to one another, as if competing to see who had been dealt the crueller blow.

As children we did not see quite so much of the jovial, good-humoured Harry Secombe because he lived so far from us, but the one thing he shared in common with Dad was the same birthday on 8 September and they never forgot to exchange greetings telegrams.

At the height of their popularity, the fan mail was stacked as high as a mountain at the BBC. Whenever a Goon called in at the studios he might well have to autograph picture postcards – and forge all the signatures of his colleagues as well. It was the only way the postcards would ever get posted.

The last series of the Goons went out on radio in 1957 though television saw their comeback in the Fred Shows two years later. Next came the Telegoons when puppets were mobilized for the animations of the Goon characters.

So as youngsters we grew up with all these voices and situations, together with many more familiar impersonations which Dad was capable of injecting into the proceedings. He was particularly fond of Laurel and Hardy, rating their talent higher than Charlie Chaplin's. It may have been because he met them in Hollywood and posed for a picture with Stan Laurel which he later proudly framed. He could impersonate them both, executing Ollie's famous phrase perfectly, 'That's a fine mess you've got me into', while fumbling with his tie. His Marx Brothers were great too; Mum made her one and only stage appearance with Dad when she played a glamorous foil to his cigar-smoking Groucho at the London Palladium.

Dad recognized the importance of being able to diversify his talents and by the mid-fifties his career was moving towards the movies. In Hollywood they were making multi-million-dollar epics with stars in the Clark Gable, Gary Cooper and Spencer Tracy mould. At London's Ealing Studios however, a cottage industry was struggling with low budget domestic comedies.

Dad was to become something of a discovery for them although he could not claim to have had much previous acting experience other than a couple of small parts. In 1951 he had played with Harry and Alfred Marks in *Penny Points to Paradise* and a year later he made *Down Among the Z Men* with Harry, Spike and Michael Bentine, based on a script by Jimmy Grafton in whose pub, in London's Victoria, the Goons were born.

It was when he was filming *John and Julie* in 1954 with Wilfred Hyde-White, whom Dad always admired as an actor as well as 'a fine English gentleman', that he became serious about acting.

He asked Mother, with all her theatre training behind her, to help him.

'What do I do with my hands?' he cried in dismay, after a day in front of the cameras. 'Where do I hide them?'

Mum coached him at home, although I doubt if anyone in the studios would have guessed as Dad didn't mention it.

It wasn't too long before his first real break came. He was signed to play a teddy boy slob acting as an aide to Alec Guinness in *The Ladykillers*. Guinness, already a respected figure of the British theatre, was to exercise considerable influence over Dad, who practically became his protégé.

But the one piece of advice the learned mentor stressed, Dad was to ignore. Guinness told him: 'Don't ever let the press know anything about your private life.'

Sadly, it was impossible for Dad to follow these wise words. Soon – too soon – he became involved with the glamour of the industry and a series of events which were to affect all our lives.

4

The Private Life of a Goon

Family reunions are part of the Christmas tradition. But the atmosphere of goodwill hung uneasily over our household, because of the running feud between the two mothers-in-law who had not even condescended to meet one another. Their differences, going back to Peg's disapproval of my parents' marriage, remained unhealed. Neither side was going to give way. Whenever it looked as though a truce had been reached, Peg would utter another remark and the wounds opened once more.

So Christmas was always a delicate period. Christmas lunch, with all its trimmings, would be served at 1 p.m. with my maternal grandparents in residence. But they would have to vacate the house at 5 p.m. for the next 'sitting' when Peg and Bill would arrive for dinner with a fresh roast turkey and plum pudding cooked and served once more by my mother.

This charade went on year after year until it was regarded as being normal routine; the only difference was that we could not talk of one set of grandparents in the presence of the other.

Peg always wanted to prove to us that she was the more affectionate grandmother. Greetings would be exchanged with a series of hugs and kisses lasting ten or twelve minutes at a time ... and we would have to repeat over and over again how much we loved her and missed her. Whenever we went to visit Peg she would again stifle us with affection. She kept a leather bag behind a cupboard in her living room which Sarah called the 'moosh' bag. Peg would collect all sorts of knick-knacks in it for us – books, cards, games and bars of chocolate.

Bill would sit quietly in an armchair and watch us rummage through the bag, smiling at Peg to see the pleasure she derived from our reaction to the 'moosh' we discovered.

It was always 'Peg and Bill'. Father called them by their Christian names because, he explained, it was a theatrical tradition. By the same token we were never to call them Grannie and Grandad. Peg, a small wiry woman with a crooked nose, liked to keep up her theatrical looks. She dyed her greying hair jet black and wore gaudy jewellery over colourful dresses and costumes. Her relationship with Dad fell into the classic love-hate one between a Jewish mother and her only son. They would row constantly, but Peg would say she was only looking after her son's interests by trying to pass on to him the benefit of all her experience. She once remarked, 'My son doesn't have to think for himself. I do it for him.' Her constant smothering made him feel emasculated and his reactions would become bizarre.

Once we were driving on the M1 motorway to the North when Peg was berating Dad from the back seat. At the press of a button he shot down the electric window and silenced her by letting a 100 m.p.h. gale into the back of the car.

Peg smoked like the proverbial chimney, getting through two packs of cigarettes a day, though Dad was even more irritated by her drinking. In later years she practically became an alcoholic and would hide bottles of gin around the house, beneath cushions and mattresses, in cupboards and closets, so that her suspicious son would not detect them. She would even fill Optrex bottles and use the eye bath as a glass for her daily 'nips'. Bill, the down-trodden husband, pretended not to notice.

Dad would often avoid, and even snub, his parents. If he was feeling in a depressed mood and didn't feel up to seeing them, he would bury himself in his photographic dark room, leaving Mum to entertain them.

Peg could only blame herself for Dad's inconsiderate atti-tudes. She had always given way to his demands as a child. Whatever misdemeanour he committed, he was forgiven. As a prank, he once pushed an aunt into the grate when she was making up the fire. She burnt her hands. But Peg didn't reprimand him. 'It's the kind of mischief any boy would get into at his age,' she said.

However, Dad wasn't slow to make use of them. He was always buying animals of some kind and whenever we went on holiday they would be asked to look after our pets.

He would pick up pets everywhere: he smuggled two guinea pigs in a bag back from France for us and in time we had quite a collection of pets – hamsters, rabbits and goldfish included. He would often become fascinated by a furry kitten or puppy and immediately buy it for someone in the family, but the moment the creature misbehaved it would be given away. We had a couple of Maltese terriers for a long period and they led charmed lives compared to the rest of the menagerie, because Dad saw 'Chussy and Tony' as the canine counterparts of Laurel and Hardy. But a pair of Labradors quickly lost favour because their insubordinate barking disturbed Dad's thinking, and a cocker spaniel barely got to know the run of the grounds before he was unceremoniously bundled over to a local farmer who had taken pity on him.

Dad, who hailed each and every pet as a future champion of Cruft's, showed no visible signs of regret at their departure. An equally fascinating range of cats, among them blue Persians and classic tabbies, stalked the household: but again Dad's affections extended to them only for a limited season. One of them only had to piddle over the carpet and got the royal order of the boot.

But it was Henry, the grey parrot, who really caused havoc. Once installed he ruled the roost. His squawking shattered what household peace there was. Peg taught him to talk when he boarded with her for one of the holiday periods. On our return, we were settling down for breakfast, when Henry decided to try out his lessons and with great clarity spoke in a way that commanded our instant attention.

'Bollocks,' said Henry.

Dad couldn't believe his ears.

'What did you say, Henry?' he asked, his dark eyes filling with hostility. Henry duly obliged.

'Bollocks,' he proclaimed once more.

'That's it!' cried Dad. 'If Peg is going to teach the bloody thing to swear then she can have him back for good ...' He gazed at our astonished faces and then addressed Mum.

'It's not good enough,' he remonstrated, 'we can't have the parrot swearing in front of the children. Anne, please tell Peg to come and collect the damned thing.'

Henry, from the safety of his cage, squawked another 'bollocks' which could have been taken either as his assent or objection. Dad thrust the dust cover over the cage. Poor Henry had made his last speech in our household.

Peg and Bill welcomed him back with open arms, initially at least. They spoilt him ridiculously with exotic packets of seeds and delights, and he was given free flight around their home. Unfortunately Peg wasn't able to teach Henry any good manners. He returned all the heaven-sent hospitality by shredding to tattered ribbons curtains, cushions and the hide on chairs. Peg spent hours patching things back together again. Henry repaid such kindness by attacking Peg as she lay in the bath. So Henry, who might have made his debut in an Alfred Hitchcock thriller at some later stage, was shipped back to Africa via the East End pet shop from whence he came.

Less fortunate were the flock of fan-tailed doves that nested under one of the gables. They were beautiful, and I can still see them now, their white wing tips shimmering in the morning sunshine. They were truly doves of peace, but sadly not as far as Dad was concerned.

Hearing some bad news one morning, I suspected a film contract that had been rescinded. Dad had to find some kind of explanation. Or blame someone.

Storming out of the house, he peered up at the doves cooing happily on the rooftop tiles.

Dad's face darkened.

'It's those bloody birds!' he yelled. 'We've got to get rid of them – they're bringing us bad luck.'

I was shuttled back into the house as he armed himself with his 12-bore shotgun and loaded both barrels. I turned on my heel as I heard the explosion and ran back on to the forecourt to see the poor birds pitching off the tiles like broken shuttle-cocks. Mum was out at the time shopping, but when she returned she shook with despair. 'Peter, what on earth have you done?' she cried.

'They were bad luck,' Dad replied, 'you must have known they were bad luck. Didn't you realize that?'

'But they were so lovely,' she cried, 'how could you shoot such beautiful creatures? What harm could they possibly do?'

'They weren't doves,' Dad protested, now trying to appease his conscience, 'they were pigeons.'

The incident made an indelible impression on my mind and it was not until later years that I was fully able to comprehend the depths of Dad's superstition.

Dad kept the shotgun in the hall as a defence against burglars. With a house and estate of that size he felt we should have some protection. Soon after buying it, Dad became like a night security guard in pyjamas and dressing gown, investigating every creak and noise. Inspector Clouseau didn't emerge until much later, but even then he didn't display much courage. Mum was always dragged out of bed to accompany him on these vigils.

She remembers a winter's night at 3 a.m. when Dad definitely heard the rustle of burglars. She was promptly roused and stealthily they made their way down the oak staircase. They heard an outside door creak. It sounded as though the intruders were breaking in from the paddock area. Dad got to the kitchen door and blasted through the cat trap without waiting to get sight of his target. Boots, many pairs, crunched the drive before Dad could re-load his gun.

'We're the police,' a man's voice cried out.

Astounded, Dad peered nervously out to find three uniformed policemen standing before him.

'Mr Sellers?' asked the police sergeant.

'Yes,' stammered Dad.

'We've had a report of burglaries in the area and we were checking the grounds for you. But we didn't think we would be shot at. It's as well you were a little off the mark, sir,' said the sergeant in charge of the party. I think the police eventually came to recognize Dad as being an eccentric local figure, best left to his own devices.

Their eyebrows must have already been raised by the week-end archery contests in the grounds of the manor when Dad would appear in Sherwood green leading a clan of bow-and-arrow wielding friends like Robin Hood and his Merry Men.

It was part of his 'self-disguise' to dress-up. He once astonished the exclusive Jockey Club in New York by attending a meeting there wearing cricket togs – in white flannels, sweater, pads, gloves and flourishing a bat.

His behaviour was often erratic during the holiday periods. One Easter we were packed and ready to leave for St Moritz, but he cancelled the trip at the last minute and tried to buy his peace by sending us two giant Easter eggs.

In the early years, when Dad's resources were limited, we would holiday on the English coast at Pevensey Bay, renting a chalet with our maternal grandparents.

Dad didn't always come with us, because he would be working somewhere, but he would appear at weekends and walk us along the beach collecting sea shells. It was difficult for him to gloss over the fact that holidays bored him. He could not get away soon enough. Even when he could afford to take us overseas, Dad was impossible to be with. Something would always be wrong and he would sulk in the hotel room while Mum took us out to see the sights. It was not unknown for him to abandon us completely and return to London as soon as he became disenchanted.

Once he nearly ditched us in Cortina. He had tried to ski but couldn't even keep his balance, had taken all his photos, bought all his gadgets and found that there was nothing more to interest him, except of course his family. He threw a tantrum, went to the airport and found that there was not another plane for a week.

Whenever Dad disappeared in the way he did, Mum would tell us, 'Don't worry, we'll stay on. We can still enjoy the holiday together. Daddy has had to go back to work for a few days.' I don't think we knew, until much later, how little my mother relished the prospect of summer holidays. Even when they were alone together, and we were left in London being cared for by our nanny and grandparents, things still didn't always work out to Dad's liking.

My mother faced an embarrassing experience when spending a quiet holiday in the South of France with John and Jackie Boulting. By the second day Dad was writing the holiday off as a disaster. He didn't like their hotel, he found the setting unsympathetic, and secretly protested to Mum that 'he couldn't tolerate John at any price'. This wasn't actually true, but Dad always felt threatened by John's intellect. He promptly walked out, taking his bag with him and checked into a hotel in nearby Nice.

This left Mum in an extremely embarrassing position. She had to apologize on his behalf and try to account for his disappearance. She also had to explain why she was still there. Fortunately, John understood my father extremely well and didn't bear any malice.

Dad's inferiority complex would always surface in the company of someone who had come through public school or university. He could be very entertaining on a certain level, but he was not always sufficiently knowledgeable on world affairs and so forth to hold his own.

There was a dinner party some years later at which Princess Margaret and Lord Snowdon were present. The conversation turned to Greek mythology, a subject that Dad knew nothing at all about. He crept out of the dining room, ostensibly to go to the loo, but Sarah heard him phoning his secretary and asking her to brief him quickly on the running topic. Dad then eased himself back into the conversation, dropping odd snippets to give the impression he was familiar with the subject. I saw him engage in this deceptive ploy on many other occasions and he would pick the brains, not only of his staff but his family too, before entering into conversation.

For him, it was a way of papering over his lack of education.

I was now six and it was at this time that I began to realize just how unhappy my parents were. Until now, Mum had managed to conceal their differences from us. I heard Wolf Mankowitz, a scriptwriter who had formed a film company with Dad, tell my mother that what Peter wanted was not a wife but a mother. She replied: 'Well I'm not prepared to be his mother. He's already got one.' She also remarked to Wolf that living with Dad was like standing on the edge of a volcano. One could never predict what would happen.

Whenever they had a row, Dad's first reprisal would be to snatch Mum's wedding ring from her third finger and throw it indiscriminately away. One went out over the rooftops of Paris when they quarrelled in their hotel room and Dad also tossed away an opal ring that he had given her as a present. A friend had told him that opals were unlucky. Of course, he was always penitent enough to buy replacement rings, but they too would disappear in time. Many sticky matrimonial moments were caused by Dad's superstitions. Two cars bumped on the drive and Dad blamed the cause on someone having left a bunch of keys on the hall table which was apparently a very unlucky thing to do.

I remember putting a cheese board on top of the fridge which fell heavily on Dad's head when he opened the door. He went mad and stormed through the house searching for a reason for the mishap, shouting with triumph when he found an open umbrella in the boiler room drying out after use.

'Umbrellas must never be opened in the house!' he raged.

Dad's film roles would also affect his daily moods. When he was working he would completely immerse himself in the new identity of the character, adapting different mannerisms, voice and personality. We hardly recognized him in these periods.

Playing a film role, searching for authenticity, would have an extraordinary, near schizophrenic effect on his own character and when he came home from the studios he could not switch off. Like the time he took on the role of a crook named Lionel Meadows, a ruthless underworld racketeer in *Never Let Go* in which he starred with Richard Todd and Adam Faith. Unable to shake off the character, he actually turned an 'evil eye' on his home and family – still playing the sinister Lionel Meadows. He was abusive and violent and we became terrified of him. If my mother uttered one word out of place he would make an immediate issue out of it.

My mother was reading a book one evening when he returned from the studio. He went through into the lounge and made a string of phone calls to his friends, which was his normal practice. When at the end of his calls he found that Mother was still reading her book, he turned on her and exploded, 'What the bloody hell is the matter with you? Why are you so miserable?'

All hell was let loose. Dad grabbed a vase and threw it straight at her. It missed her by an inch or two and smashed against the wall. Unable to control his anger he went through to the bath-room, tore a towel rail from the floor and twisted its tubular steel like a piece of rubber piping. Next, he destroyed a set of pictures that hung in the dressing room and tore every coat hook from the wall. One night he emptied a bottle of milk over her; she had to phone Dave Lodge and he came over to the house to help pacify him. Unfortunately these rows continued long after Dad had finished playing Lionel Meadows.

At this time my parents organized a party to see American singer Lena Horne at the Savoy. Mum bought a very beautiful hand-embroidered black dress to wear. They had a great evening and thought Lena Horne was wonderful. But it transpired that Mum had too many compliments paid to her, which upset Dad. When they got home he tore my mother's dress from her and in the morning when I went through into their bedroom it was lying on the floor in shreds.

It wasn't the first time that Dad had destroyed one of her dresses. Once, when she was about to go out with June Milligan for afternoon tea, Dad ripped off the pale blue summer dress she was wearing. He simply didn't want her to go out that afternoon and to him, tearing off her dress ensured that she wouldn't set foot outside the door.

Mother didn't have a mink coat in those days, but she did have a mink hat. At the height of another quarrel he ripped it apart and tore a string of pearls from her neck. The pearls tumbled over the floor like ball bearings and I helped Mum, who by now must have had a very small wardrobe, to pick them all up.

Sometimes when they argued I would catch the word 'divorce' and I would tremble. I understood what it meant. Other children whose parents were divorced would boast at school that they found the situation very agreeable, playing one parent off against the other for holidays, money and presents.

Dad always had to know what my mother was doing. He was very possessive but I found it hard to decide whether it was jealousy or a kind of malicious provocation. If anyone passed a compliment about my mother's looks, then he would throw a fit and it would provide him with grounds to question my mother's loyalty. He would deliberately stir things up and taunt her by saying she was in love with someone else.

In the middle of the night he once phoned a film producer friend and told him: 'My wife is obviously in love with you, and I gather you're in love with her. You had better come and collect her.' Mum, who remained mesmerized throughout the conversation, buried her head under a pillow in shame.

Dad sought an impossible commitment from her: my mother felt she lived in a gilded cage. As long as she was in the house, and giving him her undivided attention, then Dad would be content. If he was working in the studios he would ring three or four times a day to check her movements. If she left the house even to go shopping she would be subjected to interrogation.

We woke one morning to find that the entire lounge had been devastated, the debris scattered everywhere. This was retribution for Mum saying she wanted to leave home. Like a man suffering from 'diminished responsibility' Dad had run amok. Beautiful *objets d'art*, caringly and lovingly collected through their marriage, were now lying on the floor in many hundreds of broken pieces. Splinters of porcelain from the broken china and ornaments were embedded in the carpet. Priceless antique chairs, one or two of them Chippendales, lay shattered, as did a mahogany table. Bookcases were overturned; Dickens and the leather-bound classics were laid bare.

When I saw Mum she looked like a ghost and had bruises all over her. I started to cry.

'Don't worry, Mike. It's all right. There has been a bit of an accident,' she said, and went into the kitchen where she poured herself a glass of water.

In later years I learned that Dad had threatened to kill her that night. She took refuge in an armchair, protecting herself from his pounding blows by shielding her arms over her head and body. Finally, she collapsed in the chair, too terrified to move.

Today, I think both Sarah and I would have forgiven Mum if she had walked out on the marriage at that juncture. But for our sakes, she endured it all; nevertheless, though she could not have foreseen it, she was yet to suffer far greater emotional pain.

5

Enter Sophia Loren

Dad possessed a unique facility for being able to isolate 'domestic trifles' from his main preoccupation – his career. Little else mattered. All he needed, he said, was one break. It came in 1959 when John and Roy Boulting persuaded him to play the role of Fred Kite, a militant shop steward, in their comedy, *I'm All Right Jack*.

Critics hailed Dad's performance as 'masterly and memorable' and he gained the British Academy Award as the year's best actor, swinging the vote from three 'hotter' candidates, Sir Laurence Olivier, Richard Burton and Peter Finch. But his ambitions were far from being satisfied. Dad was more than aware that *I'm All Right Jack* could only be categorized as a comedy for the home market. It made him determined to break the international barrier.

His growing impatience was soon to be satisfied. Anthony Asquith, the director, asked Dad to play an Indian doctor in a movie called *The Millionairess*. Initially the movie did not sound as though it had too much going for it, until he was informed that the title role was going to be taken by Sophia Loren.

Dad could not believe his good fortune. Playing a leading man opposite a sex symbol like Sophia Loren was beyond his wildest dreams. Until now he had only seen himself as an ugly-looking comic. Hardly a movie star with a macho-type image. What this particular piece of casting did for his ego was reflected at home where Dad bloomed with sudden happiness, like the onrush of spring.

His first day spent at the studios with Sophia Loren was an

occasion of great delight for him. Dad rang Mum to report on it. Mum asked, 'What is she like?'

'She's ugly, with spots,' said Dad.

In fact she was the most incredible, the most tantalizing and the most beautiful woman he had ever met, he told Mother breathlessly over dinner that night, without pausing to think she might feel wounded in any way. My mother looked at Dad with an almost sympathetic expression.

'I imagine she is,' she said.

The dinner conversations became a daily report of his film scenes with her, and of their intimate conversations. Mum would bear the stories with patient humour and sometimes we laughed when he impersonated the Indian doctor he was playing. It was as if Dad's world was now clad in tinsel; he was like a rejuvenated man, constantly talking about Sophia Loren as if she were some kind of goddess.

Dad threw a party at the house and invited fifty guests, but the motive was very clear to Mum. It was his way of enticing Sophia Loren. Kitchen staff were hired, a band engaged to play in the barn so that our guests could dance into the night. Champagne and a special cuisine were laid on. We were allowed to stay up late and Dad told us that we should be deeply honoured that a guest like Sophia Loren would be coming.

For some reason I took an instinctive dislike to this lady whom Dad kept talking about. Mum thought she was as beautiful, intelligent and fascinating as Dad had described her and later said: 'What chance in hell have I got against her?'

But to me Sophia Loren seemed overbearing. She arrived wearing a yellow dress and a yellow feathered hat. After she had gone I said to Mum that I didn't like her. When she asked me why I said: ''Cos she looks like a chicken.'

It was strange. I was still a young boy but somehow I sensed that Dad was betraying Mum and directing his affections towards 'the chicken'.

I can recall feeling very protective towards Mum, on one occasion saying to her when she had to go out to dinner with Dad and Sophia Loren: 'Mum, you look like the fairy princess.'

When Dad brought Sophia to the house once more, I hid away from her at first; when I did emerge she asked me about school and whether I would like to grow up to be an actor like my father. She was sweet and charming but I still found myself reticent. When she next visited us, she played table tennis with me.

Dad explained his excessive attention to Sophia Loren by saying that every actor had to make a fuss of his leading lady and once boosted Mum's rapidly declining morale by telling her, 'Loren's got the dead needle to you.'

'Why?' she asked innocently enough.

'Because Loren is jealous of your fantastic complexion,' Dad replied. I'm sure that she wasn't deceived by token compliments.

The case was identical in later years. When Dad fell in love, it was impossible for him to disguise it. It was like an all-consuming passion that gathered momentum with the fury of a tornado. Everything in its wake was flattened: other people's emotions, their cares, needs and feelings, were crushed and cast aside.

I suspect it wasn't any different then, but I was seeing events through a child's eyes. It was only later that I was able to establish the real truth from my mother. Dad couldn't possibly keep his love for Sophia Loren a private matter; even his friends were kept posted with daily developments and yet, ironically, when any of them came to the house the subject of Sophia Loren was never mentioned for fear of embarrassing my mother.

Then Sophia Loren had some bad luck. Jewel thieves raided her hotel and stole jewellery worth £85,000. Dad, apparently more upset than the victim, felt compelled to do something.

'She can't be on her own at a time like this,' he told Mum, 'I must go and see her. She will be upset. There must be something we can do.'

There was.

Dad went out and bought Sophia an Eastern-style bracelet so that she could start a fresh jewellery collection. The bracelet cost £750 and Mum, while not a jealous person, found it rather odd that he should feel *that* concerned. The fact that he had rarely given her such extravagant presents did not enter her head.

By the summer, the frenzy of Dad's love for Sophia Loren had reached flashpoint. He was suffocated by the urge to confess all to Mum.

Wolf Mankowitz warned him he would be a fool and that he could only do irreparable harm to his marriage. But nothing was going to stop Dad from owning up. This wasn't a husband suffering remorse or wanting to unburden his guilt, this was Dad's ego running wild.

Mum remembers that night only too well. 'Dad came in and straightened his shoulders like a politician about to make a major speech in the House of Commons and said, as though he had rehearsed the line all the way home from the studios, "Anne, I've got to tell you that I've fallen madly in love with Sophia Loren." '

Mum says she did not suffer any immediate emotional shock. This only came in the passing weeks when Dad began to treat her like a Mother Confessor as his friendship with Sophia Loren escalated. He would relate the loving asides that Sophia Loren had whispered to him on the film set that day. He would tell Mum how they had kissed when camera and crew were momentarily absent from them. He would also tell of their troubles on days when they had tiffs. Mum only tolerated the situation because she did not want to see the break-up of her home. She secretly hoped that when the film was over and Sophia Loren returned to Italy the situation would resolve itself.

That day came all too soon for Dad. When Sophia left for Rome he was morbid and distraught. He told Mum: 'She'll be back. She'll be back soon. You'll see.'

In one tiny corner of her heart Mum felt saddened for Dad in his emotional plight. Any man put under the gaze of those sizzling Italian eyes might have wilted in the same way as Dad had done.

But the aftermath was getting too much to bear.

One night Dad woke up and gripped Mum's arm as if the

privacy of their bedroom had been invaded.

'Shush, don't say anything,' Dad motioned, 'I can feel her presence coming into the room. Yes, she is here with us ...'

'Who is?'

'It's Sophia ... Sophia,' Dad whispered.

Mum had taken all she could. She moved into the guest room and said resignedly: 'I've left those two together!'

Dad was now telephoning Sophia at all hours of the day and in all parts of the world telling her in every conversation a dozen times over: 'I love you, darling.' He did not care whether the family were within earshot. Mum's patience finally came to an end. Dad had been on the telephone for more than half an hour to Italy and when he put the receiver down Mum was shaking with anger.

'Do you know how long you've been on the phone to Sophia?' she shouted at him. 'What on earth is going on? Can't you see you're making an idiot of yourself? She is not going to leave Carlo Ponti for you.'

Unfortunately those kinds of outburst were much too rare. She usually suffered the insults in silence.

Dad's attitude became increasingly more aggressive. He suddenly resented his wife and family because we stood in the way of his desires to be with Sophia Loren. He was convinced she would leave Carlo for him, presuming always that she was as madly in love with him as he was with her. But when Sophia came back to London, signed to work with Dad for another two or three days to cut a record *Goodness Gracious Me* as publicity for *The Millionairess* she gave no indication of wishing to leave Carlo.

Indeed, Carlo accompanied his wife but this did little to dampen Dad's passions. He was still intent on leaving Mum for her; he was obsessed with the idea, but every avenue he pursued brought him frustration. At home he became a crazed, manic figure. If there was the least disruption to his day he would refuse to go to work. Mother was asked by the studios to exercise her influence over him. But everything he said or did was irrational. He hauled me from my bed at 3 a.m.

'Do you think I should divorce your mummy?' he said, as I rubbed my eyes and tried to gather what was happening.

'That's the only thing we can do, Mike. We must divorce. It won't make any difference to you. Sometimes you will live with your mother and sometimes with me ... you understand don't you?'

Still dressed in the pullover and trousers he had been wearing when I'd gone to bed, he was now pacing up and down the room, counselling my advice on the merits or otherwise of divorce.

Again Dad didn't consider my age: I was seven. How could I tell him whether he should divorce Mum or not?

I began to cry and my mother appeared.

'My God, Peter what are you doing? Leave Michael alone. He's got to go to school tomorrow,' she said.

A few nights later the atmosphere became even more tense and Mum sought refuge with friends, who were only too well aware of the situation that existed between my parents.

Sophia returned to Italy and Dad wore a melancholic, hang-dog expression about the house which was strangely silent for once.

It was as though Dad had been left stranded at the crossroads and now he was uncertain of the direction to take.

But feeling failure and frustration closing in on him, he had to do something to escape. The impetuous decision he now took was one that was to change dramatically all our lives and to precipitate his divorce from Mum. Without consulting her, Dad put the manor house up for sale. The first she knew about it was when an estate agent rang to ask whether a prospective buyer could come to view the place. Mum was heartbroken. She had put so much work into creating our home and had maintained it beautifully, whatever the pattern of Dad's inconsistent behaviour. Now, at a stroke, it was being taken from her. Dad wanted to move back into central London to be, he said, among his old friends. There was a new block of flats being built in Hampstead and he could buy the penthouse.

Right: My mother, Anne
Howe, photographed in
1961 at Manor House,
near Chipperfield.

Below: My father's first
Rolls Royce and my first
Austin. I was four at the
time.

Above left: Cary Grant and my father photographed on the bumper of the latter's Rolls Royce in 1959.

Below left: Tea for the Goons, 1958. Spike Milligan, Peter Sellers and Harry Secombe.

Above: Sophia Loren and my father on location at London Bridge for the film 'The Millionairess'.

Above: February 19th, 1964. My father's wedding to his second wife, Britt Ekland. On the left is my grandmother 'Peg'.

Above right: Knitting for the new arrival. Elstead, 1965.

Below right: Enter Victoria, January 1965.

Above: Britt and my father on holiday in Mexico.

Right: A doting father. With Victoria in 1967 on location for the film 'I Love You Alice B. Toklas'.

Victoria with Bert Mortimer, my father's faithful chauffeur.
The photograph was taken on location for 'Hoffman' at
Elstree.

Mum could not envisage choosing fresh decorations and furnishings all over again, but Dad assured her that on this occasion he would be employing a professional architect to design the fabric of the entire penthouse and he duly appointed a reputable London company to undertake the task. A young South African architect named Ted Levy was assigned to look after the project. The choice of Ted Levy was somewhat ironic. During his university days in Johannesburg he had been a member of a Goon fan club. Now he was to work with Peter Sellers, a man he idolized.

'I didn't quite know what to expect,' said Ted, who must now look back on that remark as the understatement of his life.

Ted's first meeting with Dad only served to enhance the idolatry. He admits that he did not give my mother, blonde and beautiful as she was, a second glance. He was totally captivated by Dad, whom he found 'witty, charming and intelligent'. He thought that my mother must count herself fortunate in being married to such a genius. Indeed, when Ted was invited by my parents to have dinner with them in a fashionable French restaurant, he marvelled at the apparent happiness of their marriage.

'Peter kept pecking Anne's cheek and squeezing her hand all through dinner. I thought they were the happiest couple in the world!' If anything, Ted was envious. His own marriage had just broken down and he was suffering a great deal. But not once was he given any indication that a similar bitterness was also being experienced by my mother, who in public would keep up appearances so as not to embarrass her husband.

We moved into a fourteenth floor suite at the Carlton Tower Hotel in Belgravia for three months while work on the new penthouse was put in hand. We loved it there. We only had to pick up the telephone to order as many ice creams and Coca Colas as we liked.

Our two Maltese terriers Chussy and Tony came with us. The amazing thing was that even though all the floors in the hotel were decorated alike, they knew exactly where our suite was. We lost Chussy in Hyde Park one afternoon. But he came wandering back to the hotel in his own time and refused to get out at the thirteenth floor when the lift attendant pressed the wrong button. He knew precisely where we lived.

The suite was referred to as the 'Sellers suite' for many years to come by the hotel staff and when the time came we were sorry to leave.

In the meantime, Dad had been putting pressure on Ted Levy to get the penthouse completed for their occupation. When persuading my mother to go out and choose the curtains, carpets and other furnishings, he asked Ted to go along with her. Dad, now nursing a sense of guilt over his feelings for Sophia Loren, also encouraged Ted to take Mum out to lunch on their shopping expeditions.

The motive soon became apparent.

'You seem to get along well with one another,' Dad observed when talking with Ted only two weeks after their first meeting.

Ted didn't quite know what to say, unaware that this was the prelude to hostilities.

Dad, in his demented mind, was already brewing the gentle poison. It poured out just after we moved into the Hampstead penthouse. Dad, after congratulating Ted on the work he had done, suddenly turned to him in a mood of anger.

Not caring that I was in the living room with them Dad ordered Ted to take my mother away.

'I don't want her,' he yelled at him.

Ted was appalled. He could not believe that his great star he adulated was saying such things. He looked at Dad as though struck by lightning. Ted had drawn closer to Mum, but as he said later: 'We were not in love and there was not the slightest question then of our living together or marrying!'

He was totally confused by the turn of events until Mum told him the truth about her marriage.

'Until then I could not have possibly suspected what was happening. In public Peter generated such warmth and sincerity,' said Ted, shocked by Mum's disclosure.

Dad, by his own hand, had thrown Mum and Ted together. Mum thought about going to Canada to stay with her brother, but that meant she would be totally deserting her family and home.

The weeks slipped away and Ted and Mum gradually started to fall in love, though at first they were unsure whether their feelings were real or whether they were perhaps playing out one of Dad's fantasies. Finally Dad agreed a divorce was the best solution, though that in itself provided something of a shock for my mother. Cavalier-fashion, Dad said that she could file the action and he would provide the evidence. He bantered on about still being in love with Sophia Loren, but then amazed Mum by telling her she could cite *her* best friend as co-respondent as he had recently had an affair with her.

'At first I could not believe that this girl could have slept with Peter. But she admitted remorsefully that it was true. It happened during the period we were staying at the Carlton Tower,' Mum later related.

Mum also told me, 'It was one of Dad's little games. He conned this girl into believing I'd left him for Ted.'

She was now faced with an inescapable truth: that there was no way she could save her marriage. So she decided to leave home – but telling Dad was a bad mistake. He burst into tears and threatened to jump from the penthouse balcony. It was not the first time he had spoken of suicide. This was always his crutch in a crisis. Mum wasn't ever sure whether the threat was real and secretly feared that he might actually do it.

Animosity persisted between them. It was a common occurrence for Dad to telephone his solicitors and tell them that he was going to divorce my mother.

Unable to get his solicitor on the line one night, Dad hauled me out of bed to tell me that he was going through with it and I would have to witness everything he said. I stood trembling in my pyjamas as Dad screamed at Mum, 'You must get out of here and never come back.'

Mum was crying and threw her arms protectively round me.

'Oh God, why do you always have to drag the children into our rows?' she wept. 'Can't you see the effect this will have on them? Don't you realize what harm it can do?'

Another terrible argument flared, unabated for hours. At one point Dad grabbed hold of Mother and started to strangle her.

'I'm going to kill you,' he said menacingly, his hands tightening round my mother's neck.

Mum did not attempt to struggle. Looking straight at him she said: 'Right, go ahead and do it.' Dad bowed down.

Mum was badly bruised and had to wear long-sleeved dresses for days in order to cover her injuries. She knew now she would have to leave home to escape his tyranny: the opportunity came when Dad flew to America for film talks. She packed her things the night before he was due to return. She knew we would be safe with Frieda, but she didn't tell us she was leaving home, knowing it would upset us. The next morning she crept out of the house. I was playing football in the garden and she came over and bent down by my side. Tears filled her eyes as she kissed me and said: 'I'm going to Grannie's for a while. Please look after Sarah for me won't you?'

I nodded and Mum climbed in her car. She was gone. Why was she carrying a suitcase, I thought. Dad got back from America to find us being tucked into bed by Frieda.

'Where's your mother?' he asked.

'She's gone to Grannie's,' I said.

'Oh,' he said, 'why would she do that?'

A few minutes later we heard him telephoning through to Grannie's home at Bovingdon. We were lying awake, listening to every word. Sarah started crying and so did I.

'Annie, you've got to come back,' he was saying, 'you can't leave me. Not now. I need you. My life isn't worth living without you. What have I got to live for?'

This time, Mum wasn't going to be blackmailed. Not even when Dad said: 'All right you may not love me, but think of the children.'

But I guess Dad had used that line too often. The only promise he managed to extract from my mother was that she would return at weekends to see us. Dad had to accept it as a compromise, because it was clear that she wasn't returning under any other condition. When the weekend came he was ready to please Mum in every way possible. He expressed pleasure at their 'civilized' approach to the agreed separation. Mum only raised her eyebrows, wondering how sincere he was.

For the next month, everything was comparatively peaceful. But on a Sunday in the following month a row sparked once more between them and Mum said she would be cancelling all further visits.

Dad pleaded to meet Mum at Bovingdon. Reluctantly, she agreed to see him. He asked if they could meet in his car at the end of Grannie's drive, which they could consider 'neutral' territory. It seemed pedantic to Mother, knowing how irrational Dad was, but she agreed. He drove into Bovingdon in the Rolls at the appointed hour and parked in darkness at the end of the gravel drive. Hearing the car arrive she walked down the drive, opened the door and got into the front seat. Dad didn't turn his head to greet her, but stared out of the windscreen as if transfixed.

Then he turned and gazed at her as though she were a stranger, and asked: 'Who are you?'

Bewildered, Mum stared back. 'Peter, what's the matter? Is something wrong?'

There was nothing to suggest he had been drinking, but his conversation was incoherent. It seemed as if he were suffering from amnesia. Mum coaxed him into the house, fearing that he was ill. When he saw her mother in the hallway in a red dressing gown, he said: 'Who's that old lady?'

In the sitting room his strange manner continued to worry Mum. As though completely befuddled he said: 'Who am I? What am I doing here?'

Mum was horrified. Sympathetically she grasped his arm, told him she would drive him home to the penthouse and get on to his doctor there. It was a three-quarter-hour journey and although Dad knew every inch of that road he kept saying that he didn't remember where he was or where they were heading. Mum helped him out of the car and into the lift, taking it up to the penthouse. But as they went through the door, Dad whirled round and slammed the door behind them. 'Now try and leave. You're never going to get out,' he cried, locking the door.

Mum was staggered. His 'sickness' had been a deliberate act, another theatrical role. But now she faced a considerable ordeal, not knowing how he would treat her, and felt more like a prisoner than a wife, when she realized there was no immediate escape. She talked to him, trying to make him see reason until the early hours; finally she telephoned the family doctor, a long suffering mortal well accustomed to Dad's moods and tantrums. But by the time the doctor arrived, Dad was in retreat. He agreed to go to bed and take some sedatives and Mum was able to drive back to Bovingdon.

Eventually he decided the divorce should proceed and went as far as assuring Mum that it would all be 'very friendly'. For a time I am sure Mum was again deceived. Dad bought a lovely little cottage back in Hampstead for her. It was in Golden Yard – only a mile away from the penthouse. He even asked Ted if he would arrange for its decoration so that Mum would be comfortable staying there.

But once again this all turned out to be a ploy to win back Mum's affections. He tried to bribe her back by giving her the kind of presents she had never seen in their marriage before . . . a mink coat and a diamond ring. But when she realized the true significance of these gifts she accepted no more.

But Dad wasn't quite finished. 'What about a new car?' he asked, but again she was strong enough to resist the temptation. She knew only too well that if she accepted any of these blandishments she would place herself in jeopardy.

Dad was getting desperate now. Solicitors on both sides were busily preparing divorce papers and I think it dawned on him that he could no longer manipulate the odds. Rejected by Sophia, he now felt that he was the injured party. The thought enraged him. When Mum and Ted went to visit Coventry Cathedral, he engaged a private detective to follow them. By now they had indeed become lovers, and they checked into a hotel on the outskirts of the city.

Biding his time until late at night the private eye burst in on them to acquire evidence of their adultery. Mum said the incident made her feel tawdry but later she was able to look back on it as something Dad might have written into a film script.

He began painting himself as a figure of desolation. In press interviews he forlornly told how his wife had run off with another man and ditched him. For Ted, who described himself as a harmless Jewish boy from South Africa, it was very flattering to be accused of stealing a great star's wife, but he did not enjoy the glory.

The evil forces consuming Dad were to make poor Ted pay a horrendous price for what Dad termed an 'injustice'. In earlier months Ted had confided to Dad how he had once been imprisoned in South Africa for his anti-apartheid activities, and had also been accused of being a Communist. Dad now came to the conclusion that Ted's recent conduct in 'wife-stealing' was tantamount to being a Communist. He attempted to get Ted barred from his professional working body, the Royal Institute of British Architects.

Dad wrote to the Institute and told them that apart from Ted's Communist politics he had also acted unprofessionally by having an affair with his wife while engaged on an assignment for him. He also said that 'Levy was unfit as a person to be in the presence of the children.'

Understandably, Ted was growing increasingly scared of Dad who once told Mum that he would get a couple of 'heavies' – stunt men from the film studios who, he said, would do anything for a 'bob or two' – to take care of him.

Dad's rantings about Ted were now commonplace at home and not even the nanny could protect us from them.

'Ted Levy has destroyed my life. He has taken your mother away from me. I'll kill him, I'll kill him,' he screamed one afternoon. Again, both Sarah and I were totally bewildered. What were we to believe? Why did Daddy want to kill Ted?

Ted, who lived in a small terraced house not far from us in Hampstead, received a visit from Dad in the early hours of a winter's morning.

'In fact it was 2 a.m.,' he says. 'I was disturbed by someone banging on the front door. I looked out of the window and saw your father outside. He asked if he could come in and see me. His voice was edgy but he seemed to be calm enough. I went down and let him in. I was still in my pyjamas and shivering with fear. In case your father should notice, I complained about the cold. I really thought he had come to kill me. I took him up to the room I used as a drawing office. We sat down at opposite ends of a long table. He wore an overcoat and he kept his hands in his pockets. I was sure he was carrying a gun. Your Dad then began telling me how I'd ruined his life by stealing his wife.

'He wore an expression of hate, anger and frustration, the like of which I'd never seen on the face of any human being before. I was convinced now that he was going to murder me. I tried to placate him by telling him that I hadn't broken his marriage, that this had occurred when he'd fallen in love with Sophia Loren and that he had already admitted sleeping with Anne's best friend. I also told him that if Anne still loved him and wanted to go back to him, then she could. I would not stand in her way. Your father calmed down with that. It seemed his energy was exhausted.

'Suddenly he looked up and offered me a cigarette. Until that point in the conversation he had called me "Levy" with near anti-semitic overtones in his voice. Now it was "Ted" and all was friendly. When your father got up and left, I collapsed into bed. My pyjamas stuck to the streams of perspiration that poured from me.'

One day Dad brought a visitor – Ted's estranged wife Barbara – to Golden Yard where Mum and Ted were listening to some classical records. Ted was dumbfounded, but the objective of the visit was transparently clear. Dad, who had only met Barbara briefly, had set out to prove to her that Ted had been cheating on her. But Ted and Barbara's marriage had collapsed months before. A psychiatrist had advised them to separate.

But now Barbara, playing right into Dad's hands, was

screaming at Ted, 'You didn't tell me the real reason for leaving me. You lied to me ...'

The whole house was in pandemonium, Dad telling Mum that he hoped she realized what kind of bastard she was having an affair with. At the height of the row Dad suddenly prepared to abandon everyone. True, his actions were never less than bizarre, but the dialogue that followed bordered on the insane.

'I want to marry Nanette Newman,' he suddenly announced, bringing the conversation to a halt. He explained he was in love with Nanette, an actress who had played his girlfriend in *The Wrong Arm of the Law* and that if he could arrange to marry her it would resolve the dilemma they were all in. Mum could then marry Ted. Nanette and her husband Bryan Forbes were close friends of my parents. Nanette had become very successful and so too had Bryan as a director.

Mum gasped: 'What are you talking about, Peter? Nanette and Bryan are happily married. Don't drag them into our sparring match.'

Dad wouldn't listen. He picked up the telephone and got Bryan on the line. Without bothering to pass the time of day, or offering even a modicum of explanation, he got right to the point.

'Bryan? This is Peter ... Look, I want to marry Nanette. Is that all right by you? I'm sure Nanette won't object,' he said, with the casual tone of someone asking a friend for the loan of a book. I imagine if it had been anyone other than Dad, then Bryan Forbes might have been struck down with apoplexy, but he coped with Dad's outrageous suggestion with impeccable restraint.

'Of course I understand,' Bryan said as though those kinds of request came every day. 'I'll talk to Nanette about it and I'll give you a ring back on the subject.'

Not surprisingly, the call never came. In a day or two Dad had forgotten about Nanette and the whole episode, but the vendetta against Mum and Ted was still seething in his mind.

By now both Sarah and I had our own rooms at the Golden Yard cottage where Mum took us with Frieda's replacement whom we called Minnie. Though we only saw Dad at weekends and during school holidays it was in those periods that he attempted to poison our feelings. When we were due to return to my mother, he would deliberately wage a tug-of-war campaign. 'There's no need for you to go back to your mother tonight,' he would say, having bribed us with new toys. 'I'm sure you are much happier here with me, aren't you.' He was not asking us, it was a statement of fact!

Often we were too scared to argue with him. Observing our silence, he would then get us to telephone and say we wanted to stay. But there would always be a row because of course it was Mum who was responsible for our daily routine. It would take us days to readjust and our school lives were inevitably disturbed.

I quickly established myself as a rebel, imitating Dad's erratic behaviour patterns in the classroom. I was unruly, undisciplined and at times quite violent. Teachers regarded me with apprehension. Mother, with genuine alarm, became·afraid to answer the telephone in case of hearing fresh complaints about my truculent conduct.

For however much she tried to shelter Sarah and me from Dad's behaviour too many elements seeped through. She blamed my rebelliousness on insecurity, and she also recognized another contributory factor though she could do little about it. Because of Dad's impetuous manner, and also the spiralling success of his career, we were always changing homes. This meant that schools too were switched with equal rapidity. Ultimately, I attended nine different schools while Sarah was shuttled through a similar number. It was hard to find and keep friends.

Sarah too had problems here, though they took a different form. She would ask the other kids whether they'd seen Dad's latest film or whether they'd watched him on television.

'I was always trying to cash in on Dad's fame,' recollects Sarah, 'I must have been an absolute nuisance. They just grew sick and tired of me and avoided me like the plague.' Equally provoking to her classmates was the fact that Sarah was delivered to school in a chauffeur-driven Aston Martin, later to be replaced by an even more resplendent Rolls-Royce. Until I was dispatched to boarding school, I too was given the same regal service by Bert Mortimer, our new chauffeur. Bert was to become a very loyal ally and, although his first loyalty was always to Dad, he was able to shield us from my father's stormiest moods.

My boarding school days began when I was about nine. Mother sent me in the hope that I would find a more stable atmosphere there. I caused havoc on my first day by constantly crying, believing that Mum, as well as Dad, had permanently deserted me. But the rebel within soon returned. It wasn't long before I was playing truant and I once ran away determined not to return. After miles of leg-weary wandering, I finally headed home to Mum's home, catching an underground train at the city boundary and paying for the fare with the shilling I still had left in my pocket. This was against all the traditions of the school and both my parents were summoned by the headmaster to pledge my future co-operation. Mother has always believed that my escapades were deliberately intended to reconcile her with Dad. Through all of this, the friction between my parents showed no sign of easing.

Mum and Ted finally decided to get married.

Dad, dogged to the end, threatened to defend and delay answering Mum's divorce petition, effectively to prevent her re-marriage. He proposed to counter file, citing Ted as co-respondent. By this manoeuvre he would appear to be the innocent party when the divorce details came out in public. It was unfair and unjust but Mum and Ted acceded to his demands rather than cross-petition which would have involved harmful publicity for the family.

They also had little money, and Mum had to pawn her one remaining ring to pay the divorce costs. It was as well that Dad didn't learn this, otherwise there would surely have been further repercussions. He was ordered to pay £5 a week maintenance for each of us children. Other than the Golden Yard cottage, Mother wasn't to receive any settlement. Understandably, Ted felt incensed when Dad said in press interviews how much money he lavished on his children and how much we mattered to him, for Ted supported us throughout this bitter period, especially when Dad fell behind with the maintenance money and clothing expenses. When Mother telephoned to remind him that the arrears totalled £2000, Dad was not co-operative.

'It's too bloody bad,' he told her, even though at the time he was earning a million dollars a movie.

Father only released the money when threatened with litigation that could have easily brought about his imprisonment for defying the court order.

Again, we did not always understand what was happening behind the scenes. There were spells, after submitting to Dad's 'brainwashing' sessions, when we regarded Ted with suspicion and resentment. It was only when we got older that we came to draw our own conclusions.

After the divorce Dad warned friends not to see or even contact Mum while she remained with Ted. The telephone went dead and Mother was snubbed and ignored by people who claimed to be friends in the past. Only two familiar voices rang through. One was Dad's publicity agent Theo Cowan and the other was Spike who asked Mum if there was anything he could do to help.

It was some time before feelings cooled down. And yet, in the end, Dad and Ted got to like and respect each other. In 1967, he invited Mum and Ted out to America as his guests, laying on a helicopter for their local transportation in California. I guess that it was a time when Dad was in one of his more generous moods.

When he was auctioning off the furniture from the Hampstead penthouse, my mother rang him and asked if she could buy a settee and three other pieces, having previously refused to take any of the household effects from him.

'How much do you want for them?' she asked.

'Oh, let's say £20,' said my father.

'Don't be silly, Peter,' said Mum, knowing the true value of the items, 'I'll give you £200 for them.'

'Done!' said Dad.

I think he came to envy the stable family life that Mum and Ted had created for us, particularly at the times when he was alone and depressed.

For with all the stardom and riches secured, Dad could never find real happiness. Not in the mansions, the limousines and yachts he came to buy. Not among the members of the Royal family and aristocracy he was to brush shoulders with. Nor could he find lasting contentment with any of his future wives.

6

A Swedish Stepmother

My father disliked his newly-found bachelorhood. He faced the world a lonely and forgotten man, his ego flattened by a divorce he had once regarded with no more importance than a game of charades.

Even after my mother's marriage to Ted, it was obvious to most people that Dad didn't seem to concede or accept its legality. He still talked of a reconciliation with my mother – something which astonished his friends – and Mum! The penthouse was now strangely silent, almost sinister, as he sat alone, listening to classical records. Well-meaning friends urged him to find fresh romantic interests to cure him of his malaise, but he instinctively feared rejection, having lost both Sophia Loren and my mother.

'Who would want me?' he kept saying, as his insecurity surfaced once again. Father, always so conscious of his looks and the way he dressed, never saw himself as a heart throb.

Yet vanity was the very essence of his profession and it was no stranger to him. Before he filmed with Sophia Loren, he had his unsightly teeth straightened and capped into 'wall to wall' line by a London dental surgeon. Often his hair would be dyed for different movies, but he usually kept it jet black to thwart approaching greyness. Baldness was no danger, his hair being healthy and thick.

His greater anxieties surrounded his weight. Jogging, long walks, exercise bikes and other contraptions were all tried in attempts to keep trim. I would hold his legs in a horizontal position so that he could do 'sit-ups' to tone his stomach muscles. He would also use a portable hand bar that could be suspended in the frame of a door. Sometimes, if he was pleased with the way things were going, he would look with admiration at his torso in the mirror and say: 'Not a bad shape, eh?'

But he seldom persevered for long – he wasn't sufficiently disciplined to continue such therapy indefinitely. Diets would also be implemented but again his lack of staying power was his undoing. When feeling depressed, he usually ate more. Often he would pillage the fridge at nights when suffering from insomnia. Sleeping pills didn't always have their desired effect when his mind, as active as an atomic generator, churned over a myriad of ideas, both creative and conspiratorial.

His suits were finely cut and tailored by Doug Hayward, the outfitter whose clients included many other actors. Mum had kept his day-to-day clothes in good order. Shirts, underwear and socks had been neatly placed on their shelves. But since she had gone, the wardrobe was looking sadly depleted with Dad having to rely on the weekly laundry deliveries for clean clothes.

For some time he could not get over the divorce. He was pensive and remote; even sceptical of his ability to raise enough charm to engage the opposite sex. He felt drained of his talent to act; there was no limit to the depths of his melancholy.

However, his strength revived dramatically when he came to film *The Pink Panther* for Blake Edwards. The mere thought of filming with two of the screen's most beautiful actresses, Capucine and Claudia Cardinale, revitalized his jaded soul and lifted his performance as the manic, accident-prone Inspector Clouseau of the French Sûreté. United Artists, realizing Clouseau's potential, instantly planned a sequel *Shot in the Dark* with the lovely Elke Sommer as Dad's new female lead.

But first he had to go to New York to shoot *The World of Henry Orient* with Paula Prentiss and Angela Lansbury. We rented a house in the romantic Gatsby territory on Long Island. It was a white, colonial-style house with beautiful grounds running down to the water's edge, where a boat was moored at a wooden jetty. Bert and Hattie Stevenson, also in the entourage, were handed the responsibility of looking after us and in the house we had a black butler and maid, Tony and Maud. With us came our new nanny, Minnie, a tall, thin and dark-haired Irish girl, but in a matter of days she mysteriously disappeared. We learned later that Dad had tried to seduce her and Minnie, in her fright, had fled home.

In spite of Dad's error of judgement in wooing Minnie, he found enough charm to captivate a blonde Swedish beauty queen he found in New York working as a fashion model.

Soon she was with us on Long Island and spent most days at the poolside in her bikini. There didn't seem to be anything more important in the world to her than her suntan, but Dad didn't seem to notice her narcissicism. She lacked any sense of humour. When I tickled her feet and pulled off her bathing cap while she was sleeping she lost her temper with me. She had little patience with children and she asked Dad why he'd bothered to have us along. Our stay on Long Island came to an abrupt end, but it had nothing to do with the crisis that was building between us and 'Miss Sweden'.

A kindly neighbour told Dad that the house we were renting was occupied by poltergeists. Until then, Dad's own dealings with 'the other world' were conducted through clairvoyants and spiritualist mediums. The manifestation of poltergeists upset him considerably. A night or two later the poltergeists struck and Dad roused Bert to witness the phenomenon. The living-room door apparently opened and closed, pictures also fell from the walls, indentations of ghostly footprints appeared on the carpet and the temperature of the room sank to a 'deathly cold'.

Without explanation we left the house the next morning and went to a hotel suite in Manhattan. It cost him a fortune for us to stay there. How Dad explained our unscheduled departure to Tony and Maud is a thought that has often caused me much amusement.

'Miss Sweden' left for Stockholm and when Dad's movie was completed we journeyed back to England where London, grey and bleak at the approach of winter, plunged him back into another fit of depression. With our return to Mum's household, bitter feelings were again resurrected over the divorce.

*

If my father needed a shoulder to cry on at this time, it was a need also felt by Janette Scott, a young actress whose marriage to Canadian singer Jackie Rae was being dissolved. Hurt, pain and all the afflictions of divorce were hiding beneath the surface when Janette met my father at a backstage West End party. Dad recognized the symptoms as common to his own and was ready to console her, although his need for sympathy was probably greater. Janette must have realized this when Dad brought her to his home in Hampstead, because he was rather adept at playing the persecuted victim. We liked Janette, she was kind and friendly and played games with us on the living-room floor.

Dad, sensing rejection once more, locked himself in the bathroom one night and refused to emerge until Bert had managed to persuade Janette to come over and talk to him.

Again, he was looking for emotional comfort. For her part, Janette wanted to keep their friendship on a calm, manageable level, but this was proving a lot more difficult than she had imagined. Her own problems seemed to take second place to those of my father.

Professional pressures did not ease the situation. Dad had signed for Stanley Kubrick's *Dr Strangelove or How I Learned to Stop Worrying and Love the Bomb*. He agreed to play three different roles; one as an RAF group captain, another as an American president and the third as a Nazi-style scientist.

Janette became a patient listener, as my mother had once been, when Dad began to unburden the problems of his working day to her. But eventually Janette felt suffocated by the demands he made on her and she left quietly for New York, telling Dad that she did not have the stamina to be part of his life. She later married American singer Mel Tormé, but that marriage also ended in divorce for her.

My father sold the Hampstead penthouse. It contained too many bitter memories for him. Seeking escape he looked once more to the countryside and found a fifteenth-century oak-beamed house in the village of Elstead, only two or three miles from the Surrey market town of Guildford. It was called 'Brookfield' and if it was possible, it was even more picturesque than our last country manor at Chipperfield. Dad hoped it would be a family home again.

Acres and acres of grounds included a lake of its own, paddocks, walled gardens and barns. But it was in need of renovation and Dad hired an army of builders and decorators. One of the barns was converted into a gymnasium, installed with changing rooms and saunas and another section was converted to a private cinema with a screen that descended from the roof at the push of a button.

Dad bought the house furnished but proceeded to rip up what he described as the 'Levy' seaweed-green coloured carpets that resembled too closely those laid at Hampstead, which had been chosen by Ted when designing the penthouse. Dad ordered the discarded carpets, which were in perfect condition, to be burnt at the end of the garden and chose others in dark red to replace them.

It was not possible to move into Brookfield until the renovations had been carried out and accordingly Dad needed to move into a hotel.

That he should be filming *Shot in the Dark* at this time suited his purposes ideally because he was able to persuade United Artists to book him into the Dorchester Hotel. He was given superstar treatment, occupying the elegant Oliver Messel suite, with its crystal glass chandeliers, chintz curtains, garden murals and original oil paintings. There was also a garden terrace reached through french doors.

Our weekends were now spent with him at the hotel and we enjoyed our visits because no restrictions were placed on us. We had the free run of the hotel on occasions and Dad, totally involved in his own world, didn't seem to register our presence.

It was on our third visit there that Dad beckoned both Sarah and me to sit with him on the sofa, saying he had some very special pictures to show us. We had seen a lot of his photographs in the past but these he seemed particularly excited about. He produced a set of pictures of a very glamorous-looking girl.

'Who do you think that is?' he asked. We didn't know. 'Is she a film star like you, Dad?' I asked.

'Yes, she is,' beamed Dad, 'her name is Britt Ekland and she comes from Sweden. Isn't she beautiful? How would you like Daddy to marry her?'

By this time, my father had already proposed to Britt. He had spotted her only days before in the foyer of the Dorchester choosing some magazines from the bookstand.

Quiet words to the concierge elicited her name and the fact that she had been signed by 20th Century Fox for the war thriller *Guns of Batasi* at Pinewood.

That she should be staying at the Dorchester was only part of the coincidence in Dad's reckoning. Only two months earlier Maurice Woodruff, a clairvoyant he regularly consulted, had told Dad that he would marry a girl with the initials 'B.E.'. Now Dad had found her ... and Bert was promptly dispatched to Britt's room to invite her to dinner in the Oliver Messel suite that same night. When we were introduced to her our instincts told us that we would get on well with her. Indeed, we thought Dad was exceptionally lucky to have found someone who looked so beautiful. It didn't occur to us that there was any disparity in their ages and I doubt if it occurred to Father, his thoughts being entirely taken up with love. But at thirty-eight years of age, he was nineteen years older than Britt.

Britt had lovely blonde hair that tumbled to her shoulders and her eyes were as blue as the early morning sky. She couldn't speak much English and her sentences were delivered in scrambled syllables. Whenever she made a mistake with pronunciation she would laugh on seeing our bewildered reaction. Dad bought her a triple banded Victorian engagement ring of emeralds, diamonds and rubies. But this was only the beginning of his generosity.

His love, as always, had to be conveyed with extravagant presents and he also bestowed on Britt a black diamond mink coat, a diamond studded gold brooch, a sports car – and a Dachsund she named Pepe. He also hired the Queen's couturier Norman Hartnell to design Britt's wedding dress for their marriage at Guildford registry office on 19 February 1964.

During the days leading up to the ceremony it seemed that

the only news of any importance in the world was Dad's wedding to Britt. The newspapers were full of it. When the day finally arrived, several thousands of fans gathered outside the registry office. Snowflakes descended like confetti from the grey skies, creating a fairytale atmosphere for the occasion. Stars and celebrities came in their thousands to the reception which Dad laid on at Brookfield, now almost ready for occupation. Sarah and I made friends with Britt's younger brother Kalle, who had come in from Sweden with his family. We handed out slices of the wedding cake, as well as titbits of information, to eager pressmen who congregated outside the gates.

In the very first week of their marriage, Dad had to go to Hollywood to start a new comedy movie *Kiss Me Stupid* for the American director Billy Wilder. But Britt had to stay on for *Guns of Batasi* and this clash of their shooting schedules made them despondent.

Dad decided that I would have to go with him to America, as if needing an envoy from the family to accompany him. I had just changed schools and made a new set of friends. At ten years of age I thought I was man enough to tell him that I didn't want to go.

'What do you mean you don't want to go? You'll do as I say,' he yelled at me.

Britt was out shopping; Peg, who was visiting us at the Dorchester, tried to pacify Dad without any significant effect. Angrily, Dad gave me half-an-hour to change my mind and ordered me to my bedroom in the suite 'to think things over'. I made the time limit last almost to the second.

'Well?' enquired Dad on re-appearing. 'What are you going to do?'

'I just don't want to come, Dad,' I said. 'It will mean missing all the things we're doing at school.'

'Right,' he stormed, 'I want to ask you one question. Who do you love most – me or your mother?'

Knowing he would be angered, I spat out, 'I love Mummy best.'

He went berserk, pushed me aside, and dashed into the next

room. He grabbed Sarah and made her stand before him.

'Now tell me who do you love best?' he screamed at her, who had already got the drift of things.

'I love you both the same,' she replied tactfully.

'All right,' snapped Dad accepting Sarah's answer, 'you can go and have some tea and cakes with Peg.'

Dad turned his wrath back on me.

'You can pack your things now. You're going back to your mother's and I never want to see you again,' he said.

In any emotional conflict tears would stream to Dad's eyes, and now he was crying as profusely as I was. He buried his face in a handkerchief and disappeared into his bedroom; Bert dutifully came through to help me pack. Into the car were piled my clothes, books, toys and gadgets – everything in the suite that I possessed. Sarah, crying too, collected her things. She said she would come with me, because she didn't want to stay without me.

Dad emerged once more, sobbing, to say how much he loved me yet now I was leaving him forever. Sarah could go too, but the next time she visited him she wouldn't be able to bring her brother. Bert frowned uncomfortably through it all. He said, 'Don't worry, Michael. Your father will get over it and see you again, I'm sure he will.'

Our sudden arrival at my mother's home caused her some alarm, until she learned what had happened. 'You should know your father's moods by now, Michael,' she chided me.

I took refuge in my room and opened the bureau drawer in which I kept a collection of Dad's pictures. Some were film stills, others came from the family album. I daubed the photos with a thick, black pen and then tore them up into tiny pieces. I can still remember the feeling of rage. I replaced these pictures with some of Sarah and me and placed them all round the room.

That night I cried bitterly, thinking that Dad would keep his promise never to see me again. Mother told me at breakfast that she had spoken to Dad, that he hadn't meant what he said and I was to forget the incident.

He left for America alone. He had rented an apartment

for Britt in Chelsea and engaged a secretary for her. Britt was worried about him. Six thousand miles away in California, he was becoming increasingly jealous and would check her daily movements by telephoning friends. Eventually he talked Britt into quitting *Guns at Batasi* and joining him in California. Britt's three weeks' work on the movie had to be scrapped and Dad paid out 60,200 dollars to the film company in compensation.

It was Easter and my birthday was approaching. Dad felt it was time to repair the rift between us. He called my mother and asked if Sarah and I would like to go to America for the holiday and see Disneyland. Mum encouraged me to go. 'Besides, Michael,' she said, 'the opportunity of seeing Disneyland is too good to miss.'

Nevertheless, I was still feeling apprehensive when our plane landed in Los Angeles and Bert picked us up from the airport. What would Dad say about having disowned me? He would surely make some remark. But he greeted us at the house he had rented, and the episode was never even mentioned. It was as though it had never occurred.

The house was marble floored and luxurious. It sat on top of Beverly Hills among a colony of Hollywood stars. Our neighbours were Cary Grant, Steve McQueen and Shirley Maclaine and in the coming days we were to see quite a lot of them. It was Cary Grant who was to ensure that Dad's stay in Hollywood would not pass without due celebration. He gave a star-studded party and although we felt slightly bewildered by the glamour of the occasion, we noticed several faces from television and cinema which were very familiar. Cary Grant ran his hand through my curly hair and told Dad he had a fine-looking son, while making a similar fuss of Sarah.

We were allowed to stay in the legendary star's house for the party, scoffing candies from a buffet table dripping with delights and weaving our way among the beautifully dressed stars. We were introduced to many of them, including Samantha Eggar and Nancy Sinatra, but the encounter that thrilled me most was with Eddie Byrne, the actor who played 'Kookie' in the television series *77 Sunset Strip* and I asked him for his autograph.

Children of our age would have been happy enough to get to Disneyland by road, but Dad hired a helicopter to take us there in style. It was the first time that Britt had flown in one and it was our first flight too. This was the icing on the cake, for Disneyland itself was a wonderful fantasia with Mickey Mouse, Donald Duck, Goofy and countless other Disney creations parading before our eyes.

In the euphoria of such happiness it was impossible to imagine that Dad was about to suffer a series of heart attacks that were to take him to the brink of death. He had always been obsessed by the dread of having such an attack – more especially since the death of his father Bill who had died the previous year from a heart attack while undergoing surgery.

There was an occasion when Dad, appearing in the West End show *Brouhaha*, complained of chest pains when Mum was driving him home one night from the theatre. He was sure he was suffering a heart attack. But when he got home and a doctor was summoned, the pains were diagnosed as no more than indigestion.

Yet Dad would return to his secret dread time and time again. Spike Milligan said, 'Your father was always searching for a bloody heart attack as if it were a letter that he knew had been posted and hadn't arrived.'

We stayed at the Disneyland hotel for two nights and then returned to Beverly Hills. We were tired, but excited by the holiday. When we went to bed, there was nothing to suggest that Dad was ailing in any way.

He was joking with us, as he closed the door on our adjoining rooms.

'Good night. God bless,' he said finally. 'Sleep tight.'

We slept through until the middle of the night when a sudden commotion in the hallway disturbed us. I heard Britt's voice frantically calling Bert for help.

'Come quickly,' she was pleading. 'It's Peter. He's not well...'

We heard Bert crossing the hallway and Britt phoning for a doctor. Although we didn't gather it then, that much feared heart attack had finally arrived.

Dr Rex Kennamer, a heart physician, came straight out to the house and Britt, suspecting that we were awake, looked in our rooms to reassure us that Dad was going to be all right. She said the doctor was giving him tablets so that he could sleep.

We saw Dad the next morning. His face looked strangely grey but he put on a smile for us and said: 'It's nothing to worry about, kids. I wasn't feeling well. I might have to go down to the hospital later this morning for a check-up, but Britt is coming with me and I'll be back'.

An ambulance arrived an hour or so later and Dad was taken out to the Cedars of Lebanon Hospital. We waved to him from the steps of the house as he was rolled out on a trolley.

'Your father is going to be okay,' said Britt, 'but it's possible that they might have to keep him in hospital just for tonight so the doctors can complete their tests. Anyway, if he is not home tonight, he will be tomorrow . . .'

Britt came back from the hospital late that night, saying that Dad was perfectly well and that he would be home first thing in the morning. We accepted the situation as only children can. We didn't see it as a crisis but it developed into one when at 5 a.m. the next morning the night sister at the hospital rang Britt to urge her immediate return to the hospital.

Dad was unconscious. In two hours he had suffered seven consecutive heart attacks. Britt spent the whole of the next day at the hospital at his bedside. He had been placed in the intensive care unit and wired to life-support systems. One of the doctors told Britt to expect the worst because only a miracle could save her husband. When she returned to the house she tried to hide the truth from us, but her eyes were moist.

Britt called our mother and arranged for us to leave on the morning flight back to London. She must have reckoned that if Dad was about to die, then it was better for us not to be there. Poor Britt. She had only been married to Dad for forty-six days.

We got the plane to London and at Heathrow were confronted by a barrage of photographers. Mother met us at the customs barrier. As flashbulbs popped, Sarah asked her what was going on.

We learned that he was still alive, but only by the thinnest of threads and the hospital bulletins were unchanged. For five days his condition remained 'critical'.

The newspapers were already carrying elongated biographies that might have passed as obituaries. Television news commentaries were making Dad's fight for life their lead story. But I don't think we yet grasped the gravity of the situation. As children we had become accustomed to the media's interest in Dad's activities. It was hard for us to differentiate between this crisis and any other occasion when he was in the news. When he was divorced from my mother the newspapers were smothered with stories and when Dad married Britt the news occupied the front pages. Whenever he made a movie, there was always something in the columns about him. So even when the papers were carrying the headlines 'Peter Sellers on the Brink of Death' in bold, black type, we were inclined to believe it was not really true – something which would bitterly affect us all.

But in the household a sudden dilemma arose.

Dad's accountant Bill Wills called Mum and urged her to pay the outstanding instalments on the insurance policies Dad had taken out for us, so that they would not be declared lapsed in the event of his death. While appreciating the practical necessity of eliminating this risk, as seen by the accountant, Mum found the experience sordid and upsetting.

And the miracle came, as we knew it would. Dad's face, lit up in a smile as he left hospital, appeared on the front pages. Sarah asked my mother, 'Why did they all make such a fuss, Mummy? Look, there's Daddy. And he's laughing.'

7

Royal Days

Back now from America and his terrible ordeal, Dad strolled on the sunlit lawns of Brookfield with the gratitude of a man whose life had been spared, to see his home and family once more.

Hand-in-hand we walked with him to the lake and there he hugged us close and whispered: 'My children, I never thought I would live to see this day ... I am the happiest man in the world.' After several weeks in hospital, he had been allowed to return to England on a promise to doctors that he would spend the summer months recuperating at home, without stress or strain. He had also given assurances that he would no longer smoke – usually he got through a pack a day – and that he would keep a daily check on his weight to ensure strict control. Various pills were also prescribed for him to stabilize his condition and replace his lost energy.

Everything was blissfully happy – at least for those first few days. Unfortunately, Dad had made some disparaging comments about Hollywood to film critic Alexander Walker who published them in London's *Evening Standard*.

'I've had Hollywood in a big way, luv,' Dad had remarked in a careless moment. Those who had befriended him in Hollywood felt insulted and Billy Wilder, who condemned him as being more difficult to work with than Marilyn Monroe, sent him a rueful cable: 'Talk about unprofessional rat finks'.

Dad tried to correct impressions by taking out a whole page advertisement in *Variety*, declaring that he had no criticism of Hollywood *per se*, only as a place to work in. It wasn't strictly true. His sympathies were far removed from Hollywood. To his way of thinking the superficial standards that prevailed there were epitomized by a television interviewer, who neglecting his homework, addressed my father as 'Mr Peters'. Dad also loathed the Californian jet set, the parasites of his own profession who posed as producers, putting together multi-million-dollar deals while quaffing other people's champagne. He would describe this particular breed as 'herns'.

'Listen to their conversation when you get them in a group,' he would say, 'and all you hear is a drone ... hern ... hern ... hern.' Dad didn't like the way Americans packaged their lives either. Every product was 'homogenized, pasteurized, sanitized and sterilized' if it wasn't 'jumbo sized, economy sized or deep fried' not forgetting sandwiches which were 'open faced ...' Dad adopted the labels and would use them in all sorts of contexts.

His real detestation however remained Hollywood, and it stayed unaltered throughout his lifetime. It was only with great reluctance that he ever filmed there again.

Dad's recovery was slow. But gradually he was able to see more of his friends and his adrenalin seemed to run almost normally when Spike, Graham and David came down to the house.

Another visitor was aviator Tommy Sopwith who flew to Brookfield in his helicopter. Grabbing white sheets from the bedrooms, we laid them out as markers in the field when we heard the chopper's engines roar above us. Tommy invited us aboard for a joy ride and suggested paying a surprise visit to some friends only three or four miles away. But a navigational error on Dad's part brought us into a stranger's back garden. An elderly couple having afternoon tea were astonished at the sight of Peter Sellers climbing out of a helicopter on their lawn asking for directions.

Within weeks of being back at Brookfield Dad bought a new Ferrari so that we now had four cars in the garage. Among them a Rolls-Royce for which he had managed to secure a personalized number plate. Its registration was PS 1872. Dad wanted to acquire PS 1 and traced the registration to a car owned by a dour Scottish lady. He offered her £1000 for the car and its licence plate but she declined, and still refused to part with it when his bidding reached £2500.

It must have been very hard on my mother at this time. She was expecting a baby and while we were excited at the prospect of having a half brother or sister, we were more interested in what was happening at Brookfield. Sarah would repeatedly tell Mum how wonderful Britt was and this must have been hard to take at times. Sarah would recount days when Britt had taken her for walks in the countryside around Elstead and found coins hidden under fallen leaves by the fairies.

She asked Mum why we had to stay with her five days of the week and with Dad and Britt only two.

Mum's wardrobe was also compared with Britt's.

'You ought to see Britt's clothes,' Sarah said, 'she's got hundreds of dresses, a mink coat, even a mink bikini – and her *shoes* ... she must have thousands of pairs, I couldn't count them.'

Later Sarah was given a fur coat by Dad at Britt's instigation. When Christmas came round we didn't celebrate the occasion like normal families: after lunch with Mum and Ted in Hampstead, we'd then be driven by Bert to Elstead for more turkey with Dad and Britt.

Mum would feel anxious, knowing we were allowed to run wild at Brookfield without any discipline being exercised on us. Sarah got quite tipsy at the age of seven by drinking the wine from unfinished glasses after a dinner party one night. No one noticed what she was drinking and only when she started hiccupping was her condition realized. She slept very soundly that night.

We never observed set hours for going to bed and no one worried if we were still up at midnight. There were no rules. As long as we didn't impinge on Dad's time and enjoyment we knew that we could do as we pleased.

I had learned how to humour him by only saying what was necessary to keep the peace; in later years I was able to develop this technique with some skill. I was like a barometer at gauging

Dad's moods and could detect them by the tone of his voice. If he called out 'Michael' – then I knew that trouble awaited: if it was 'Mike' then I knew all was well.

My mother gave birth to Kate on 17 August: Dad sent some flowers and had actually gone to see her during her confinement. Ted didn't object. Dad too had news to impart: Britt was pregnant, but he said he was urging her to have an abortion. 'I've got Michael, I've got Sarah. I don't want any more children,' he told Mum. She was appalled.

Britt was aggrieved at the suggestion of terminating her pregnancy for no valid reason other than Dad's aversion to the increased responsibility; she rang Nanette and Bryan, who had stayed close to us as family friends. Nanette, who had two youngsters of her own, was aghast at the pressure that Dad was applying to Britt and she got Bryan to reprimand him.

Dad was always so changeable. He immediately turned course and a little later became demented by the possibility of Britt losing her baby. Suddenly we were being warned that our noisy behaviour would disturb Britt. One day Dad telephoned Mum and said: 'Michael and Sarah are coming back to you. They're driving us crazy. Britt will lose the baby if you don't have them back.'

Mum, just out of hospital and with Katie to nurse, could not help but think that Dad was being unreasonable, and that Britt was unaware of it. Mum had come to consider Britt a good stepmother for us. She had found a very warm and human side to her nature, much more than the glossy starlet image allowed.

When Kate was four months old, we had another half sister, Victoria, to share our lives. Victoria was born in the Welbeck Street Clinic in London on 20 January 1965, and among the telegrams of congratulation that poured in was one from Princess Margaret and Lord Snowdon and another from Prince Charles. The Royal family, including the Queen, Prince Philip and the Queen Mother, were devout Goon fans and Dad, as one of their favourite artists, had become a personal friend.

Lord Snowdon, who was always closer to Dad because of their mutual interest in photography, had taken pictures of Britt at

Kensington Palace. These appeared in the *Sunday Times* before their marriage and Dad called my mother to draw her attention to them, because he wanted her to approve his new bride.

Tony and Princess Margaret were more regular visitors to Brookfield than other members of the Royal family. On their first visit Dad demonstrated how I should bow and Britt taught Sarah to curtsey. But at the witching hour we got stage fright and hid under the kitchen table. We were drilled to be on our best behaviour. I was expected to put on a proper suit and tie and Sarah would wear the frilliest of her dresses. We were very nervous and considered Victoria lucky to be able to look out on the scene from the safety of her cot. We had to be very careful what we said and could not speak to a member of the Royal family without first being spoken to. Then we would have to preface our words with the customary 'Your Royal Highness'.

Once, we went on a picnic with the Royal couple to Windsor Great Park. It seemed like any other family gathering and when Sarah and I had finished our lunch we slipped away to play catch in the woods. Dad came chasing after us. 'What the hell do you think you're doing?' he cried.

I said, 'What do you mean? We've finished our lunch.'

'Oh no you haven't,' he said firmly, 'you're in the middle of it. You can't disappear from the table when Princess Margaret and Lord Snowdon are still eating. Come back at once.' We soon picked up correct etiquette after that.

Dad was persuaded by Tony to take up water skiing on the lake at Windsor and he bought a wetsuit and all the necessary skis and equipment. But he found it was a difficult sport to master and kept diving beneath the surface. Had it not been for Tony spurring him on, I am sure Dad would have lost interest sooner. Tony made a special double-length ski-bar for the tow rope so that he could accompany Dad on the runs and show him where he was making mistakes. But eventually my father gave up in despair. Water skiing came much more easily to Britt. She was as sure on water, balanced on a pair of skis as she was on the snow slopes of St Moritz where we were to take our winter holiday.

Princess Margaret and her husband came to film shows at our Elstead cinema which could seat twenty guests; the movie that caused most amusement was one shot by Dad and Tony of the family at large. It was given its premiere at Kensington Palace on the occasion of the Queen's 39th birthday and rescreened at Elstead many times. It was real burlesque with Princess Margaret impersonating Dad impersonating ... Princess Margaret, while Tony filmed the whole sequence. Dad also played a one-legged golfer and Britt starred as an old movie sex siren.

Prince Charles was also a guest at Brookfield and in casual sports jacket and flannels put in an appearance for the Goon reunions. Britt organized the dinner party with salmon, duck and other exotic dishes prepared by our new chef and the best French wines were brought from the cellars.

We were allowed a day off school for the occasion, but Sarah hid in the stables the whole time and didn't meet the Prince, much to Dad's chagrin, whereas I was reminded that I had shaken hands with the future King of England and would live to treasure the memory forever. I saw him once more in fact: playing polo at Windsor Great Park. At Christmas we received a personal card from Buckingham Palace from him, illustrated with one of his own water colours. The Prince loved the Goons probably more than any other member of the Royal family except for the Queen Mother. She always had a special place in Dad's affections.

During the grouse and pheasant shooting season Britt and Dad would wear tweeds and fleece-lined boots and Dad would often spend days out on the Royal estates with the various parties, dressed in full shooting gear, a deerstalker hat, hacking jacket, breeches and boots. He had also bought himself a £1200 Purdy twelve-bore shotgun.

Like Princess Margaret's son David, Viscount Linley, we had to remain at home during the shoots but Dad would return in triumph at dusk with a brace or two of pheasants that he had shot: these would be passed to the chef to prepare for dinner.

Princess Margaret and Tony came to another party at Elstead and Dad gave me a box of tricks so that I could provide the cabaret. I was far from being properly rehearsed but Spike and Michael Bentine gave me a helping hand behind a collapsible screen and at the end of the evening Princess Margaret was telling Father that Tommy Cooper (a well-known English 'magician') would soon be facing competition.

The Queen and Prince Philip entertained Dad and Britt at Windsor Castle the following Christmas. The Queen was always amused by Dad's antics. On another of his visits she had opened her drawing-room door to find him skating along the corridor on one of her son's trolleys. She joked with him. 'You'll find it's much safer to ride one of the horses out in the paddock, Mr Sellers.' I doubt if Her Majesty knew of Dad's equestrian activities, such as they were.

At Elstead, he had stocked the stables with a whole string of horses and employed grooms to run the show for him.

My horse was Steptoe; later on it was her foal Candy which belonged to Sarah. Britt rode out on Sungold and Dad's horse was named Hercules.

We all rode pretty well except for Dad, whose courage was sapped by the formidable sight of Hercules, who must have stood all of seventeen hands. Yet he would boast that he was always out, over meadow and dale, leaping ditches and dugouts.

'You won't find a better horse than Hercules,' Dad cried to many a fascinated listener. But in reality, the stable girls and grooms conducted a running wager on whether the day would ever arrive when he would actually climb into the saddle for he would always find some excuse not to go out with the morning ride.

When Princess Margaret and Tony were with us, Dad was too vocal about his prowess on Hercules and almost found himself committed. But as Hercules was being saddled for him, and the stable girls waited with bated breath to see him appear in his jodhpurs, he was saved by an alibi in the nick of time.

'I think I'd better scrub the idea,' he told them, with a careful measure of disappointment in his voice. 'You go out by all means, but I'd better not risk it. I'm starting a new movie tomorrow and I've got to be careful about insurance. I know the chances are only remote, but if I were to have an accident . . .'

Princess Margaret was understanding. Dad breathed again.

Accidents, of course, did occur. Sarah, whose love for horses was stronger than any other member of the family, was thrown badly and the horse's hoof gashed open her leg. The scars are still visible today.

But a more tragic event occurred. Both Steptoe and Candy had to be put down by the veterinary surgeon when it was discovered that they had both developed tumours. We did not know of the animals' plight until Dad took a call in America, where he was working at the time. We were staying with him and Sarah listened to the conversation. The news came as a great blow to her.

Victoria, now a toddler, was given Sarah's tiny palomino pony Buttercup to learn to ride on. She would go out on Buttercup in a special basket saddle and her confidence quickly grew so that she could soon manage the pony without assistance. She became very attached to the champagne coloured pony but when she was four years old, Dad in a moment of largesse, handed Buttercup on to Tony and Princess Margaret's children. Victoria was very upset and kept asking Britt where Buttercup disappeared to after it had been collected by horse box.

Dad often gave things away without thinking about other people's feelings. If he bought a gift, then he felt entitled to reclaim it at any time. When Victoria was old enough to understand what had happened, it wasn't in her nature to hold it against Tony or Princess Margaret. Indeed, her earliest memories of the Royal couple were happy. They gave her a fluffy teddy bear which she adored and would take to bed with her. And when she lost one of her baby teeth, Tony slipped a £5 note under her pillow: at Brookfield the fairies lived up to their aristocratic breeding!

Whatever social pleasures Dad engaged in at that time they

were not allowed to interfere with his need to return to work. After five months at home he was impatient and restless; the actor's natural yearning for expression stifled. Eventually, the doctors advised his gradual return, feeling that it might be more harmful to his health if he was allowed to vegetate at home, in deep frustration. Dad's comeback was as gentle as the doctors wished it. His initial role, necessitating only three days' filming, was in a television production, *Carol for Another Christmas*, shot in New York for UNO.

This prepared the way for something much more challenging. While insurance companies at this juncture were loath to offer cover for my father in any major film, Charles Feldman was one producer who was willing to take a risk with his own money in casting Dad for *What's New Pussycat?* with Peter O'Toole, Romy Schneider and Woody Allen.

If Dad's health had suffered a reversal during shooting, Feldman would have lost a personal fortune of £150,000, but his gamble, however calculated, came off. Dad's performance as an eccentric woman-crazed psychiatrist in the movie was a triumph. We went to Paris to see him filming on alternate weekends. Britt took us out to see the sights and we went to the top of the Eiffel Tower. Dad's confidence was restored and any doubts he harboured that his talents might have diminished were dissolved.

But now he was faced with the kind of problem that really needled him. Britt, with Victoria being cared for by a Swedish nanny named Inger, was also ready to resume work. Britt was determined to fulfil her ambitions and was much more resistant to any suggestion from my father that she might shelve her career in favour of his than my mother had been.

Dad was desperately jealous of Britt: he felt that a younger and more handsome man might make a play for her and that she would be especially vulnerable on a film set without him. Whenever Britt was offered a movie, the script would be carefully scrutinized by Dad who would then do everything in his power to talk Britt out of accepting the part.

She was offered a movie with Dean Martin. I think Britt was

keen on doing it, but my father was not happy about the screen-play. It involved some fairly passionate love scenes.

'Do you really want Dean Martin breathing bourbon fumes all over you?' said Dad, eager to find any flaw or defect in the script or co-stars, rather than admit to his own nagging jealousies.

There was only one way to appease Britt, while ensuring that he was able to keep a protective eye on her, and that was to become a 'husband and wife' team and work on movies together. Dad argued that if Richard Burton and Elizabeth Taylor could manage it, so could they. Britt didn't have any objections and she happily signed with Dad for two consecutive films that were to be shot in Rome. The first of these was *After the Fox*, in which Britt actually played my father's sister, and the other movie was *The Bobo*. Within a matter of weeks they left Brookfield for Italy.

When we visited them in the holidays we went by train, because there had been a plane crash somewhere and Dad, superstitious to the core, wasn't taking any risks. News of a crash always had that effect on him. He insisted we cross the Atlantic in the Queen Mary on one occasion in preference to taking a plane.

But now we were in Italy, which became yet another home to us. Dad had rented a shuttered villa in Rome set among a grove of olive trees, on the ancient Appian Way. We had a housekeeper and servants and of course Inger, whose main responsibility was Victoria. Tony Curtis was also filming in Rome at the time. He had taken a similar house only two hundred yards away, and Neil Simon who wrote the screenplay of *After the Fox* lived opposite us.

The paparazzi, Rome's infamous pack of photographers who trail celebrities to snap their least indiscretions, were intrigued by the sudden infiltration of so many stars on the Appian Way. No one could step outside the door without a shutter lens clicking. Britt enjoyed provoking them. She scootered out on a Vespa she had been given for doing a television advertisement and the paparazzi pursued her relentlessly.

Dad was in a state of high tension, as he was prone to be when contemplating a new movie. He would find fault with everything and everyone and from the moment the cameras rolled on *After the Fox* there were bad vibrations. Not detecting this undercurrent we were captivated by the set, which was an incredible replica of Rome's most famous thoroughfare, the Via Veneto, and all its shops. We hung outside a toy shop with our eyes glued to the windows.

In the meantime Dad was already falling out with the director, Vittorio de Sica. In the past he had admired the work of Italian directors, but their use of humour, especially in the case of this movie, was very different. The clash of wills reverberated.

The movie was being made under the aegis of Brookfield Productions, a company that Dad had formed with a close associate John Bryan, who, as the nominated producer, was now sitting in the hot seat. They had signed a six picture deal. Ironically *After the Fox* was to be their first and last. The two partners were constantly opposed over company policy and John refused to listen to Dad's suggestion that de Sica should be replaced.

The backlash was felt on the Appian Way.

Dad's increasing dissatisfaction was now directed towards Britt. 'You're a lousy bloody actress,' he screamed at her one night. 'Can't you get one scene right? Why don't you listen to what I tell you?'

But jealousy was still the root cause of his anger. Britt had dared to glance at a young Italian actor on the set and this had caused Dad's hackles to rise. At the height of the row he threw a chair at her and Britt climbed through a back window to escape. She ran across the Appian Way in her nightdress to find refuge with Neil Simon and his wife. By now we were all awake. The servants and Inger began switching on the lights, hoping thereby to quieten Dad down. Neil Simon rang and spoke to Dad, who left the house in his dressing gown to collect Britt. She came back on his arm sobbing and as they returned indoors we heard Dad crying too. He seemed to spend most of his life creating rows and then patching them up. Sometimes the process could be very costly for him.

When the film moved to a location on the breathtaking isle of Ischia we were booked into the Hotel Regina Isabella where Dad and Britt took one suite and we shared another. Britt invited her mother and two of her three brothers to join us for part of the stay. This did not exactly improve my father's temper. They would all chat away in Swedish to one another and Dad would claim to be forgotten. Again, ill-feeling between Dad and Britt erupted. Dad, rather than go sunbathing on the free days of the work schedule, would sulk in the suite.

Sarah's affection for Britt meant she would side with her when blame for the constant arguments was apportioned.

She would often say to me: 'It wasn't Britt's fault. It was Daddy's ... Did you hear what he called Britt?'

I could remember similar rows that Dad had with my mother and I told Sarah that he used to call Mum a bitch too and that it didn't mean anything.

But in each fresh quarrel that ominous word 'divorce' would resound all over the house and we would shiver, knowing its consequences only too well.

Sarah wasn't able to contain her secret anxieties forever and she questioned my father before he set out for the studios one morning.

'You're not going to divorce Britt, are you?' she asked.

Dad, in unusually good humour that day, appeared surprised at the suddenness of the question.

'What on earth are you talking about, Sarah?' he said. 'I wouldn't dream of divorcing Britvic. Why should I want to do that?'

Dad had always called our stepmother 'Britvic' whenever he felt in any way loving towards her, but our instincts as youngsters told us that Dad was only glossing over the cracks as he had tried to do before.

This marriage, like his last, was deteriorating in an identical pattern. Disenchantment and disharmony clouded most days.

Britt, normally bubbling with spirit, was low and despondent.

She would play lots of games with us and take us out for walks and for picnics, but Dad was more absent now and invariably when he came home another feud between them would develop.

Things were distinctly chilly at the time of their second movie, *The Bobo*. It was a light-veined script in which Dad was cast as a singing matador and Britt as his seductress, Olympia.

Only a day or two before shooting began Dad got his solicitors to write to Britt and tell her that he intended to file for divorce. It was suggested that while they were working on the movie together Britt should arrange to take separate accommodation.

The letter also frankly stated: 'Your husband intends to work with you in the same manner as he would with any other actress and he trusts you will reciprocate his intentions.'

Only a day later Dad relented and repaired his rift with Britt with a profusion of kisses and the usual gifts. He went out and bought all sorts of trinkets to give to Britt to show her how mistaken he was in thinking that they should separate when he loved her so much. One of the gifts was a gold Cartier watch. During their next serious row he was to stamp on it with the heel of his shoe and throw the particles down the loo. But for a week or two, while the production of *The Bobo* was assembled, there was relative peace.

This time we had taken a house on the Appia Antica. It was slightly smaller than the last one, but it had the statutory swimming pool and that was fundamental to our contentment if we were to keep out of harm's way.

It was not long before Dad and Britt were again at logger-heads. But now Dad became increasingly violent. Furniture and belongings were smashed and the damage didn't perturb *him*. Once he overturned the bed that they had slept on and Britt's teeth were chipped when one of the castors hit her mouth. Like my mother before her, Britt tried to save the marriage and stretched her patience and endurance beyond normal limits.

Welcome respite from the almost daily friction came when Dad, on a trip to Genoa, decided to buy a brand new yacht costing £150,000. Dad named it *The Bobo* after the movie and it was fitted out with every possible modern seagoing device, radar and automatic pilot included. Sleek and white hulled in design, it had six berths with three double suites.

We were quite breathless when we saw *The Bobo* for the first time. Dad told us that we were going to sail around the world in it and we believed him. Everything else in our young lives took on a minor significance compared to life on *The Bobo*. We were ready to set out on adventures like Jacques Cousteau, and were convinced we would be seeing whales and sharks and experiencing all sorts of hazards. Meanwhile we had our share of adventures in exotic spots like Capri, San Remo and Monte Carlo. I went for a spin in the super-powered Boston 'whaler' that trailed *The Bobo* as a tender. I hit a wave at high speed and the boat flipped over in the water. Luckily, I was thrown clear, since I could have been shredded to pieces by the roaring propellers. Bert came to the rescue and plucked me out of the water, but as I climbed aboard *The Bobo* my father gazed over my shoulder at the upturned Boston and said sadly, 'What have you done to my boat, Mike?'

That was Dad. He once crashed a car and climbed out unscathed. He rang Mum and told her, 'I'm sorry, but I've written off the jalopy.'

She asked, 'But what about *you*? Are *you* all right?'

'Oh yes,' said Dad, as though the thought hadn't occurred to him. 'I'm okay ...'

'Then why worry about the car?' said Mum in exasperation.

Dad was more proud of *The Bobo* than he had been of any of his regal cars. During the long hot summer seasons, cruising in Mediterranean waters, the yacht was to become the scene of countless cocktail parties that would last from noon till dawn. Dad, not usually high in the popularity polls, suddenly became the focus of attention.

The yacht's three-man crew found they were more usefully employed opening champagne bottles than manning the boat's huge diesel engines which lay dormant for most of the time.

We sailed to Sardinia to rendezvous with Princess Margaret and Tony, who were staying as guests of the Aga Khan. Sarah later told Mum that we had met the Earl of Cannes. Only by means of elimination was Mum able to understand that she meant the Aga Khan!

Sardinia was a high point in our calendar. Tony felt that at twelve years of age it was time I was taught how to ski and he proceeded to give me lessons under the critical eye of Britt and Princess Margaret. Victoria was learning to swim with Sarah and Inger and although she fell and cut her chin she wasn't deterred. She was soon splashing about in the warm blue waters alongside the yacht.

But in time, the enjoyment of being aboard *The Bobo* began to wane. Dad was already getting bored and making excuses to go to Rome or to fly back to London for weekends. We also had to return to England in time for the new school term.

While we had been in Rome, Peg had died and the shock hit Dad pretty hard because when he first heard that his mother was in hospital with a coronary, he ignored the suggestion of returning to London to see her. When he finally left, it was too late. He was filled with remorse and for weeks after the funeral he was deeply depressed.

He felt he could have contributed so much more for his mother in her twilight years, although he felt he had perhaps done more than most sons, having provided her with every comfort in life. Since Bill had died he had also given her a chauffeur-driven Bentley, so that she could do her shopping at any time and be taken out for afternoon rides into the country-side.

She would often stop outside Mum's house and tell the chauffeur, taking a sly dig at Britt, 'That's where my son's first wife lives. What a darling sweet girl she is.'

Sometimes Peg picked us up from school in the Bentley and this would particularly embarrass me because she would always lean down and kiss me. My friends would poke fun at me and say tauntingly: 'So who is Grannie's boy then?' But we also missed her very much and now that we were home once more we felt that a familiar face was missing.

Dad did something very strange within a few days of getting back. He brought Peg's clothes from her apartment and burnt them in a pile in the garden incinerator. Britt looked shocked and asked him: 'Peter, why are you doing that? Why don't you give them to Oxfam or some such church organization?'

Dad's lips tightened and his eyes flashed hostility. He stalked past Britt without saying a word. It might have been that he was trying to obliterate all memory of Peg, but if that was his intention, it was only a momentary delusion.

Dad was to become very sentimental about Peg. He would light a candle to her memory every Friday. When Sarah happened to mention how Peg had predicted that she wouldn't live to see another Christmas, Dad was again plunged into acute depression and cancelled a visit we were going to make to the film studios the next day to see him work.

On the living-room dresser he kept a framed picture of Peg and my father became hysterical when Britt accidentally knocked it over. The accident occurred when they were again in the middle of a quarrel and slapping each other's faces. Britt's return swipe knocked off Dad's hornrimmed spectacles and caught Peg's picture. It crashed to the floor and seeing it all in shattered pieces Dad burst into tears, sobbing that Britt had ruined his favourite picture of Peg.

'We'll never be able to replace it,' he moaned.

That particular row was to prove grievous to my father in more ways than one. He had just been awarded a CBE and the next day was due to be presented to the Queen at Buckingham Palace to receive. Britt had scratched his face and the next morning he had to call in one of the studio's make-up artists to powder over it.

'Luckily,' hissed Dad at Britt on his return from the Palace, 'the Queen didn't spot it. And, fortunately, neither did the photographers.'

8

Son of Fame

Our schooldays were as turbulent and traumatic as any other aspects of life under my father's rule. His responsibility as a parent extended to our enrolment into private schools, fitting us out with appropriate uniforms, and paying our fees.

But his contribution ended there. Anything else, like showing interest, helping with homework, attending speech days or concerts, and offering general encouragement were not forthcoming. Thank goodness we had Mum and Ted to rely on.

I was more of a rebel at school than either Sarah or Victoria. My kindergarten days passed without incident and my school reports at The Hall School in Hampstead looked fairly promising. But when my parents were divorced and I was sent to Ibstock, a preparatory school at Roehampton, seven miles south-west of London, I began to demonstrate my dissatisfaction with all that was happening around me. I cried tears of anger and desperation on my first day there, feeling my parents had abandoned me.

Eighteen months later, my father dictated I should go to a more fashionable boarding school. Frensham Heights, which was much closer to Elstead. I was now eleven and my new friends at school were impressed to learn who my father was. Once he came and collected me in his gold-coloured Ferrari and they got him to sign his autograph in their exercise books.

They assumed, of course, that because my father was rich I would always have a lot of money to throw around. They thought I was joking when I told them that Dad gave me £1 a week pocket money and that this would be withheld if I ever upset him.

My crisis days at Frensham's began when I started stealing things. At first it was fairly innocent, pinching biscuits and goodies from the school kitchens. But then I pocketed a master's cigarette lighter because I was now in a gang which surreptitiously smoked at break periods in a far corner of the playground. I escaped with a warning for this misdemeanour, but swiping our gardener's wages from his home was something very different.

Dad called the police to track down the thief and when he discovered it was me, after all of Brookfield's staff had been fingerprinted, he was horrified.

'Why in the hell did you do it?' he stormed. 'You've had everything you've ever wanted. Now you steal from me. Why? There must be an answer.'

I couldn't find one to satisfy him, except to say that he hadn't given me any pocket money for two weeks and that the boys at school thought I was 'loaded'. I had spent the £14 wages on pop records that I'd bought in Farnham with a friend. I offered to repay the gardener's wages out of my pocket money week by week and when Dad's temper cooled down he accepted the offer.

I had a bad time at Frensham's. The other kids would break anything I had: personal possessions in my room would be vandalized and even rulers and pencils were snapped into pieces. One or other of the kids would say: 'You can afford it. Your Dad's rich.' Even the teachers seemed to think that I had been born with a silver spoon in my mouth.

The headmaster said I was 'wild and unsettled', and called my parents in to discuss the situation with them. I can still recall that particular day, for my mother came out to Brookfield and met Britt. She said afterwards that Britt was concerned and sensible about my behaviour and had promised to do all she could to help.

With the school lying so close to Elstead, I saw no reason why I should be a full-time boarder. So some nights I would secretly slip away and return home on the bus. Dad didn't question my presence, assuming that I had been given permission. But when my moonlight flits were discovered I was again hauled before the headmaster. This time, he read the riot act and said he could no longer tolerate my conduct.

That afternoon I was due to go to the dentist.

Dad warned me that something was going to happen, but told me not to worry about it. I asked him what it was. His reply was as unique as any of his Goon-like classics. 'That's what I am telling you, Michael,' he said, 'don't worry about it.' I was expelled and as Dad advised – I didn't worry about it. But for my mother it was much harder to accept.

The headmaster at Frensham's suggested that I should have psychiatric treatment and appended this recommendation on my final report like a big, black mark. This made my mother's task in finding another school that would accept me much more difficult. Father had put my name down for half a dozen schools before I was born. As well as Eton, Harrow and Westminster, he had fortunately registered my name with a more modest establishment: King Alfred's, at Golders Green, where Sarah in later years was to join me in the co-educational system. But before I was accepted, the principal insisted that I should undertake the psychiatric treatment my last school recommended, so Mother arranged appointments for me with Dr Miller who passed me on to a child psychologist.

My visits to him usually resulted in a game of chess and he told my mother, in one report, that I was 'an insecure child lacking the attention of his father'. Later, as my conduct at school showed no signs of improving he diagnosed that I was going through an identity crisis and that my disruptive practices in the classroom were made in order to get attention.

The psychologist was getting closer to the truth. I no longer wanted to be Peter Sellers' son. I craved for my own identity. What had Dad done for me? Did he really care about me? Whenever I talked about school to him, he was always too busy to listen. His own activities and pursuits left him no time to spare for anyone else, not even his children.

I was asked to arrange the stage lighting for the school's

fiftieth anniversary pageant. It meant remaining in school over a weekend that I had promised to spend with Dad. When I told him about the project, feeling he would share in my excitement, he was peculiarly off-hand.

'Tell me the truth, Michael. You don't love me. You don't want to come to see me. Why invent excuses?' he bellowed. 'If that's how you feel about me then I have no wish to see you again. Is that understood? Stay at school. Stay wherever you like. But don't come home to me.'

I felt totally confused. What did I have to do to keep on the right side of my father? Could anything please him? Dad had suggested I might like to go into the theatre when I left school. Surely, being asked to do the lighting for the school play was the first step forward? A tutor, seeing how pensive and withdrawn I was in class the next morning, asked if anything was wrong. For the first time I felt anger burn within me, and I told him that my father had kicked me out of home. I didn't want to betray my father, but I felt it was time the school got an inkling of the truth.

When I was thirteen, like most of my chums in the class, I was smoking pot. It was easy to get. Dad was smoking it too, and he kept the grass in empty film canisters in the house. There was so much of the stuff that I knew he wouldn't miss a little. It was like his pills – he had thousands of them – and I would help myself to amphetamines or Mandrax sleeping pills.

But at school pot was always the favourite and we would roll joints in the neighbouring park.

My mother found out what was happening. She suspected that the source of our supply was from pushers, haunting venues where the day's big pop groups played at weekends. Some of it certainly came from there, but she did not guess that I was also poaching grass from Dad's hidden sources.

I went missing for a night, sleeping at a friend's house, and I forgot to call my mother. She broke down in tears when I got home the next morning and demanded to know where I had been. And Ted gave me a roasting too for causing her so much anxiety. She then told me she knew I was smoking pot and threatened to see the headmaster. She did, and caused a terrible furore. I was suspended for three weeks and faced with expulsion. Dad was summoned urgently to the school and sat with my mother in the headmaster's study as the report was read out to me. Dad looked in my direction and said in an admonishing tone that I must never smoke pot again.

I nodded my head, evidently with sufficient repentance to secure my readmission to King Alfred's for another term's battle.

My father, I knew, was being hypocritical and I stupidly thought that this gave me the licence to act the same way. (Ironically, a few months later, he gave a lecture at the London School of Economics and came out on the side of the pro-marijuana movement!)

By this time, my psychologist was more harassed than my headmaster. I got black-listed once more when I threw a pencil case across the classroom and hit a girl in the eye. Luckily, she was not badly hurt, but I was sent home for the rest of the day. Again the psychologist put this down to my identity crisis and looking back, I am sure he was right.

I wore a long, old overcoat at the time that I bought in a secondhand shop which my mother said Fagin would not have been seen dead in. I also refused to go to the hairdressers and my lank hair hung down over my shoulders like twists of straw. Mum asked me why I dressed that way and she says my answer rather summed up all the things the psychologist inferred: 'When people see me,' I said, 'they say, "There's that boy with the long hair" rather than, "there's Peter Sellers' son"'.

But some of my friends would still take delight in telling others who my father was and I hated it. The psychologist said that it was all part of my inferiority complex. There was really no need to disguise myself. I didn't resemble Dad in any way. My colouring was as fair as my mother's and I had inherited her blue eyes.

In my teens I was already six feet tall (I'm 6ft 2ins today). My height has always been one of the mysteries of the family.

Maybe, as Dad once suggested, it had something to do with the great Mendoza!

At times, my friends had good reason to tease me. When I was fourteen, Dad gave me a car as a birthday present; a mustard-coloured 850 cc Mini. It was brand new from the factory and had a special steering wheel and other equipment. Dad may not have been interested in my education generally but he clearly wanted to teach me to drive. We would go out all over the Elstead estate and when I came to take the official driving test three years later I passed with flying colours.

However, I imagine my car caused some resentment at school, although I tried hard not to boast about it.

At King Alfred's, I wasn't alone in having famous or unusual parents. There were one or two other children of famous people attending as pupils. Jazzman Humphrey Lyttleton's kids were there and so was Kathy Kubrick, daughter of Stanley Kubrick, who had been the director of two of Dad's films. Kathy was in my class for a while and I had a crush on her. She was a brunette and very pretty and we started going out together. She invited me home to dinner and I thought I was polite and said all the right things in front of her parents, but her father appeared to be extremely possessive of her; after I left he telephoned Dad and said: 'Keep your son away from my daughter.' Having heard of my transgressions at school he felt sure I would be a bad influence on her. Dad, to my surprise, dismissed the call lightly and was tickled pink by the thought that I was suddenly showing an interest in the opposite sex.

It was at this stage that Dad gave me a list of subjects that I should pay special attention to in my education but I tossed the piece of paper away without bothering to read it. I thought it was too late now for Dad to direct the way my education should go. I had never been academically minded and when I finally left school at the age of eighteen, having now won approval at King Alfred's, I just managed to pass three 'O' levels in woodwork and technical drawing, history and art. I also got CSEs in science and maths.

Dad wanted me to be a film director, but I am afraid I didn't live up to his expectations. When eventually I became a carpenter, spurning the glamorous life-style that he wanted me to follow, he simply asked me when I was going to get a 'real' job.

Sarah caught up with me at King Alfred's when she was eleven. She was tiresome in those days. While I was trying to play down the fact that I was the child of Peter Sellers, Sarah was doing the reverse.

'My father is Peter Sellers,' she would boast, 'didn't you see his film on television last night? It was great, wasn't it?'

I would shudder and growl at Sarah to keep quiet. Gradually she came to this conclusion herself when she saw that she was creating a barrier of jealousy that was reducing her popularity.

Sarah suffered more than I did from lack of communication with Dad. We could talk to my mother, and take our problems to her at any time.

Sarah painted Dad's portrait in water colours from one of his photographs. She took several weeks completing it and put a lot of work and painstaking effort into it. She presented it to Dad on his birthday and he thanked her for it. But the picture disappeared. Sarah came to the conclusion that Dad didn't care for it enough to hang it up in the home.

Sarah also went through a phase when she ducked out of lessons but overall she was much more dedicated and disciplined than I. She got four 'O' levels out of six but Dad was too uninterested to ask her how she fared. She then got three 'A' levels and was considering reading history at university.

She mentioned it to Dad and he replied: 'What do you want to do that for?' His appalled voice indicated that it was the most ridiculous suggestion he'd ever heard.

Sarah, at that point, knew she had to make her own decisions and her own way in life. She went on to study art first at Camberwell and then at the City and Guild in Kennington. She always sought Dad's approval but as I myself had experienced, his interest in what she was doing was vague.

Yet when Dad was away, and he telephoned, we would always have to take turns to tell him that we loved him. When

A publicity still taken at the Dorchester Hotel in the year of the marriage to Britt Ekland.

Above left: Elstead, where we spent so much of our childhood. The right wing was added by my father and built in the same Tudor style.

Below left: Lord Snowdon and Britt in Sardinia, on the Aga Khan's yacht.

Above: One of Princess Margaret's frequent visits to Elstead.

Ringo Starr bought Elstead from my father and in turn sold it to Stephen Stills. On this occasion Stephen had invited us to visit him at our old home.

Left: With Britt during the 'Yoga Days'. Santa Monica, California, 1967.

Below: Liza Minnelli and my father in 1973 when they had announced that they were to be married.

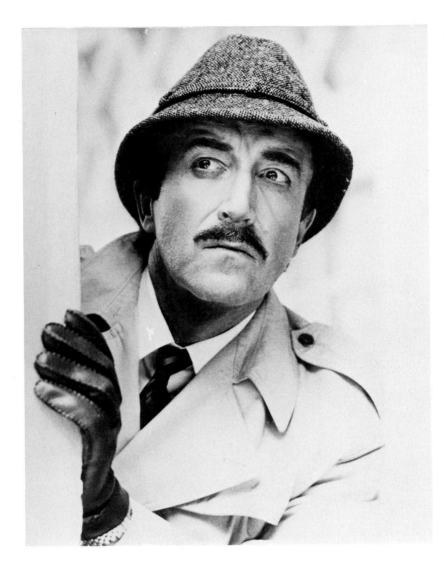

Clouseau.

friends came round and heard our conversations we would find it embarrassing to be heard saying, 'and I love you too, Daddy,' before putting down the receiver.

Sarah gradually learned how to humour my father, by weighing all her words very carefully before uttering them.

She once started praising Ted and the new house with a swimming pool and billiards room that he had bought for Mum, and she found that Dad was jealous of our family life, and the fact that Ted could now give us a home as luxurious as he could. Dad seethed with anger and played his familiar line, saying Sarah didn't love him and that didn't she realize that Ted was only her stepfather?

Sarah's countenance was always pretty jolly, despite all the unrest at home. She could be stubborn, argumentative and emotional at times but she wasn't anywhere near as quick tempered as Dad. With dark hair and brown eyes, she had a likeness to him, but as I've said, Victoria had a stronger resemblance. She has most of Dad's features, except for the aquiline nose – hers is more like Britt's. She has also got Dad's colouring and I would say she was the most recognizable as a Sellers among us.

Victoria's earliest memories are, of course, at Brookfield. She remembers jumping up and down with us on the trampoline that Dad erected in the grounds and she recalls the chicken hut and the geese, the ducks and the fields beyond. In her pastel pink bedroom along the corridor she slept at nights with the electric light on. She thought that Brookfield with its creaking floorboards was haunted.

She would often run along to her mother's bedroom and spend the rest of the night there, too afraid to return to her own room because of the 'noises'.

Dad would call her 'Toria' when he was feeling affectionate towards her. But he took little more interest in her than he had done with us. She was Britt's responsibility and if our stepmother was out for the day then Inger the nanny would take over.

Victoria had barely started school when Dad and Britt

were already talking of divorce and she grew up in the belief that divorce was a normal procedure. It wasn't until she was eight or nine that she also realized that we were only her half-brother and half-sister, although this didn't make any difference to her love for us or to our love for her. In the coming years, our hearts cried out for Victoria, who became a 'tug-of-love' child, torn between Britt and Dad, who didn't really consider Victoria's feelings; his sole aim was to oppose anything Britt suggested. There were bitter battles over the schools she should attend, and where and when she should spend her holidays.

Poor innocent Victoria was the victim of Dad's malice as he took revenge on Britt and the lawyers' letters that were exchanged between the two must have cost tens of thousands of pounds. Victoria would start at one school, only to find that she had been transferred to another. She went to school in Sweden, in America and in England. She spent one term as a pupil in my old school at Ibstock. There, Dad went to see her and ordered her to get her hair cut. She did. When Britt visited her a day or two later, she got a pair of scissors and cut her hair even shorter. She told Victoria she looked stupid with a fringe. On seeing the result Dad went mad, because Victoria was left looking like a bear.

'Don't listen to what your mother says,' he raged at her, 'only listen to me...' But hard though these times were, Victoria's agonies had only just begun.

9

Divorce from Britt

My father's marriage to Britt was crumbling by the day, if not by the hour. But their futile attempts to salvage the remnants went on for several painful months. They tried all sorts of cures. They bought a very elegant flat in Clarges Street, Mayfair, with art nouveau furnishings and decor. It was to be their town house where they could more conveniently entertain their friends.

They decided that they should no longer suffocate one another; that their marriage could be revitalized by working on separate projects. Dad deduced that in the past they had perhaps made the mistake of being too close to one another. His new approach sounded good in theory, but in practice it was to become a nightmare, as we discovered when we flew to Los Angeles where he was filming *I Love You, Alice B. Toklas* in which he played a lawyer who turns flower-power hippie.

We stayed in yet another rented house on Beverly Hills, but Dad was in the doldrums once more, pacing the rooms as though carrying the burdens of the world on his shoulders. It was not only his aversion to Hollywood that was antagonizing him. It was the knowledge that Britt was filming in New York, having signed to play a Quaker-girl-cum-music-hall-stripper in *The Night They Raided Minsky's*.

Every evening he would monopolize the telephone, questioning Britt about her day's shooting schedule and wanting to know who she lunched with and where she was going for dinner.

Dad was torturing himself in his jealousy of Britt and it brought disaster on the set of *Alice B. Toklas* where his moods caused constant conflict. The smallest things upset him. A script girl came on the floor wearing a purple sweater and Dad called a halt to filming until she was removed. 'Purple is an unlucky colour,' he declared to the amazed crew, 'I refuse to allow purple on any set where I work.'

He gave orders for the set to be 'closed', which ostensibly meant that the press was barred. This set up a rift between Dad and the established columnists. Joyce Haber of the *Los Angeles Times* wrote that: 'Peter Sellers was behaving like a brat.' And she reported that he had threatened to pull out of the movie unless the entire crew was changed because too much information about him was filtering out of the studios.

Against this unrest, he tussled with Britt, insisting that she fly out to join us at weekends. So she would take the last flight out of New York on Friday nights and the last one back on Sundays. Sometimes her co-star in the movie, Elliott Gould, would accompany her, as his situation was the reverse of Dad's. Elliott's wife Barbra Streisand was in Los Angeles working on *Funny Girl*. Occasionally, the two families dined together, and we were invited out to Elliott and Barbra's beach house at Malibu.

By the spring there was an amnesty. We headed back to Europe. Dad proposed we should all settle in St Moritz for a while: his accountants suggested he might like to think of Switzerland as being an eventual tax haven.

Britt's younger brothers Kalle and Bengt came over and the household suddenly rang with voices and high spirits. Dad actually encouraged our organized parties to local discotheques. I borrowed his clothes, which now fitted me, so that I could wear something new each time we went out.

We were in St Moritz for my birthday and Spike's kids came over with his wife to join the celebrations which Britt organized for me. But that night, for some inexplicable reason, Dad started to sulk and went to bed as I was about to blow out the candles on my cake.

As a peace gesture to Britt, Dad had promised to buy her a new Ferrari but when it arrived, he showed distinct reluctance to hand the keys over. It was clear that he wanted to keep the Ferrari for his own use and Britt, guessing that this was his motive, bought herself a Lotus.

It was in the summer, aboard *The Bobo*, that Dad informed us that he was going to divorce Britt. We could not mistake the sad resignation in his voice, as he told us that he would never marry again. 'Marriage is for cretins,' he said ruefully. 'Why should I need anyone else?'

He sighed, 'I wouldn't advise either of you ever to get married. Marriage simply doesn't work.'

Sarah afterwards said defiantly that she would marry one day despite Dad's discouragement.

His marriage to Britt effectively came to an end in Rome. Making a last ditch attempt at yet another reconciliation, they were staying at the Excelsior Hotel. A bitter row broke out between them over dinner and it carried on until the early hours of the morning. Other hotel residents complained about the noise as Dad ripped up Britt's clothes, stamped on her wedding ring and smashed her cassette radio into a hundred fragments. He then called his Italian agent and asked him to collect Britt as though she were a bundle of laundry, saying that his marriage was over. It was 4 a.m. in the morning and Britt was lucky to find another room in the adjacent Flora Hotel.

She was granted a divorce, on the grounds of mental cruelty, in London on 18 December 1968, along with a £30,000 settlement. She was given care and control of Victoria with joint custody.

Dad's reaction was exactly the same as that at the end of his first marriage. He didn't accept the fact that he was divorced. Britt was staying at the Dorchester just prior to her departure to Sweden for Christmas. Dad offered her the Clarges Street flat to stay in. She had Victoria with her and it was convenient in the circumstances. She was led to believe it was all going to be very 'civilized' – and accepted his offer. She even went out to dinner with him in a party that included Warren Beatty, Julie Christie, Roman Polanski and Sharon Tate.

But at the end of the evening Dad was feeling morose and did not seem to understand why or how their divorce had come about. Just as Victoria was going to bed in the Clarges Street flat, he suddenly threatened to kill Britt. Taking down the double-barrelled shotgun that he used on the royal pheasant shoots he pointed it at Britt, his finger coiled on the trigger. Britt stalled him.

'Don't be silly, Peter,' she soothed him. 'What reason have you got for killing me? The divorce is over now and if you kill me you will be the one who will suffer most. You will end up in prison for the rest of your life. Your career will be in ruins and you would never see Victoria again ...'

Dad apparently stood immovable in the doorway, still brandishing the gun, while Britt kept on talking to him, playing for time, saying how seriously he was putting his whole life at stake. Finally, she walked over to him and slipped the gun out of his trembling hands. Dad crumpled on the sofa and burst into tears like a child, burying his head between his hands. After that, we did not see Britt for a long, long time. She went to Rome to film and fell in love with an Italian producer, Count Ascanio Cicogna, known in the playboy world as 'Bino'.

In his spitefulness over their affair, Dad threatened to have Victoria made a ward of court if Britt lived with Bino. He hired a private eye to spy on them.

Bino bought a yacht, *The Rebit*, twice the size of *The Bobo*.

Dad was convinced that Bino had been talked into buying the yacht by Britt; and he was delighted when news came from Rome six months later that Bino's financial empire was in a state of collapse and *The Rebit* had been confiscated by creditors. But Dad was not totally without sympathy. When Bino committed suicide in Brazil a year later he was genuinely saddened by the news.

One afternoon I had gone with him to see his tailor Doug Hayward. Outside he suddenly said: 'Come on. We're going to Frank Sinatra's flat in Grosvenor Square.' I couldn't work out the purpose of our visit, but Dad seemed to know exactly where the flat was and once we got to the residential block he took a lift up to the penthouse.

He rang the bell and a nervous-looking fair-haired girl answered the door. She was quite thin, almost waif-like in blouse and skirt. I didn't think she was particularly pretty, but when Dad introduced me I managed to distinguish the name: it was Mia Farrow, who had once been married to Frank Sinatra. She looked strangely intense but she invited us in for tea.

She began talking to Dad about films and I started looking through the records in Sinatra's cabinet. I didn't see any of his there, though he had a huge number of jazz records.

Dad too had a collection at Elstead of more than 2000 – his favourites were recordings by Stan Getz, Oscar Peterson, Errol Garner, Glenn Miller and Count Basic. Mia said she would like to come down to Brookfield to hear some of them.

Mia's warmth emerged on her visit to Brookfield. She was fascinated by the house and walked with us through the grounds. Both Sarah and I wondered whether she was contemplating marriage to my father; it was to be a natural reaction whenever he brought new female friends to the house.

The newspapers were now speculating on a romance but when Mia disappeared back to America, her name wasn't mentioned again.

Dad decided to sell Brookfield. We weren't told since it seemed beyond him to consider that we too might have sentimental feelings about the place we had called home. He claimed it held too many memories for him. He was selling the house for £70,000 to Ringo Starr, having filmed with the Beatles' drummer on *The Magic Christian*. Dad had also met John Lennon who had offered £150,000, but he wasn't going to gazump Ringo and kept his word, even though he was again losing money on the deal. He had made at least £50,000 worth of renovations at Brookfield since we had been there.

Ringo came out to Brookfield to discuss the purchase and he played drums on Dad's old set in the studio. Ringo expressed surprise finding them there, not realizing that Dad had begun his career as a drummer. They got along well together and became close friends, enjoying pulling practical jokes on one another. But then practical jokes were a good way of killing tedium on film sets. Harry Frampton, Dad's make-up man, was always involved in the subterfuge.

A favourite trick was to 'rope up' a crew by knotting their coat belts together. Dad once posed as a Chinese waiter and persuaded a Swedish girl reporter that he was more interesting to interview than Peter Sellers. When one of Ringo's friends visited the film set he was the unsuspecting victim of the 'wallpaper hanging' act when empty cigarette packets, match boxes and other odd articles were taped to his back.

Graham Stark was always a victim for film set pranks. On one of the *Pink Panther* movies, scenes were deliberately halted so that Graham would have to refill his pipe. Tobacco was replaced by marijuana and Graham was stoned out of his mind at the end of the day's filming and unable to fathom out why the morning after. Dad and Blake Edwards also hoaxed Graham into sending for some newly discovered German virility pills – he did not realize that the advertising sheets he was shown were 'dummies' specially printed to dupe him.

Ringo's experiences on *The Magic Christian* were no less frenetic and he emerged from filming wearing a bigger grin than before. But Dad didn't. Having financially invested in the film he lost his shirt on it and no royalties ever came through.

During my schooldays the Beatles were practically everyone's heroes and I remember having a Beatle suit made for me. Dad claimed that before the Beatles were really known he was asked to invest in their careers. It would have meant an outlay of £2000 at the time but he had decided against it. Now he was ready to remedy that error by forming a property development company with George Harrison. George's business manager Dennis O'Brien also happened to act for Dad and soon they were exploring ways and means of expanding the new company.

Their first enterprise involved buying real estate in the

Seychelles and Dad flew out to East Africa for various abortive business talks. Another project involved a hotel deal with the Canadian government and various other offers were mulled over. Inevitably, Dad lost interest when he didn't see any immediate results and eventually resigned his directorships.

But George Harrison's life-style became a very strong influence on my father at this juncture. Sarah called these the 'yoga' days. We would visit George at his mystical Victorian house at Henley-on-Thames. In its basement was a grotto from which one could take a rowing boat out on the adjacent lake.

George had previously introduced Dad to the Indian sitar player, Ravi Shankar. A guru was found for him and my father would now go about the house wearing kaftans and chanting the scriptures. He would also burn incense and pray before a picture of Buddha. Every morning he would adopt various yoga positions and learned to stand on his head, which he once demonstrated in the cocktail lounge of a Jumbo jet at 30,000 feet. He befriended two young Americans who were members of the Hari Krishna sect. Shaven-headed and white robed they drove to the house in a Mercedes limousine. One of them produced a bag of glittering stones from a ruby mine that had been bequeathed to the cult by a convert. It was as well Dad didn't have a diamond mine among his assets, otherwise he might have been tempted to make a similar donation.

Dad's dedication during the yoga period meant special diets and macrobiotic food. Some of the salads were very pleasant but whenever Victoria came to the house she would complain because there was nothing substantial to eat!

Dad sometimes dressed in hippie clothes and bought a whole range of denims to fit the part. He brought two friends, disciples of the same guru, to Portugal to visit us on holiday with Mum and Ted. They spent all their time standing on their heads and cooking vegetarian food, but Dad abandoned them to us when he returned home.

His final disenchantment came when he asked Ravi Shankar to arrange a recital for his friends. Ravi's minions sought a substantial fee for the evening's entertainment and this astounded Dad because of the financial support he had given to Ravi in earlier months.

Dad's love life once more took precedence. Zsa Zsa Gabor's daughter Francesca Hilton, who was only 21 at the time, was often on the telephone line to him and I would take her calls. I first met her at the Playboy Club in London when he was appearing in cabaret with Sammy Davis Jnr (Sammy was a close friend of Dad's).

Sammy had brought his show *Golden Boy* to London and later in his dressing room at the Playboy he introduced Dad to Francesca. She came down to Brookfield before Ringo moved in, but I think my father was a bit cautious about her, fearing that her loquacious mother might have something to say on the subject of their relationship and thus might present him in a bad light in the newspaper columns.

Dad's next love was a Pan American hostess, Alice Joyce, who was invited to entertain his guests at home with her demonstration of one of the airline's safety procedures. At the end of one champagne-soaked evening, Dad actually proposed to her but Alice, while flattered, didn't take it seriously. This may have been a mistake on her part because Dad was in fact ready to enter marriage again despite his condemnation of the institution as a whole.

My father had still not recovered from the divorce and he continued to be infuriated by Britt, who was now apparently being escorted by the Queen's cousin, Patrick Lichfield.

Dad had only met Lichfield briefly, but hated the mere mention of his name. We were driving home one night when he thought he saw Patrick crossing the road. Dad drove straight at the figure and swore: 'There's that bastard Lichfield. We'll knock him down.' When we got closer and Dad saw he was mistaken, he growled, 'pity!', as we swerved past at high speed.

He still wanted his revenge on Britt for all their past troubles. She was now 'Ekland' in all conversations and for good measure was 'a lousy actress', 'a gold digger', and later 'a professional girlfriend who was an amateur at everything else'.

Victoria was always tearful when her father described Britt in these terms. 'Why do you call Mummy such names?' she kept asking.

In the meantime, marital problems had also beset Princess Margaret and Tony. They were now thinking about separation and Tony was seeing Lady Jacqueline Rufus Isaacs, now present at most of Dad's parties.

He usually trod very carefully in his contacts with the Royal family during this period. His admiration and respect for Tony as a friend saved him from making a fool of himself over Princess Margaret.

'I was always very very fond of her,' he confided to me, 'and now that we were both free agents there didn't seem to be any reason why I should not have an affair with her. I wanted to but couldn't. I knew I would never be able to look Tony straight between the eyes again without feeling guilty.'

Princess Margaret entertained my father at Kensington Palace one evening. He said she was wearing a low cut gown and after dinner all the servants disappeared. They were alone. They were sitting talking to one another when suddenly Dad realised how attractive Princess Margaret was.

'My God' he thought, 'if I don't behave myself I'm going to end up in the Tower.'

Later Dad fantasised to me: 'I didn't know what the protocol was on these occasions! Besides there wasn't a copy of Burke's Peerage to hand.'

The Princess asked to meet Warren Beatty which was a relief to Dad because it meant they could keep their relationship on a friendly basis.

When Warren was in town a month later Dad rang him and said that 'someone special' wished to meet him.

Warren, his interest aroused, enquired who. But Dad told him it was a secret.

Dad arranged to collect Princess Margaret for dinner in his Rolls-Royce and then to pick up Warren from his hotel in Park Lane. When he climbed into the car and recognized his blind date he gasped: 'Jeezers, Pete, ain't that something? I'm glad to make your acquaintance, Ma'am.'

Warren certainly came to Europe with a reputation as a womanizer. Earlier in the year he had stayed aboard *The Bobo* and I remember trying to sleep one night beneath the top deck over which Warren was sliding with one of the bikini clad glamour girls who had brightened the sights of the day.

Dad's friendship with Tony Snowdon was one of mutual respect and shared interests. Dad admired his work and the way he put together picture spreads for *Paris Match*, the *Sunday Times* and *Vogue*. So inspired was Dad that he too acquired the first of several *Vogue* commissions to photograph the children of famous people. Dad got many of his friends to co-operate including Michael Caine, Stewart Granger and Jennifer Jones and was persuaded to include one of his own children in the series.

Sarah, posing in a long white cotton dress, flew the family flag very well. But the assignment turned sour for Dad when he came to photograph Walter Matthau. He was a strange man and for some reason seemed to take offence. He couldn't hurry through the session fast enough. As he left he crashed his Mercedes on a post and Dad went to commiserate. But Walter merely said 'It's nothing,' even though he had ripped the whole of one side off the car.

Sarah also felt inspired to take up photography and it was then that Tony wrote her a six-page hand-written letter of instruction for beginners which helped her a great deal.

Having left school, it was time to think about my own future. Dad would have been happy if I had chosen to go into the theatre and did his best to persuade me into it. I was actually given a small part in *The Magic Christian* as a young hippie in an Afghan coat and I was paid £30 for five days' work.

My debut however had been made in *Mr Topaze* when I was

only six years old. I pretended to be a pupil in a classroom, with Dad as the teacher! I was also cast as a musician lying in a bathtub in a scene for *There's a Girl In My Soup* but found myself envying Dad's part a little more – sharing a nude bed scene with Goldie Hawn!

Dad was very patient with me. Blake Edwards invited me to work on the video equipment of *The Return of the Pink Panther*. My initial enthusiasm however quickly waned. For three months I just hung around on the set, with less to do than the clapper-board boy.

When we were little we used to know film sets better than our nurseries. Dad had arranged for us to be around during the making of most of his movies. We knew how the cameras were loaded and operated, how the lighting was arranged and the skill required to select and assemble the props.

Induced by Dad I once made a home movie with friends at school and it had been good fun. Dad had even edited one of his short feature movies, *The Running Jumping Standing Still Film* on the wall of my bedroom. But I was still a long way from wanting to take up the profession seriously.

My first job on leaving school was with a local Hampstead radio-electrical company, installing hi-fi equipment. But Dad got me placed as a sound engineer in the Oxford Circus recording studios run by George Martin, who not only produced Dad's albums, but also those of the Beatles. Spike's son Sean worked there too, and for a time we shared a flat together.

We worked with many of the day's top bands. I even got to play bass guitar myself and my name was credited on various albums. I proudly showed the sleeves to Dad but he wasn't particularly impressed. Sean and I were regarded as the terrors of the studio, but eighteen months later we both wanted to escape from the pop/drug scene and started a decorating business together, before I decided on my career as a carpenter.

Sarah was not smitten with show business either. She had a small walk-on part in *Hoffman*, and in one of the *Pink Panthers* she was seen as a fairground booth attendant. She thought she lacked the confidence to become an actress and she also felt that she would be living in Dad's shadow, suspecting she would always be known as Peter Sellers' daughter. Her final thought was that there were too many discontented people in ˙show business, people who never seemed to be able to find happiness.

Victoria on the other hand grew up liking the idea of becoming an actress and today she is still thinking in those terms, having sung with a pop group in Los Angeles during weekend breaks from school. It could yet be that the name of Sellers will be one to be reckoned with again.

Miranda's Pedigree

The first time I saw Miranda Quarry, who was to become our second stepmother, was at a dinner party in a Chinese restaurant in London. Dad was holding court in the presence of Warren Beatty and Polish film director Roman Polanski with the usual retinue of jet-set glamour girls. My eyes rested on someone new in the pack: a pretty, fair-haired girl whose hand was firmly on Dad's arm. With her free hand, she was trying to manipulate her chopsticks but without success – partly, I realized, because she was stoned. Someone in the party, and I suspected it was Dad, had been coating the biscuits with a certain brand of honey shipped from Italy by a lady who persuaded her bees to pollinate amid the blossom of marijuana plants. The little jars of honey were assumed to be 'a gourmet's delight at the time and thus avoided the detection of Scotland Yard's Drug Squad. They were difficult to find and expensive to buy.

Miranda, whose fair complexion required only the lightest of make-up, was of a classical English mould; one of the debutante breed whose aspirations in society were helped by the fact that her stepfather was Lord Mancroft, the former Conservative cabinet minister.

Dad beckoned me to sit down and introduced me to her. She giggled, 'Peter, I didn't know you had a teenage son.' Turning to me, she said: 'Would you like to try some of our honey? Put some on the crackers. It's lovely.' Dad nodded consent, though only a few days before he had been lecturing me once more on the dangers of becoming a 'druggie' when I admitted to him that I had taken LSD.

When I next saw Miranda, aboard *The Bobo* in the South of France a month or two later, she apologized for her behaviour in the restaurant and said, 'I'm sorry if I gave the wrong impression of myself. I don't normally act that way.'

By now Dad had changed the yacht's name to *Victoria* and later *Maria* was added. She finally became registered as the *Victoria Maria* which may have been the only public compliment he ever paid to one of us.

The summer season arrived and the water ski equipment was cleaned and polished. The speedboat on the aft deck was made ready. We sailed first to Cap Ferrat to see David Niven and his wife Hjordis. We then tied up in Monte Carlo, alongside a rather larger and more luxurious yacht that belonged to Sam Spiegel, the Hollywood film mogul. Dad had met Miranda through Spiegel and one of the guests aboard the Hollywood tycoon's boat was Kathy Green, an American musician's daughter, who was in her late twenties. I formed a friendship with her which infuriated Sam, who no doubt felt that he was about to lose another of his guests.

Sam – we called him 'Shorts' because he favoured a pair of Bermuda-style shorts that started at his knees and came half way up his chest – sent a cryptic message through his skipper that the less I saw of Kathy the better. We ignored it. At 16 years of age it was no more than an infatuation on my part, and Kathy, who was very down to earth, objected to the implications. She wasn't one of the starlet breed who stretched out on the sun decks ready to sleep their way to success. Monte Carlo that summer would not have been the same without her.

Miranda, conversely, didn't like it on the boat and would often prefer to book into hotels on the quayside. She was scared of the water. One day Dad called on the ship's radio and sent a message for me to go to Cap Ferrat to pick him up. I took his Riva speedboat *Bluebottle II* to keep the rendezvous at the *Voile D'or*. I arrived there and waited off shore for 90 minutes but there was no sign of him. So I got through on the ship-to-ship radio to discover Dad had changed his mind but hadn't bothered to let me know! He had gone out to lunch with Miranda, joining a party with Leslie Bricusse, Tony Newley, David Niven and Roger Moore.

Dad, unsure as ever about marriage, somehow kept the relationship with Miranda in a state of limbo for two years. But it survived all the usual qualms, tantrums and suspicions.

Once they were out in his silver Rolls-Royce and got themselves into a hiatus that was to have disastrous consequences. Dad parking the Rolls became so incensed by something Miranda said, that he deliberately crashed the car. He drove into another Rolls and then reversed into the car behind. The police were called and Dad was arrested and taken to Gerald Row police station in Belgravia where he was held until 6 a.m. before solicitors were roused to arrange his release, which came on the assurance that Dad would pay for all damage he had caused. No charges were brought against him and in that he was fortunate. All three cars were badly damaged and Dad's own Rolls-Royce, one he had purchased from playwright Terence Rattigan, was a mess – its coachwork dented front and rear.

Dad didn't talk to Miranda for some weeks after the incident. Indeed, we could have been forgiven for thinking that we wouldn't see Miranda again, for Dad started wooing Britt once more and actually persuaded her to join his party for the royal premiere of *The Magic Christian*.

Sarah went with Dad and was presented to Princess Margaret. I accompanied Britt. Reaching the West End cinema, I was ready to turn and run when I caught sight of the crowd that was gathered on the pavements, with a three-line array of photographers. But Britt steadied my arm, put on a winning smile and whispered to me to remain calm, as I tried to skate unnoticed across the red carpet rolled out for the stars. Britt didn't give Dad any opportunity to repair old alliances that night. There was no longer a future between them.

Stricken by loneliness, Dad decided to repair his friendship with Miranda, but this time she wasn't going to settle for anything less than marriage. When Sarah saw the newspaper bill-boards announcing 'Sellers to Marry Miranda Quarry', she was sure that the press had got it wrong for once. 'They're not even on speaking terms,' she told my mother.

I was also taken unawares. I'd gone to Venice to join *The Bobo* for the last leg of its summer cruise. As I stepped on to the boat, a dishevelled Dad was disembarking in a hurry. I asked him where he was going as I tossed my bags into the cabin.

'Back to London,' he said.

I was bewildered. 'But you've invited me for the holiday,' I reminded him. He shrugged: 'Well, the boat's yours. Get on with it. Don't worry about me.'

Dad was pursuing Miranda. By coincidence I had bumped into her at Venice airport. She was looking very upset – having left the yacht only hours earlier. I guessed by her expression that she and Dad had been having a row.

It emerged later that they had discussed marriage. Miranda wanted to fix a definite date and now Dad, scurrying to London, was ready to agree. The first thing he did, back in London, was to call Caxton Hall to arrange the ceremony. It was kept very quiet and Dad and Miranda exchanged matching wedding rings. Sarah went to the wedding and cried. She didn't want Dad to marry Miranda because she suspected we were resented in some way.

Neither Sarah nor Victoria was invited to be a bridesmaid, but Miranda's two favourite Pekinese dogs Tabitha and Thomasina were prominently featured in the pictures and Bert Mortimer was Dad's best man.

Only hours before the ceremony, Dad had telephoned both my mother and Britt and actually laid blame on them for the fact that he was being forced into marrying Miranda.

Mum told him he was suffering from an attack of nerves and that he would soon make the adjustment, while Britt simply encouraged him and wished him every happiness.

Miranda had certainly called the shots, if Dad was to be believed. Still besieged with tax problems, Dad had been giving thought to making his future home abroad. At first they rented a house in London's Cheyne Walk, Chelsea, and occupied it for a year. Miranda liked the house to be run in the traditional manner. She and Dad held court upstairs; children and servants were relegated downstairs.

Miranda's. parents insisted that Father should take out a £100,000 insurance cover as his health was still questionable. No doubt these were just two of the requirements laid down by Lord and Lady Mancroft, who strongly objected to the marriage. They were not happy about the fact that Miranda was marrying a man who was 22 years older than herself. They were even less enthusiastic about the fact that Father was an entertainer with a working-class background. Fame was not a substitute for blue-blooded breeding. They wanted Miranda to marry into the aristocracy, preferably someone with a title. Miranda ignored the protests. She argued that if Dad was accepted by the Queen and other members of the Royal family, then it was unlikely that society would ignore him. Eventually her parents gave their reluctant approval.

Miranda found the celebrity world fascinating. Dining with stars like Michael Caine, Warren Beatty, Julie Christie and playboy boss Victor Lownes furnished her with the kind of titillation that society thrives on. But she wasn't always so good at putting a name to a familiar face. She asked Henry Fonda who he was at one party and the legendary Hollywood actor sighed deeply and walked away in disgust.

Dad would sometimes lose patience with her at moments like this and when she ventured to defend the violence of Sam Peckinpah's films, she found Dad's views were directly opposed to those she was expressing. Unfortunately, Dad concluded the discussion on a rather violent note: by punching a hole with his fist through the papier-mâché wall in the Aretusa restaurant where we were lunching. Waiters scurried to our table and asked Dad if anything was the matter. 'Yes,' groaned Dad, rubbing the pained knuckles of his hand. 'How can my wife support Sam Peckinpah? What does she know about the film business?'

Miranda tolerated Dad's erratic life-style. She loved the

parties, the champagne and the first-class trips to New York, Paris and Rome. I came to the conclusion that she was the caricature of a classy English lady who couldn't ever step down from her social pedestal.

Miranda was with Dad in Paris when he first dabbled in 'acid'. He had a bad trip and Miranda had to nurse him through it. He became very touchy about the experience, vowing he would never touch LSD again. Like Miranda, he was happier smoking pot and we indulged to our heart's content aboard *The Bobo* when she was at sea. By now, Dad more or less accepted the fact that I was also a pot-smoker.

Once, leaving the yacht in a hurry for London, he handed me a container stuffed with Acapulco Gold and asked me to toss it overboard rather than risk taking it through Customs.

Dad expounded early in the marriage on the theory that his own world would integrate amicably with Miranda's. He wanted to sample the rarified atmosphere of the lives of the landed gentry and Miranda held his passport to it. For a time it was a romantic enough notion: dinner parties in Belgravia homes, champagne and picnic-basket days at Royal Ascot and Henley, glittering nights of ballet and opera at Covent Garden. But ultimately Dad got bored with it all. His basic down-to earth attitude, his need to say precisely what he felt at any time, could not long be restrained. Soon his dislike of the stuffy, pretentious life style of society people was to emerge. Society gadabouts in their cravats and showy sports cars were now put down by him as 'chinless wonders', while Belgravia's social set became the 'Eaton Square Mob'.

At this period, Dad's level of patience and tolerance was running pretty low. His career had hit a very rough patch. His last four films had flopped badly, including the ten-million-dollar *Casino Royale* in which he played the bogus James Bond. None of the major studios wanted to invest in his talents and he didn't have too many sympathizers. His slanging matches on film sets with directors like Robert Parrish, De Sica and Joe McGrath didn't generate much friendliness towards him. There was also his confrontation with Hollywood producer Walter Mirisch on issues affecting the way the industry should be run.

Dad was described as an 'asshole' by those Hollywood protagonists who were ready now to plug a hole through his career. Not that he was unaware of his enemies. He kept what he called a 'shit list' of producers, directors, newspaper columnists and critics aligned against him. But it was his former allies who turned coat that caused Dad the most pain. One afternoon he came home crestfallen because an old friend had deliberately avoided him. 'When you're bad news,' despaired Dad, 'no one wants to know . . .'

Friendship wasn't Dad's strongest point at the best of times. Spike, Graham and David, not to mention Bryan Forbes, all suffered the foibles of his unpredictable temperament. To be a friend of Dad was like running an assault course with no finishing line. They must all have known they were going to be insulted and abused. Anyone who could stand up after that kind of treatment and remain loyal to him was indeed a true friend.

Big stars like Sammy Davis Jnr, Orson Welles and Elliott Gould who might have been lasting friends, were also exasperated by my father's complex behaviour. Sammy was the closest, enticing Dad out on night club forays that lasted until dawn. This meant, for Dad at least, spending the whole of the next day in bed recuperating – but for Sammy it was a routine exercise. After a couple of hours' sleep he was revived and ready for action once more.

'I can't live in Sammy's nocturnal world,' complained Dad, when it was apparent their friendship was cooling.

Orson Welles was totally mystified by Dad's strange ways. Though they began as friends, Dad didn't want to work in the shadow of Orson's gargantuan presence on *Casino Royale* and this led to bitter conflicts which went unhealed. His friendship with Elliott Gould, on the other hand, just drifted into obscurity. There wasn't any particular reason, except that Dad just couldn't be bothered to keep contact. Most friendships with other artists declined this way.

But if Dad was resentful and suspicious of his associates at this time, then he had to thank two of his older friends who were now to resurrect his career. John and Roy Boulting managed to talk Mike Frankovich into casting Dad alongside Goldie Hawn for the Columbia comedy, *There's a Girl In My Soup*, the film in which, as I have said, I was also to play a small role.

The Boultings convinced Frankovich, who had earlier called Dad a 'sonofabitch', that the genius of Peter Sellers was parallel to that of Charlie Chaplin. The film was crucial to Dad's financial affairs: he was going to get 350,000 US dollars plus 10 per cent of the profits. His role in the movie as a woman-chasing gourmet was the nearest he ever came to playing himself.

Dad was already counting his coppers. He decided to sell *The Bobo* which was costing £75,000 a year to maintain. The French-born skipper Captain Jerome Varello wasn't very happy about Dad's decision, but there was nothing he could do.

Dad also sold the Clarges Street apartment in Mayfair and his cars went under the hammer too, the Ferrari and Rolls-Royce among them. The only one he retained was the Mercedes which was a second-hand model he bought from Blake Edwards.

It was Blake who had a hand in determining our move from London to Ireland. He had been making a picture there with his wife Julie Andrews and they had filmed some sequences at a stately home close to the village of Maynooth, just over an hour's run from Dublin. Dad made some enquiries. The mansion stood in 1000 acres. Through the summer months it was open to the public. Even if it had been for sale it would have been well beyond my father's means. But on the estate, attached to the mansion was a coach house which was vacant at the time. Dad and Miranda went to see it and fell in love with it.

It was a high-ceilinged period house which looked out over the grounds. They were told that if they bought it they could also rent rooms in the East Wing of the mansion whenever they had guests. The idea appealed to them. For Miranda it was perfect. She had strong family connections in Eire and knew as many titled folk there as in England.

Dad was equally delighted: the Republic was a tax haven for writers and artists who were classified as 'exempt'.

So the move to Maynooth was made; the estate was idyllic. Miranda was in her element in these surroundings. In sheepskin jackets, silk scarves and fur-lined boots she blended perfectly into the countryside and might well have been mistaken for the squire's wife by the tourists who flocked to the estate during the summer months and paid their 50 pence to look round the house. Later, Sarah and I acted as guides.

The rooms of the coach house were more modest than those of the larger house, but Miranda created a pleasant atmosphere by furnishing it with Chippendale and flowered curtains. She also found an Italian artist to paint the ground floor loo with nudes and phallic symbols. Fluorescent paint was used on the wall-to-wall mural, which was lit by an ultra-violet lamp.

When we stayed on the estate we occupied the guest rooms in the mansion and so did Bert. But the servants, two maids and a housekeeper, lived out.

Miranda was not able to drive because she was used to having a chauffeur so she found Bert invaluable on shopping jaunts to Dublin, to collect provisions when deliveries weren't on time. The fabric of life was in keeping with the traditions she was accustomed to. Our weekends were spent out with noble lords and ladies and their beloved polo ponies or visiting stud farms to purchase more horses for the paddocks. In some ways Miranda was very disciplined and frowned on the bad habits of the young. Indeed, she went so far as to tell Sarah that she hated children; did not think they should be seen or heard. She repeated to us the rules of her own childhood, where she was only allowed to see her parents at breakfast time and in the evening when the governess would take her through to the drawing room to bid good night. She also wanted to mould Sarah and Victoria as young ladies who might one day be considered as debutantes and dressed Victoria in frilly ribboned dresses, though when at home she was allowed to wear sweaters and jeans. Miranda also considered that she was too thin and would urge her to eat creamy cakes.

She thought we were all slovenly, not only in dress, but in the way we spoke and in our deportment. Even though I was sixteen and had helped Miranda to organize her London flat, she was equally critical of me. She urged Dad to see that we all took elocution lessons and also suggested sending Sarah and Victoria to finishing schools in Switzerland. So Dad wrote a list of complaints about our general behaviour and our inability to speak the Queen's English properly, sending a copy to Britt and Mother. Their reaction was identical – why this sudden interest in our education? And there the matter rested.

If Miranda seemed to resent us, then I imagine it was due to the fact that we were the children of Dad's previous marriages. There was a rare, if not unique occasion, when Miranda, just before marrying Dad, telephoned him to discover he was having afternoon tea with us and his two compatible ex-wives!

She was annoyed because he showed some reluctance in leaving us to keep an appointment with her.

'I don't see my family that often,' he said tersely.

It was pretty clear to us that Miranda wasn't thinking of having any children of her own. Not at that stage, at least. But she talked of her 'babies': a menagerie of five dogs, two cats and ten parrots who were housed in cages in the flower room but were allowed the free run of the house. The smell and the noise were unbearable, but she didn't seem to notice. Sometimes the dogs would bound into the house covered in dung and I would tell Miranda that she should have to put them out because of their filthy state.

Her puritanical rules about children were relaxed when it came to the animals. They were treated much more royally. Often the dogs would be given fillet steaks to eat, while we would be offered scrambled eggs or baked beans for dinner. She also cooked the animals roast chicken and we were not allowed to go anywhere near the oven. Dad would filch a chicken leg unaware he was eating the pet food! For some reason, he assumed that chicken constituted the family menu and Miranda didn't lead him to believe otherwise! She doted on the animals, most of which were named after Beatrix Potter characters, including a cockatoo who was called Jemima.

It wasn't too long, of course, before the animals began to wear down my father's nerves. We were constantly falling over them but even when we gently pushed them aside we would invoke Miranda's anger. All of us were asked to take the dogs out for long walks and the temptation was always to lose one deliberately. Once I persuaded Bert to drop off one of the Pekinese when we were a few miles out from the estate, but it still managed to find its way back. Ironically, I was one of the search party that Miranda rustled together to look for her 'darling, missing little baby'.

The parrots, despite creating mass destruction in the home, were also treated with similar affection. But their squawking was deafening and they would unnervingly descend on people's heads at dinner.

Dad, unable to quieten the cockatoo, attempted to strangle it but the bird's flapping wings prevented him from tightening his grip on its neck. We thought Jemima would be able to count her blessings for a merciful escape, but the next morning she was lying dead in her cage. Dad wore an expression of guilt. Probably she died from a heart attack – at least, that was what he said in Miranda's presence.

Dad's patience with animals was limited. It could expire at any time. Especially if he lost interest in them, or they became a nuisance. Miranda acquired a Shih-tzu puppy when we were on a visit to California. It was allowed free licence about the house we were renting. I was swimming in the pool one afternoon when Dad and Miranda, on the verandah nearby, began arguing and the Shih-tzu was the cause. 'What in the hell do you want another dog for?' roared Dad. 'Haven't you got enough?'

Suddenly the sliding doors to the verandah opened. An outstretched hand appeared like the jib of a crane being mobilized to discharge its cargo. I caught sight of the poor unfortunate Shih-tzu being held aloft, now poised over the edge of the swimming pool.

The luckless puppy sank into the depths of the pool. As it

submerged beneath the surface, I swam across to that side of the pool and pulled the wretched animal to safety.

To please Miranda, Father smuggled the dog into Dublin via London's Heathrow, risking arrest by customs officials. (By then he was a committed tax exile.) It was a terrible gamble to take. The puppy was given a sleeping pill but woke in its holdall as it was taken through Heathrow's corridors to the transit lounge. Luckily, no one heard the dog yapping before it went back to sleep. In the terminal, a friend picked up the holdall and walked out with it, so avoiding the necessary quarantine restrictions. He later took the dog into Dublin to be reunited with Miranda and the menagerie.

Miranda rarely accompanied Dad on the sixty days a year that he was legitimately allowed back into London. 'My babies don't like flying,' she would say.

On the first occasion Miranda returned alone to London, Dad got so fed up with the animals around his feet at Maynooth, that he arranged their passage to Heathrow in the hold of a cargo plane. He then alerted Miranda, saying: 'Your babies are waiting for you at Heathrow. You'd better get out there and collect them.' When next Miranda was staying in London she fell sick with meningitis and Dad spent all the days he could at her hospital bedside.

When Victoria came in from America she was given another of the rooms in the east wing of the mansion. Four of the dogs expected to sleep on her bed as usual. Victoria, who was only five years old at the time, was disturbed, and could not sleep. She went in search of the loo but could not find one and began screaming. Bert who was occupying an adjacent room went to her rescue. Miranda was unsympathetic and although it was clear she was frightened, Victoria had to remain in the big house. Victoria could not understand why Miranda would not allow her to sleep in the same house as her father.

Miranda surprised us, however, by throwing a birthday party for Victoria. The irony was that Victoria didn't know any of the one hundred and fifty children who were invited. They were carefully selected and were the youngsters of the elite.

'Everyone brought me a present, but I didn't know any of the children's names,' Victoria remembers. She posed for pictures astride a toy reindeer with a boy who was also celebrating his birthday. Everyone was in fancy dress and the tables were laid out with fizzy drinks, cakes, jellies and sandwiches.

Sarah's schooling became a touchy subject once again. Dad insisted that she should come to Maynooth after staying on holiday in California with Blake's daughter Jenny Edwards. He thought she should go to school locally, or even in Dublin, in preparation for the proposed Swiss boarding school. Sarah was then attending King Alfred's in London and was happy there. She told Dad that she wanted to go back to London to be with Mum and Ted. That only made matters worse. When she protested she would lose all her friends, Dad said: 'Oh you'll get over it. You'll make new friends here.' Fortunately, Mum rang and spoke to Dad. She told him his ideas for Sarah were preposterous and that she should return to London in time for the school term at King Alfred's. Only then did Dad give way.

Sarah always thought that Miranda was 'snooty' and her cold, detached manner must have given this impression in the eyes of an adolescent. When she was thrown from a moped after leaving a champagne party Sarah scarred her leg and stomach badly, but Miranda didn't appear perturbed by her injuries, nor did she go to Sarah's room to visit her. Yet if one of the dogs got a cold then the vet would be instantly summoned! The animals were always given priority to children.

Sometimes we would have play readings. On one occasion the family was invited to one at the Guinness home. Dad was an instant choice for these kinds of parties, and his children were expected to show the same kind of acting flair. But the Guinness party was a dismal flop. I stumbled over my lines and Dad, with Miranda's encouragement, forced me on with the part despite the growing embarrassment I felt as everyone's eyes fixed on me from around the fireside.

Dad was still pleading lean times. For Christmas he gave us £10 each in notes, telling us that it was all he could afford as he was hard up. We would have found that easier to accept had he not given Miranda's sister Jessica a Pentax camera and all the accessories.

He also promised to buy me a car for my seventeenth birthday. I was then playing at odd gigs on my guitar with a pop group and I thought it would be better to have a van to get around in, with all the equipment that travelled with us. Dad agreed and a van, which wasn't going to be any more expensive, was duly ordered. But then he changed his mind. The first indication I got of the van's cancellation was from the garage where it had been ordered. When I asked for an explanation, Dad just sighed and said that he could not afford it.

Again, I would have been prepared to have accepted his answer but then I learned he had bought a saloon car as a present for another of Miranda's sisters. Dad's flamboyant extravagances at this time were for outsiders. His family didn't count for all that much.

He was always generous to Miranda's sisters. Her elder sister Venetia was married to Captain Fred Barker. Dad and Fred formed a helicopter aerial photographic company using a new shockproof camera, unaffected by vibration. He actually filmed a promotional trailer for the new company, which looked set to flourish in some style, but once more Dad found it difficult to devote adequate time to it.

Slowly but surely Dad began to tire of Ireland. But he tired more of the long round of social parties that Miranda inveigled him into attending. He began to admit that he didn't like her friends: he labelled them as 'prize bores' and that more familiar phrase 'chinless wonders' crept back into his conversation.

Once accosted at a party and asked his profession Dad replied, 'I'm an actor.'

'Yes, old boy,' answered the aristocrat patiently, 'but what do you actually *do?*'

Dad yearned to get back to England and to meet up again with his old friends. He longed to see Spike, David and Graham.

It was doubtful if they would have been welcome at Maynooth. Spike as a celebrity might have been acceptable, but nondescript actors like David and Graham, under Miranda's social laws, didn't qualify. Arguments not only about friends but on other issues too began to boil over into bitterness.

Another winter of discontent was upon us.

Dad's Secret Child

Dad became a virtual recluse. Every passing day brought increased loathing of Ireland.

He would sit brooding, morose and listless. Nothing would stir him or arouse his interest.

His marriage to Miranda was as treacherous at root as the cattle grid at the far entrance of the estate. But Miranda was strong willed. She wasn't going to concede or bow to Dad's depressed moods. Nothing was more important to her than the social calendar. It was just too bad if Dad was bored with nobility. He would have to suffer it in silence.

One big event loomed near: an important society dinner in Dublin, for which Miranda had organized a party of friends. Dad had no intention of attending and on the preceding afternoon he took a pair of scissors and chopped off his hair. Uneven tufts were left sprouting from his head, giving the appearance of a mangled cat. Miranda was aghast when she saw what he had done.

'You can't go like that,' she screamed.

'No, darling,' said my father coolly, 'of course I can't. Why do you think I cut it that way?'

A day or two later, when more bickering broke out between them, Dad threatened to shave his head to the scalp like Telly Savalas.

'Maybe that's what I'll do,' he nodded, 'I've always wanted to be a monk.' Unhappiness persisted and the friction mounted.

Sometimes it appeared that Dad deliberately set out to ruffle Miranda when she least suspected his motives. When, on a rare occasion, we drove into Dublin he asked me to take over the steering wheel while he slept on the back seat. He knew that I hadn't passed my test. Miranda, sitting in the front passenger seat, protested.

'Don't you think you had better drive now, Peter?' she kept saying. 'What if we get stopped by the police?'

Dad snorted.

'Michael is perfectly capable. He's been driving since he was ten years old. I'll take over when we get to the city boundary,' he said, shutting his eyes in token sleep.

But the animosity and the rows grew more fearful.

Before Dad had left England his friends had gathered together at a farewell party organized by Miranda at San Lorenzo's restaurant in Knightsbridge. Everyone at the party had signed a '*Ciao* Peter' message in a handsome leather-bound book that he was to keep as a memento. Alas, the book was to be torn to shreds on his next clash with Miranda, when I was present. He tore out chunks of the book by the handful and tossed them to me. 'Tear them up. Every goddam page,' he yelled.

Miranda ran from the room in tears. But more was to come.

Dad seized the wedding album from the same cupboard and began tearing up their wedding pictures.

'That was the most terrible day of my life,' he ranted, 'why did I marry her? . . .'

Bert was summoned and we all went through to Dad's bedroom where Miranda was lying weeping on the bed.

'Take all of my wife's jewellery and throw it into the lake,' Dad ordered Bert. 'Look, there's her jewel box over there. Just do as I tell you – take the lot and dump it . . .' Bert breathed heavily and looked glumly at Dad and then at Miranda whose head was buried in the eiderdown. Bert took out the jewel box as Dad instructed and we left the room while Miranda sobbed. He had the good sense to take the jewels to the safety of his room. Experience had taught him that Dad was quite likely to change his mind when he cooled down and Bert didn't relish the thought of skin diving in the lake to retrieve the gems.

A week or two later when Miranda had served her penance the jewels were returned to her, in the way that Dad had given us back the toys he confiscated from us as children.

The months droned wearily on, without any visible signs of improvement in relations between them. A stranger who telephoned the house and asked for Miranda raised Dad's suspicions.

When Miranda returned to the house that evening after a day's shopping in Dublin it was to face an inquisition. 'Who was the stranger who called?' demanded my father.

Without the slightest evidence he accused her of having an affair.

Miranda pleaded her innocence but Dad wasn't going to accept her protestations.

'I want proof of your innocence,' he raged.

The inevitable conclusion he reached was that she was guilty of all the accusations he had wildly levelled against her. Miranda was nonplussed. In their more loving and tender days Dad would become 'Muffins' to Miranda and he would pet her. But now he started abusing her.

Suspicion remained unabated in Dad's mind. I discovered a spare telephone line that could be plugged into the estate office switchboard and Dad asked me to 'bug' the telephone in the house so that he could listen to Miranda's calls.

I was sickened to think that Dad would stoop to these lengths but I did as I was told because in my heart I hoped that he would find that the accusations he made against Miranda bore no foundation. She did not particularly win my approval as a stepmother, or as the perfect wife to Dad, but I did not like seeing her as the victim of baseless suspicions.

But Miranda's innocence did not save the marriage which was clearly on the rocks. Little remained to be salvaged.

Dad left Ireland for London without any qualms and rented a place in Eaton Mews.

Feeling lonely and depressed he accepted an invitation to go to Germany and Austria and asked me to go with him. It was like playing lapdog to him until he met a beautiful German model in Munich who had apparently been one of his long-standing fans. Her company was like a tonic and the distress he felt at the failure of his marriage was briefly pushed aside.

But while in Vienna he suddenly remembered it was his wedding anniversary: Interflora were called in to send some red roses to Miranda. He also arranged to see her and booked a flight out to London. But if these gestures were intended to effect a reconciliation then it did not work out. A legal separation between them was agreed ensuring automatic divorce two years later. When Miranda gained her freedom she was to marry Lord Nuttall.

'That's what she always wanted,' said Dad cynically, 'a title ...'

Dad tried to pick up the pieces once more, but neither the reappearance of Francesca Hilton or the freshness of Sinead Cusack, a young actress who starred with him in *Hoffman*, interested him or could divert him from the post-marital malaise that we had seen him decline into twice before.

Dad talked about ending his life but I told him not to talk in such a way. He sighed and said he had once seriously contemplated suicide but ruled against it for his children's sake. In these dispirited periods of his life, when he experienced strong feelings of rejection, my father would embark on nostalgic pilgrimages. Once more we were taken back to Portsmouth to see the old homestead where Peg and Bill once lived; we were obliged to visit his old school house in Highgate and the pub where the Goons were first formed.

Some weeks later, when I was lying sick with fever in Mum's house, Dad burst in from another of his sentimental journeys. With him he brought a schoolday sweetheart – the girl who bore his illegitimate child.

I had learned of this family secret only six years earlier. I was having dinner in Knightsbridge with Dad and one of his friends who was a doctor. When the conversation turned to children, Dad said in matter-of-fact tones that as well as Sarah, Victoria and myself, he also had an illegitimate daughter whom he had not seen since her adoption. I looked up from the table surprised by this sudden revelation, but I didn't actually believe the claim as Dad was prone to exaggeration and would invent stories to fit situations like slotting pieces into a jigsaw puzzle. Only later was I able to substantiate the story. I felt pretty shocked to think that we had a half-sister somewhere that we had never met or even knew about.

But now this girl's mother stood over me. I guess she was 45 or 46 – around Dad's age. She was kindly and rather matronly-looking with mottled eyes and greying, mousey-coloured hair. She was nicely dressed and bore the look of an honest person who worked hard throughout her life. She was far removed from Dad's brigade of dolly birds.

Dad introduced us and as I propped my head up on the pillow, he said: 'Well, this is my son. I thought you might like to meet him . . .'

I saw tears in the woman's eyes. I could imagine what she was thinking. She was trying to form a picture of what her daughter might look like, knowing that she would be six years older than I was.

'Yes, Peter,' she murmured sadly as she collected her thoughts, 'he's got a lot of your features.' Then she smiled at me and said, 'I'm sure he is a good father to you, Michael.'

12

Liza with a Z

Dad started work for the Boultings on a new comedy at Shepperton studios with the unlikely title of *Soft Beds and Hard Battles*. It was set in occupied France, and Dad was persuaded into playing seven different roles, though they were all military autocrats of differing countries and uniforms.

Roy and John Boulting were, in their dealings with my father, like a pair of intrepid prospectors ready to burrow through mountain rocks in a blizzard to strike gold. They employed wit, wisdom, tact, discretion, diplomacy and patience to lay bare the genius in Dad's soul. Only by these skills could they regulate his tantrums, antagonism and his natural scepticism.

They also insured against every possible and conceivable hazard, but even the clauses ranged under 'an act of God' could not cover the tempestuous field of Dad's emotions. If he was in love, then inspiration would flow from him like the purified waters of a spa fountain. But on his first day at Shepperton they must have exchanged uneasy glances; Dad was still feeling low.

Storms gathered and the rains fell. But to the sheer delight of the Boultings a rainbow suddenly appeared in the sky: her name was Liza Minnelli, as dazzling and brilliant as her mother Judy Garland had once been.

Liza was appearing at the London Palladium in her spectacular show *Liza with a Z*. Every night, after the last curtain, she went out on the town. Someone brought her to a party that Dad was throwing for his show business friends in the mews cottage he was renting in Belgravia. She sang and danced at the party.

It was, in Dad's own words, love at first sight. 'We clicked like magic from the moment our eyes met,' said Dad, 'and Mike, have you seen Liza's eyes? They're like big brown saucers. How could any man escape when she turns them on you in the way she did to me?'

No one could recall two stars falling so instantaneously in love with one another. Their blinding passion was so strong that it burned the front pages of the world's press. Unblushingly, out in the streets, in restaurants and at people's homes, they were swapping kisses, squeezing hands and laughing and joking with one another. They wanted everyone to know how much they were in love. No secrets were held back.

Only three days after they met, Dad rang my mother and said: 'Anne, how would you like me to bring over Liza? Yes, *Liza Minnelli*. We're going to marry and I'd love you to meet her.'

Mum laughed. All the past injuries she had suffered were long healed. She'd found happiness and contentment with Ted and now she could smile at Dad's outrageous antics, because they no longer involved her. She was able to see and sample them through the eyes of a spectator standing safely on the sidelines.

Having consulted my mother prior to marrying Britt and Miranda, Dad now wanted the same approval for Liza. It was as if he needed her reassurance that he was doing the right thing. He duly brought Liza over to Mum and Ted's place in Hampstead around seven o'clock for cocktails. They were very impressed by her. Her big smile and bubbling personality were infectious.

She wore a plum-coloured track suit and Dad, in his standard grey suit, sat on the sofa holding her hand. They were like two teenagers in love for the first time. When Mum went through to mix some more drinks in the kitchen Dad followed her through.

'I think she is great,' said Mum, 'I do hope you'll be happy this time.'

'Yes,' said Dad wistfully, 'well, I did love her mother's old films.'

One morning a furniture removal van arrived outside the door of Mum's home. 'I think you must have come to the wrong house,' she said to the removal men, 'we're not moving ...'

'No, ma'am,' said the foreman, 'Mr Sellers has sent us over for the piano.'

Dad was taking Sarah's rosewood Knight upright piano so that Liza could continue to rehearse her act, having now moved into the Eaton Mews cottage with him. Our half-sister Kate, who was then learning to play the piano, had to go to a friend's house to practise.

Dad, totally besotted with Liza, wanted to do everything to please her. I was wearing a new check trench coat that Liza happened to admire. No sooner had she mentioned it, than Dad despatched Bert to the shop where I purchased it and bought her one.

'Here, Michael – you give it to Liza,' he said. She was touched by the gesture.

Liza certainly appealed to us as stepmother-elect. Sparkling and open in her conversation, she didn't talk down to children, but treated them like adults.

Sarah went with her to Shepperton Studios to see Dad at work on his new film and they got on famously. Victoria also liked her and Liza gave her a necklace as a present. She was kind also to Kate, sending her thirty-six autographed photographs for her friends. I admired her greatly too, and instinctively I knew she would be as famous as her mother had once been.

There are advantages and drawbacks in being the offspring of the famous. As a child Liza had experienced both, in much the same way as we were now doing.

She said she had always wanted to go on stage, so she was happy following in her mother's footsteps. But she had not traded on the name of Garland.

'I loved my momma dearly,' said Liza, 'but I didn't use her ticket, I had to do it my way. Sure, Momma helped a lot. Her name opened a lot of doors for me but after that I was on my own.'

I appreciated all that Liza said but I told her that I didn't think my future lay in the same direction as my father's.

'I'm sure you'll make it whatever you decide to do, Michael,' she said encouragingly. 'I think you've got your father's determination.'

We were all prepared for Dad to marry Liza. They had exchanged engagement rings, but some delay to the nuptials was anticipated as Dad's divorce from Miranda had still not come through.

Liza and Dad were now into the third, exhilarating week of their romance. Only then did I begin to detect that something was amiss.

Dad began to complain that he couldn't ever really see Liza on her own. She was always surrounded by an entourage of friends and advisers, who would rarely leave her side. Manager, secretary, mother's friend, musicians and dancers from her Palladium show all flocked around her.

'They swarm over her like honey bees,' said Dad, now wearing a frown, 'and I have to keep telling Liza about them. What do we need all those people hanging about for?'

'How do we get rid of these people when we marry?' he asked Liza.

'Get rid of them?' said Liza, shocked by the suggestion. 'These are my friends, Peter ... they're always gonna be my friends. I just can't cut them off dead. If we're going to marry, then you're gonna have to accept them.'

Dad said later that this episode was the turning point of their relationship, but for Liza it came when she consulted the London clairvoyant Fredrick Davies who predicted on a radio broadcast that she would not marry Peter Sellers.

When later she asked him to explain his pronouncement the clairvoyant read the Tarot cards and confirmed his earlier prediction.

Dad was infuriated that Liza had gone to a clairvoyant of her own choosing and argued that he knew the most knowledgeable clairvoyants and astrologers in the world, which for once, wasn't an exaggeration.

'Why didn't you tell me?' he said. 'You could have gone to one of mine and I would have come with you. We can still do that now. It's not too late.'

'But it is, Peter,' said Liza, now convinced their marriage would not succeed. Two days later she issued a statement saying the affair was over.

Dad rang Spike and Graham and his other friends as if he was in mourning. 'Why didn't she go to my clairvoyant?' he said.

In his distress, Dad also called me.

'I've broken with Liza. Can I come and talk with you, Mike?' he said, his voice strained and empty. I had some friends round at the time. It was typical of Dad to choose an inconvenient moment, but I could not put him off. I quickly told my friends to disappear and got ready for Dad's arrival. I knew it was going to be a long night.

He poured out his heart to me as though our roles as father and son were reversed.

'It would have worked,' Dad kept saying, 'but we just couldn't ever talk without one of her friends butting in. Imagine our home. It would have been full of friends, who she would have thought were helping her. I told her she didn't need people like this. That we could manage our own affairs ...'

Dad's regrets hung over the room almost as thickly as his cigarette smoke.

He stubbed out one cigarette and lit another.

'I loved her, Mike. I really did,' he whispered, 'and I love her now ... that's why it hurts so much.' I remember tears coming to his eyes.

I drove him home around 4 a.m. London is inhospitable at that time of the morning. It was still dark, the street lights bathing the pavements. It was cold and Dad turned up the collar of his coat, his shoulders hunched with the dejection of a man burdened with all the troubles of the world.

I returned to Eaton Mews for breakfast. Dad had not gone

to bed. He was still in his overcoat, on a kitchen chair, poring over the morning newspapers. He was gently crying as he looked at the headlines relating how he and Liza had parted after only one month together.

'I suppose they will say I was a fool,' said Dad, as I handed him a cup of coffee. 'Well, I don't care what they think. When haven't I been a fool?'

It was not always easy to feel sympathy for my father, but this time I really felt for him. He needed words of encouragement.

'There are plenty more fish in the sea, Dad. You haven't done too badly so far ...'

In the summer of that year, I struck up a long friendship with a Californian girl whose flatmate had been my father's lover on occasions; this girl insisted on passing on to me the secrets of my father's sex life. I was on the point of telling her that she was being indiscreet but then thought that my father would have been flattered by this unsolicited testimonial to his prowess.

Now nearing the peak of his fame, Dad liked to create the impression that any woman was his for the asking. It was a fantasy. He certainly had a predilection for young women and for blondes; and often I found that the girls he was taking out were younger than myself.

'I like young, beautiful girls,' he would say, 'and I'm in the position to be able to pick and choose them.'

Sarah was cynical about that kind of boast. 'Can't Dad see they are gold diggers?' she would say angrily. 'Any girl is going to be bowled over by someone as famous as Dad, the provider of furs and sports cars, the means of entry to the jet-set. He's frightened of mature women because he knows they won't tolerate his eccentric behaviour.'

It was an opinion that Victoria came to share and one that I could not easily dismiss from my own mind. Only too clearly, we remembered the days as youngsters when Dad would take us out for a car ride, saying that he was going to buy an extravagant present for some new girl-friend. We would have to wait patiently in the car parked outside Cartier's or Garrard's while Dad disappeared inside to buy a gold bracelet, watch or trinket.

When he climbed back into the car, he would just pat our heads and say: 'Where do you want to go now?' Invariably, he spun the car round and we were taken home for tea.

Dad's breed of women didn't appeal to me very much. Among them, Britt was the exception and I formed a closer attachment to her than any of the others. I could easily have passed as her boy-friend at the age of 15 when I was more than six feet tall and escorting her to discotheques and on ski runs in St Moritz, when Dad wasn't around. But as I grew older I realized that Dad's style of life was beyond me – and that his women were also. I was young, but I had no riches or social standing. And I wasn't famous. I was happier with girls within my own reach.

Way outside my reach was the next girl in my father's life. Her name was Christina Wachtmeister, the daughter of Count Wilhelm Wachtmeister then Sweden's Ambassador to the United States. Dad had met her some time before but now their friendship was to develop dramatically. He telephoned me and asked me, out of the blue, if I would like to take a holiday with him in Acapulco. I laughed.

'What time do you want me at the airport?' I asked, immediately telling my boss in the hi-fi shop that I was going on holiday.

'Tomorrow. At 11 a.m.,' said Dad. 'We'll be gone for about a fortnight.'

I didn't realize it then, but Dad was using me as a decoy. Suddenly conscious that Miranda's divorce petition was about to be filed, he was at pains to keep a low profile. Our travelling companion was the Countess Christina. To her friends she was simply known as Titti. She possessed typically Swedish good looks – high cheekbones and ice-cool blonde looks. Her family was obviously wealthy but she wanted to make her own way in life and worked successfully as a fashion model.

I recall first seeing her with Dad on the night The Who's pop opera *Tommy* opened at the Rainbow Theatre in London.

Now, at the airport, Dad whispered to me: 'If anyone asks, she is with you.' I looked admiringly at Titti and smiled. I was only too happy to oblige.

Our trip to the Mexican playground took an endless eighteen hours but the hotel into which Dad had booked us was magnificent. Brightly painted bungalows, luxuriously fitted, dotted the surrounds of the main hotel and we could motor all over the resort in candy-striped jeeps. The sea shimmered in the blazing sunshine and from the hotel we had breathtaking views of the coastline.

All day long we lazed by our own individual pools or on the beach. We also rented one of the yachts in the harbour for trips out to sea. Dad was relaxed and happy – happier than I had seen him for many, many months.

It was not often I saw him get drunk but this was one occasion when he was ready to cast his cares aside. The exotic tropical drinks were too tempting for him and in a local night club he actually climbed on to the stage to join the flamenco dancers, to a roar of approval from those people in the audience who recognized him. Titti and I were hysterical with laughter as we watched him, clapping his hands above his head and swirling like a matador in time with the dancers.

That night we had to carry him home from the club and drive him back to the hotel slumped in the back seat of the car.

In this euphoria of holiday bliss, Dad had thrown all caution to the wind in veiling his relationship with Titti. As the decoy, my role was at an end.

But on the morning Dad was trying to throw off his hangover, we were stricken with panic when we learned that Miranda's sister Victoria was in Acapulco.

Dad sobered fast when he heard the news. Victoria and a friend were travelling all over South America. By coincidence they had come through Acapulco to discover that Dad was staying at the resort. They traced us to our hotel and left a message, which Dad cagily returned. But as a gesture of courtesy, he had no option other than to invite the pair over for drinks.

'Now remember, Mike, you've got to play it as though you're with Titti,' said Dad going through the whole charade again before Victoria's arrival. Titti was amused and told Dad not to worry.

'I'll make such a fuss of Michael,' she said, stroking my hair, 'that no one will ever guess the truth ...'

Victoria and her friend duly arrived and spent the evening with us. They were having trouble with their accommodation, so Dad found them rooms in a neighbouring hotel and instructed the manager to forward their bill to him.

He made much of his fondness for Victoria, but maybe he was merely buying her silence, since my pose as Titti's boy-friend was to wear pretty thin over the next few days.

I would call Titti 'darling' and so would Dad. Then he would kiss her. Victoria and her companion must have wondered what was going on. If this in itself wasn't suspicious enough, a regular miscalculation of our room numbers would occur when ordering drinks and meals.

One evening Victoria beckoned me aside and said: 'Look, I know what's going on. Titti is with your father, isn't she? Don't worry, the secret is safe with me. I shan't rush home and tell Miranda. You can trust me to be discreet.'

My subterfuge with Titti was exposed, but when we got back to London, my father for some reason tried to pair me off with her sister Anna. I was flabbergasted. Anna was a year or two older than Titti. How could I possibly go out with someone who was the elder sister of my father's girl-friend? It was too disconcerting and I didn't like the idea of two sisters comparing notes.

Dad was in love with Titti and I was surprised that he managed to delay a single day after his divorce officially came through from Miranda before he proposed. When Titti didn't give a definite answer he got his newly appointed secretary Sue Evans to telephone her for him to try and persuade her. This was his safeguard against rejection.

Titti thought that Dad was being faint-hearted and wasn't willing to give him an immediate answer.

Dad couldn't understand why Titti didn't accept his offer. He enquired of Sue, who had taken an office in his apartment at Roebuck house, 'Isn't she in love with me?'

Sue was probably the sixth or seventh secretary who had joined Dad since he was abandoned by Hattie. Hattie Stevenson had quite remarkably suffered him over twelve traumatic years. He sacked her on innumerable occasions, but always found himself in the invidious position of having to beg for her return. Finally, Hattie was forced to make her own decision to quit when Dad refused to grant her the holiday dates she requested.

Sue was to inherit all of Dad's problems, tantrums and complexities – sorting them out would require superhuman understanding.

But business letters, calls from film studios and arranging meetings were of less significance than keeping tabs on Titti. To work for Dad was a round-the-clock operation. He wouldn't think twice about ringing up Sue in the middle of the night.

Dad, as ever generous and expansive when in pursuit, arranged a dazzling social life to ensnare Titti. When Royal Ascot came round, he took a flower-decked private box with crates of champagne. If she wasn't impressed by that, she was certainly carried away by the thought of Cary Grant joining our party.

The ever youthful Cary, slim, suntanned and flannel suited, provided the necessary draw. He gave a special greeting to Bert, who was once his chauffeur. But he waited until Titti was powdering her nose to congratulate Dad on his choice of girl. 'She's just a dream, Peter. Congratulations. Where did you find her?' he exclaimed. With Cary's compliments to encourage him Dad accelerated the chase for Titti. But, immediately, he once again became over-possessive.

He wanted to see Titti every day and when he wasn't with her, he wanted an explanation of her movements. The familiar niggles began to creep through. We were in California where Dad was having his usual round of film talks. Titti was with us and was enjoying herself: she'd met both Ringo Starr and George Harrison at the recording studios in Los Angeles where

Ringo was cutting an album with The Band, who usually backed Bob Dylan.

Dad's relations with Titti were in good shape until the day she asked him to reimburse her for the money she had spent on some rolls of film she had bought for *her* camera. He was flummoxed. It was such a small, ridiculous thing. 'Why can't you pay for it yourself?' Dad remonstrated with her. 'You've had your flight paid for and your hotel. What more do you want? Can't you afford a few rolls of film?'

The whole episode got under Dad's skin. If Titti had asked for a Rolls-Royce or a Mercedes he might have turned round and bought her one. But to give her a couple of dollars for some rolls of film? Dad must have thought that he was being taken for a ride.

'Is this all I mean to you?' he said sadly. 'Is this the price of your love?'

Unfortunately, Titti didn't let it rest at that. She asked Dad to compensate her with £6000, which she assessed was her loss of earnings as a fashion model while devoting her time to him.

I was surprised that Dad didn't end the relationship then, but he didn't seem to worry about this set-back. Within a day or two he was cosseting her with his usual affection.

We flew from California to New York. Dad sprawled out on the plane to get some sleep and I chatted with Titti. She looked incredibly beautiful in her favourite silk shirt and satin trousers. I had seen the abrasive side of her character, but now she was genuinely trying to find some means of reaching a better understanding with my father.

'How is it possible to cope with him, Michael?' she asked me. 'One day he is so wonderful: the next he sulks for no reason. What is a girl to do? I say things I shouldn't because I have to defend myself. But I just wish he wouldn't make big issues out of my little chance remarks. How can I begin to understand him?'

I laughed at her naivety. 'It would be impossible to begin to answer that question. It would need a seminar to attempt to explain Dad's complexities,' I said.

In New York we managed to get back to normal. Dad and Titti appeared to be getting on quite well once more and their romance continued to flower. There was no lessening of affection and the bouquets, presents and trinkets continued. Marriage was still very much on my father's mind.

Sue would be persuaded to ring Titti and delicately broach the subject so that Dad could gauge what her answer might be.

'I know that Titti is 100 per cent right for me,' Dad told me.

I raised doubts.

'But Dad, you said that about Liza Minnelli ...' I reminded him.

'Maybe,' snapped Dad, annoyed by my mention of a past encounter, 'but remember I've known Titti almost two years now. So how can it be wrong? We wouldn't have gone this far if it wasn't going to work.'

I really couldn't argue. As if to strengthen his case, Dad showed me a set of nude pictures he had taken of Titti in the shower.

'Now can you see why I want to marry her, Mike? Isn't she beautiful?' he said.

Neither Sarah nor Victoria particularly wished to see him marry Titti, who consumed all his time, energy and thought. Oddly enough, Victoria only thought of Titti as being the girl-friend of Britt's brother Bengt, for they had had a long affair.

Upon Victoria fell the real brunt of the relationship. At nine years of age she was forced to trail Titti and Dad on their party rounds, when no one could be found to stay in and look after her. At home she could not have friends to stay and had to be careful not to make a noise. Dad was still practising yoga and quiet was obligatory.

Wearing only his underwear each morning he would stand on his head or take up the lotus cross-legged position, issuing chants in the direction of an altar arranged in a corner of the sitting room. A statue of Buddha, incense and a porcelain three-headed elephant symbolizing the Eastern gods were arranged on it.

Dad once went to Northern Ireland on a peace mission with

his guru, but his yoga days were numbered. Soon the altar, the kaftans and velvet prayer cushions disappeared without trace from his house, as though they had never existed. Titti was far more important in Dad's thoughts than any Eastern mysticisim at this point and she commanded every ounce of his attention.

Nevertheless, she kept stalling the question of marriage, although she appeared willing to follow him wherever he went. Together they jetted to Cyprus for Dad to film *Ghost in the Noon Day Sun* and to rent a villa surrounded by sweet scented lime trees. It was a romantic enough setting for him to propose marriage.

But then the relationship plunged into an abyss. They were dining in a taverna in nearby Kyrenia when a handsome young Cypriot started casting Titti admiring glances. They did not go unnoticed by my father who could not contain his jealousy. He accused Titti of encouraging the Cypriot and after heated words he stormed out of the restaurant back to the villa to pack her clothes.

When the taverna clientele next saw Dad he was tossing Titti's suitcase through the door like a caber. It crashed on to a table, shattering wine bottles, glasses and crockery. He thought he had caught Titti but from beneath the debris appeared a pair of eyes, innocent but fear-stricken, belonging to a complete stranger. Dad realized his mistake. Clouseau might have been forgiven for saying it was a case of mistaken identity, but Dad found it far more than that as waiters and manager surged around him. Meanwhile Titti, who had switched tables in Dad's absence to join her admirer, watched the extraordinary scenes with a mixture of delight and desperation. The end of the relationship was near.

Some weeks later, Titti failed to turn up for the Swiss preview of *The Return of the Pink Panther*. Regarding the film's opening as one of the most important moments of his life Dad took Titti's sister Anna instead. So much was at stake with the success of the new Panther film. Would the public still love the bumbling Inspector Clouseau after such a long absence?

Disputes over editing and production had resulted in two of Dad's more recent films being dumped in the archives without a public screening. One was *The Blockhouse* which he shot with Charles Aznavour in the Channel Islands and the other was *Ghost in the Noon Day Sun* with Spike Milligan as his co-star. Spike and Dad were accused of turning the film into a Goon-like spectacle and the director Peter Medak was left doubting whether the two should have ever been paired together and allowed so free a hand.

Clouseau was needed to change Dad's fortunes and at the time of the preview in Gstaad he placed much emphasis on the outcome. We were all telephoned and the family presence demanded. Sarah, who was then in preparation for her 'A' levels, doubted that she would be able to come.

'Can't you make the effort for once?' he yelled. 'Is it too much to ask? This is the most vital moment of my life ...'

Sarah got permission to miss school and we were ready to meet the flight schedules set for us. But then Dad decided that he wanted to stay in London an extra day to attend an Alice Cooper pop concert; so everyone's plans had to be altered to coincide with his. We arranged to fly with him on the Friday morning – to discover he'd left without us! When we reached Switzerland he was engulfed in a blaze of publicity and in fact we saw very little of him.

But the film got rapturous acclaim and once more his career revived triumphantly. In Dad's mind it was something of a vindication. Whenever critics slammed one of his films – and he was always susceptible to criticism – he would begin to question his own ability to play a role.

Riding high on this plateau of success, he returned to London hoping to repair the rift with Titti which had caused her to miss the preview. He was in such a hurry to disembark at Heathrow that he forgot to say goodbye to us. But going in search for Titti was really a lost cause. She had abandoned all hope and had no intention of re-establishing the relationship.

Dad retreated to the sanctuary of Roebuck House to lick his wounds. Once more he was overcome with loneliness and

Miranda Quarry (now Lady Nuttall) – the third wife. They
were only married for two years.

Above: In the garden at Elstead, at the time of
'What's New, Pussycat?'

Above right: Sarah and I on location with Ringo Starr for
'The Magic Christian'. Richmond, Surrey, 1968.

Below right: 1970, on location for the film 'A Girl in my
Soup, with Nicky Henson, son of the celebrated Lesley
Henson.

Above left: An unusual shot of my father in Los Angeles, 1964. This was just before his first heart attack.

Below left: The backyard at Elstead was occupied by this unusual array of vehicles on a memorable occasion when Tommy Sopwith came to visit us. The helicopter belonged to Tommy.

Above: With Spike Milligan at the Round House. He and my father did a turn during the course of one of Michael Parkinson's shows.

Three photographs taken at my wedding,
July 1979. Right: Father and Son.
Below left: Ted Levy, Katie
– my half sister, my mother. On my left is
Sarah. Below right: Theo Cowan, my
parents and the bridegroom.

Above: A photograph I took of my father at St Moritz in 1968.

Above right: The house at Gstaad, now occupied by Lynne Frederick and David Frost.

Right: The fourth and last wife, Lynne Frederick arrives at Heathrow for the funeral.

depression and would call us on any pretext, engaging us in long conversations.

Often he would complain that we didn't see him enough, that we were disloyal and uncaring. Accustomed to such a reaction, we simply felt that he ignored us when it suited his convenience.

Luckily, a trip to New York cropped up and Dad was able to shake off his mood. We accompanied him and stayed at the Plaza Hotel which was pretty full at the time. A note was waiting for him and when he read it his face lit up with excitement.

'What do you think?' he asked, thrusting the note into my hand. 'Have a read ...'

It was from Elvis Presley's former wife, Priscilla. She was also staying at the Plaza on the top floor and her note was an invitation for Dad to join her for a drink. 'I love your films and I would very much like to meet you,' Priscilla wrote. Dad's American press agent David Steinberg gave a word of caution.

'She may have left Elvis, but they've still got ties,' said David, 'otherwise she wouldn't be surrounded by bodyguards.'

Dad looked up. 'Bodyguards?' he enquired.

'Yeah, protecting her up in the suite,' said David.

Dad, who was always boasting he could get 'the boys' to take care of someone, had a particular abhorrence of bodyguards. Especially if they were on someone else's payroll. Nevertheless, he could not resist the temptation to get the measure of Priscilla.

He wasn't disappointed. She was as glamorous as her pictures suggested. Dad reported she wore an off-the-shoulder black dress, which left nothing to the imagination. 'But I didn't see any bodyguards,' he said, 'unless the guy who was serving the drinks was one of them ...'

David nodded.

Priscilla was persistent. Another invitation came down the next day for Dad to join her once more. Ever charming and courteous, Dad accepted, but made elaborate plans to make his exit if things weren't to his liking. Both David and I were briefed to make urgent set time calls to him in her suite – these would provide valid reasons for taking his leave.

On our second call Dad seized the opportunity and took the lift down to the foyer to join us.

'It's all a game,' he said looking ruffled by Priscilla's apparent Presley persona.

We laughed.

On our return to London Dad befriended the actress Patricia Neal's daughter, Tessa Dahl, who was only eighteen. Tessa was flattered and gave the impression that she was going to organize Dad's life for him. She established herself in the apartment at Roebuck House answering telephone calls and the door bell with great self assurance. But this time, thankfully, Dad recognized the danger signs and asked Tessa to leave. Although Dad knew the agony of being spurned, he didn't show much consideration when it came to giving the marching orders to someone else. He just told Tessa to go. And closed the door.

13

Communion and Cocaine

We were cosseted in luxury at the Palace Hotel in Gstaad (the Swiss resort), the snow-capped Alps silhouetted against the brilliant sunshine. Skiers were out all over the slopes and in the distance we could see the cable car ascending the mountain pass. But Dad stayed brooding in the hotel suite, meditating about the less agreeable areas of his life and the need for spiritual salvation at the end of it all.

'We must pay our dues,' he said, getting carried away by this urge for atonement.

In London he had often talked to his friend Father John Hester, the Soho priest who looked after the problems and needs of artists. Father John lived in hope that Dad would not have to search any further than the Christian faith, but he knew that was probably too much to expect. Being a Protestant was not enough for Dad, who could be Jewish, Moslem, Hindu or any other religious faith on a given day. His beliefs were an amalgam of all teachings, faiths and cultures. If someone offered a cut-price, special-offer, gift-wrapped religion that guaranteed miracles and a personal audience with the Maker, then Dad would apply for instant enrolment. Now that his kaftan and yoga days had gone, once again he felt compelled to find spiritual strength.

He remembered a bearded Catholic priest whom we had met on our earlier travels in Central America. The priest, suffering from an incurable disease and given only weeks to live by doctors, had made a miraculous recovery and told Dad that his survival was brought about by constant prayer.

Dad was deeply moved by the priest's simple faith and now, in Gstaad, his thoughts captured by a new spring of religious consciousness he felt the necessity to talk to him. Telephone calls were placed across the vast continents of the world in order to trace the priest. The exercise carried more urgency than Dad would even show when discussing a multi-million-dollar movie. Finally, he located the holy man and persuaded him to fly to Switzerland on a first-class air ticket that would be arranged for him.

Three days later the cleric appeared in Gstaad; two extra suites were taken in the hotel. One was put at the priest's disposal and the other transformed into a chapel. Only days before Dad had been placing orders with room service for champagne, caviare, club sandwiches and cartons of cigarettes. Now he was galvanizing porters into preparing the rooms for communion. The priest, a round-faced man in his late fifties, was quietly impressed by my father's spiritual feeling and holy Communion was arranged in suite 721, now resembling a chapel, at 7 a.m. the next morning.

Feeling that this was something personal, I didn't intrude on Dad's plans. I thought I would keep to myself and let Dad get on with it. The night before the communion service, I went out to a disco and didn't get back until very late. At 6.30 a.m. the ringing telephone woke me. It was my father.

'Michael, are you getting dressed?' said Dad.

'What for?' I asked, my head throbbing.

'What for? You know what for. Holy communion ...'

'But Dad,' I protested, 'I'm asleep. That's nothing to do with me ...'

'Of course it's got something to do with you. What in name's sake do you think I flew the priest over here for? I'm not going to celebrate communion on my own.'

'Yes, Dad,' I replied uneasily.

Dressed in sweater and slacks I went up to suite 71. Dad opened the door and frowned when he saw how I was dressed. I gathered that I should have put on a grey suit like the one he chose to wear. He shook his head in dismay, but the priest then beckoned us both forward to start worship.

We were solemnly kneeling in prayer when we heard passing our door the excited voices of members of a skiing party on their way out to tackle the crisp mountain slopes at dawn. It would have been beyond the wildest imaginings of any one of them to have guessed the proceedings within suite 721. But neither Dad nor the cleric seemed put off by the commotion and the Communion went on without further interruption.

A day or two later the priest flew back to Mexico. I have no doubt he was certain that he had left behind two potential candidates for Catholicism.

My maternal grandfather died at this juncture and Dad's talk about death at the time upset Sarah. He told us that Grandad would be well taken care of, telling us how he had been able to maintain communication with Peg 'on the other side' through a spiritualist medium. Sometimes he talked as though Peg were still alive. It emerged that Dad would 'consult' Peg in special sittings he conducted with Doris Collins, a medium who came into favour after the death of Maurice Woodruff. He would frequently conduct a three-way conversation with Peg by telephoning Doris in London from any part of the world. She would fall into a trance under which she possessed the rare ability of being able to dial out Peg 'on the other side'.

He was always susceptible to the utterings of fortune tellers, palmists, crystal-ball soothsayers, astrologers, tea-leaf readers and others who claimed all sorts of mystical powers.

Most mornings he would read his horoscopes in the newspapers, choosing to forget those which were in any way disheartening. Things of the occult fascinated him. Practically every house we moved into was supposedly haunted and he actually had the mews cottage in London's Belgravia exorcized to rid it of evil spirits – having of course seen the film *The Exorcist* at some earlier date. Indeed, on the night he saw that particular film he refused to return home because he felt the house was too spooky to stay there alone and booked into the Inn on the Park feeling safer in the livelier atmosphere of a hotel.

But now in Switzerland, we were getting back to a degree of normality after our religious purge. It was as well the priest from Mexico was no longer on hand, because he might have been shocked by the things that began to filter back into Dad's life. His friend Roman Polanski threw a party in his rented chalet at the resort and Dad was inspired by what he saw: Roman seemed to have enticed every long-legged maiden out of the mountains.

It was a party decorated by the 'beautiful people' as the newspaper columnists always described them, and I got in on Dad's coat tails. At 20 years of age I was ready to be initiated and Dad was equally ready to initiate me. He encouraged me to meet the girls that he thought I might like.

Someone produced some 'grass' and Dad got me busy rolling joints until someone arrived with cocaine. I was then equipped with a razor blade and asked to cut the cocaine on Roman's marble table into pieces for guests to sample at their random. I thought that I would sample the cocaine myself; this was to be my last experience of drugs. Looking round at the 'beautiful people' I felt repelled by their behaviour.

Life continued in a similar way. Dad threw what was described as 'the social event of the season', taking over a Gstaad night club for a dusk to dawn party. Stars jostled to get through the door. Our table was reserved in a corner and Elizabeth Taylor and Richard Burton joined us. They were good friends of my father's but by the time the night ended I felt doubtful about the future of their relationship.

The band was loud. Very loud. The amplifiers flanked us, drowning the conversation. Elizabeth was annoyed and got more cross as the evening wore on. Finally she dispatched a message to the band asking them to quieten things down. The musicians threatened mutiny and Dad, taking exception to Miss Taylor's action, ordered the band to play as loud as they liked. As a further token of his displeasure he took over the drums himself, belting hell out of them in a way that might not have had the approval of Buddy Rich but certainly deafened the club and Miss Taylor into surrender. She beat her retreat at that point – it seemed that Dad had punished her sufficiently.

Our spree moved to America and Dad's humour, never too good in Hollywood, did not improve. We went for a drink in the Polo Lounge of the Beverly Hills Hotel. It is the favourite place at cocktail time for movie stars, producers and the usual hangers-on. A waiter came over and politely asked me to produce my ID card which young Americans are issued with to prove they're 21 or over. For some reason Dad took offence and started bawling at the waiter.

His language was very descriptive and the Polo Lounge ground to a halt as his temper gathered fury. The manager was summoned from his office and Dad repeated the insults from beginning to end, not caring who was listening to him. In the end I managed to drag him through to the vestibule and into another bar of the hotel.

Dad had good reason to vouch for my age. Under a trust fund that matured when I was 21, I was receiving £20,000. Similar trust funds were also created for Sarah and Victoria on their coming of age. Dad had laid down the funds when we were youngsters on the advice of his business managers. Ostensibly, it was a legal tax loophole for he was able to divert the interest on the capital into his personal account.

14

Sarah Picks Lynne Frederick

Sarah was at Dad's apartment in London at Roebuck House early one evening when he showed her some photographs of two girls. They might have been fashion pictures he was submitting for *Vogue* because Dad was a regular contributor to the magazine.

But Sarah guessed that there was something special about these particular pictures as Dad peered at her over his horn-rimmed specs.

'Which girl do you think is the nicest?' he enquired, almost too casually. Sarah studied the photographs carefully. Both girls were in their twenties. One was blonde, the other a brunette.

'I don't know,' said Sarah, 'they both look nice. Who are they? ...'

'No, no. Just choose one,' said Dad. Sarah picked out the brunette wearing a scarf round her neck.

'Maybe this one,' she said, 'but it's not really being fair. You can't judge someone until you've met them. How can you make allowance for personality, background and intelligence? Come on, Dad, who are they? Should I know?'

Dad smiled gingerly.

'Not really. They're just a couple of girls I happen to know and I can't decide between them.'

'Decide what?'

'The one I really want to go out with,' said Dad.

Sarah didn't know it then but from the two photographs she had picked out our new stepmother.

'That's Lynne,' said Dad, 'she's very nice but she's a bit suburban.'

Lynne Frederick had waist-length deep brown hair as a child actress. But now, at 21 years of age, she was a brunette in the modern style with highlights streaked through her hair. Her almond-coloured eyes to me shone with undisguised ambition. Dad's meeting with her was another masterful production by Dennis Selinger who seemed to have the knack of restoring romance in Dad's life when it was most needed.

Dennis organized a dinner party when Lynne just happened to be one of the many guests, sitting strategically two or three places from Dad so that their eyes would not fail to meet. She had once been David Frost's girl-friend and according to the gossip columnists she had come to Dad 'on the rebound'; Lynne's interpretation was more simple but whatever her past, Dad was obviously excited.

Sarah accompanied him on a trip to Bond Street where he bought Lynne her first trinket and from that moment we knew that it would only be a matter of time before Dad proposed to her.

I was not particularly enthralled with the idea. Dad's love life was getting past a joke. If his emotions weren't becoming damaged then his image surely was. How could he expect the public to take him seriously if he didn't conduct himself in a more mature way?

I told him frankly: 'Aren't three failed marriages enough? Live with her if you have to, but for heaven's sake don't marry her. If it went wrong you would be a laughing stock ...'

My first impression of Lynne didn't do much to alter my views. She was not exactly my idea of sweetness and light. It didn't concern me that she lacked the good looks of Dad's past wives and girl-friends, but those innocent eyes, certainly her strongest feature, didn't deceive me. She appeared to want to dominate all conversation and be the centre of attraction.

I'm afraid we weren't very kind in our judgement of Lynne when Dad gathered our final verdict on her. Sarah thought she wasn't too bright and Mum and Ted, whose opinion was sought after dinner in a Chinese restaurant, were subdued in their praise and told my father that they thought she was a nice enough girl. But our views didn't really count for much, because whatever our opinions, they would be of purely academic interest. In the end, Dad would certainly make up his own mind.

His ardour continued unabated even when Sarah blithely announced that she was dating a boy much older than Lynne.

'How old?' searched Dad, playing the protective father.

'He's 33,' replied Sarah.

'Thirty-three? But you're only 18. Don't you realize that?' Dad reprimanded.

'Well, look at it this way,' shrugged Sarah, 'you're 49 and Lynne is 21. You've got twenty-eight years dividing you. There's only fifteen years between us.' Dad groaned, lost for an answer. Setting us an example was never his forte.

Sarah's boy-friend was also named Peter and what was more, he was a photographer. For this reason, he was acceptable to Dad initially, when Sarah first introduced Peter to him.

All might have been well but Peter, on this, his first meeting with Dad, remarked, 'So you're the old man? Sarah is always wondering what you're up to.'

Sarah bit her tongue, knowing that Peter had gaffed.

Dad resented nothing more than being called 'the old man' even though the term was generally accepted as an affectionate one. Peter produced a portfolio of his pictures for Dad to see. Sarah thought they were lovely, and Lynne praised them too, but Dad got out some of his own prints to compare them and said, 'Look at the quality of these. I wouldn't ever put out anything as grainy as that ...'

Dad liked to believe that he had the best photographic equipment in the world and for the money he lavished on it, that was probably less of an exaggeration than most other claims in his life. He also felt that he had the best advisory service in Tony Snowdon whose work continued to appear regularly in the *Sunday Times*.

Dad's relations with the Royal family, however, took quite a blow on the West End premiere of his new Inspector Clouseau movie *The Pink Panther Strikes Again*. Lynne wanted to be presented to Prince Charles who was attending. She wasn't content with just going to the premiere. Because of his long-standing friendship with the Prince Dad didn't envisage any problem. But the committee organizing the gala limited the number of people that could be nominated to be presented to His Royal Highness. They ruled that as Lynne wasn't married to Dad she could not reasonably be permitted to be among that number.

Dad responded angrily, demanding Lynne's presence. But for once he found that even the powers of United Artists could not elevate Lynne's name to the presentation ranks. Even his last, dogged attempt at blackmail proved futile.

'Don't expect me to play Clouseau ever again,' raged Dad, 'if you snub Miss Frederick – you snub me.'

Prince Charles was severely embarrassed by Dad's decision to boycott the premiere and later made it known that he thought my father had been misguided.

Whether this accelerated Dad's decision to marry Lynne is a moot point, but in the mayor's parlour in Paris on 18 February 1977 – less than two months later – Dad married Lynne. He was in France for tax reasons and our understanding was that Lynne would not have gone there with him unless they were indeed to be married.

When eventually I saw Dad he asked me if I wasn't going to congratulate him.

'What on?' I asked.

'On my marriage to Lynne,' he said bristling.

'Congratulations,' I said, dry lipped.

Sarah flew into Paris the day after and got to the hotel as Lynne was on the telephone to a friend. As my sister walked in the door Lynne said, 'I've just realized that I'm stepmother to three children. My goodness!'

The significance of that remark was not lost on us, because from that point on Lynne regarded us as 'children' even though I was nearly four months older than her and all three of us were of her generation.

Sarah was told the reason that none of us was invited was

to keep the ceremony secret from the press, a factor stressed by Dad in a letter to Victoria.

But of course attempts to keep the ceremony under covers caused far greater publicity than if Dad had issued gold-edged invitation cards to all and sundry. It leaked out to the press a few days later.

Lynne seemed to bask in the glory of it all until her mother Mrs Iris Frederick, a casting director for Thames Television, went into print saying: 'How could my daughter marry someone like Peter Sellers with his track record? The marriage is doomed from the start.'

Mrs Frederick was obviously appalled by the publicity and took her daughter to task in *Woman's Own*, a British weekly magazine. She said she was tired of Lynne dragging their lives through the newspapers and making it all a public affair. 'My own marriage ended unhappily when Lynne was two,' wrote Mrs Frederick, 'I tried to compensate for her having no father by devoting all the time I wasn't working to her. Perhaps if I had married again she wouldn't have gone on choosing men twice her age as boy-friends – looking for a father figure I suppose. She flitted from one to another like a beautiful butterfly.'

Dad told me he had known his new mother-in-law in earlier years as a close friend and I could not help but wonder whether Iris felt spurned in some way, having seen her daughter marry a man she once regarded as a hero. However, Dad certainly did have a bad track record and there was a considerable age gap between him and Lynne. Enough to upset most mothers whatever the circumstances.

Dad was naturally taken aback, but remained philosophical about Iris's outburst.

Dad's tax situation enforced yet another move from London and one I am certain Lynne contemplated before agreeing to marry my father. They bought a £100,000 villa in the South of France which stood on the water's edge in the holiday resort of Port Grimaud. Once more Dad was not satisfied with the house as it was. The whole place had to be gutted and rebuilt; a balcony was added to the main bedroom and the floors were laid with marble tiles. Kitchen and bathrooms were also streamlined regardless of cost.

Dad loved the idea of a new home and a new marriage. It was always like starting a new chapter in his life when all previous events, happenings and links with the past could be discarded. That was why, in times like this, we were a nuisance to him because we were part of his former life. We didn't really figure in his future.

Lynne was already talking about having children and spoke at length with Sarah about it. Dad was present all through the conversation but when Sarah asked him if we were going to have any more sisters or brothers he noticeably evaded the questions. He was conscious of his age and the thought of having a large family was distant from his mind. Instead, he gave Lynne a Yorkshire terrier – which in her absence was occasionally booted from the room for his misdoings.

However, Dad wanted to look 'young' for his bride. This induced him to have the puffy bags appearing beneath his eyes removed by cosmetic surgery. His 'double' chin worried him more and this was taken care of by the same process in Los Angeles, when the operation was conducted after an intravenous Valium injection. When it was over Dad invited me to inspect the cosmetic surgeon's skills. 'What do you think?' he asked, raising his chin for me to see.

'That looks fine,' I replied.

In fact there was a slight scar but Dad used make-up to cover it. Until it healed he was quite sensitive about it.

Much more of a worry to Dad was the growing deterioration of his heart condition. Every plausible excuse was advanced against having open heart surgery and now, in the early summer of 1978, he thought he had found the answer. Once again, the basis of his new theories was grounded in the obscure world of mysticism.

In the Philippines there was a group of psychic surgeons who claimed miracle cures even for cases regarded as terminal. Dad, who said he was satisfied with his investigations into the

Filipinos' claims, totally ignored the evidence of a British television documentary exposing these surgeons as tricksters whose practices were condemned throughout the medical profession.

Only the most desperate of patients, it was said, were driven to consult these 'psychic surgeons', who conducted their 'surgery' by invisibly passing their hands into a patient's body and plucking out the diseased tissues.

Some friends of mine who learned of Dad's intentions to go to the Philippines telephoned me and urged me to dissuade him from making the trip. I got in touch with him and told him bluntly that many people had already testified that the Filipinos were fakes and that he was only deluding himself by believing they could possibly be genuine.

Dad didn't want to listen.

'You tell your friends to keep their noses out of my private affairs,' said Dad angrily. 'I don't meddle in their lives. So tell them not to meddle in mine'.

'But Dad, these people know what is happening in Manila. They only have your best interests in mind ...'

I was wasting my breath. Dad was going to go, whatever I said. I hoped that Lynne might talk some sense into him, but her view was that nothing could be lost in going to Manila and seeing for themselves how the Filipinos worked. So they set out for Manila and we knew that once they were gone Dad would be easily persuaded on to the operating table.

News came soon enough from Manila that the operations were 100 per cent successful. Dad had taken a series of twenty-eight operations in all and said that he was totally fit and well again. Of course we heard more about it all on their return to England.

'Everything was absolutely genuine,' said Dad, who had a deceptively healthy glow from the suntan he had also acquired in the Philippines, 'and I didn't feel a thing.' He pulled up the sweater he was wearing and said, 'Look, there's not a scar. They made their own incisions just by touching my chest with their hands. I didn't feel a thing. I didn't have an anaesthetic and I could see what was going on all of the time.'

Lynne had photographed Dad's operations and she now produced a set of colour pictures to prove their authenticity. She also had two operations to cure a back problem.

'They really are incredible,' said Lynne. And glancing at Dad she said, 'Aren't they, darling?'

'Oh yes,' he said, 'these people are performing miracles. One day the medical profession will recognize their work.'

We felt embarrassed and sickened as we listened to Lynne and Dad unfold the saga over dinner at Mum and Ted's. Dad said that one of the surgeons had placed his hand into his chest and removed some fluid that apparently was causing his heart problem.

'Now, I just don't feel a thing,' said Dad.

Mum and Ted hid their feelings, though, like us, they suspected that Dad had been duped.

The pictures that Lynne produced were sufficiently gory to lead one to believe that the surgeons were indeed severing parts of the body with their bare hands, but the television programme had shown that the 'operations' were conducted by sleight of hand and the removed 'human' tissues came from pigs and other animals. My mother asked Dad if he still had to take his pills.

'Oh God, no,' said Dad, 'what for? I'm 200 per cent fit now. I've thrown all the pills away . . .'

Mum was horrified. We all were.

Dad raved about the Filipinos' skills to Ivan Waterman, London *News of the World* columnist and told him: 'These surgeons are genuine. Everyone will soon see that the work these men do is quite unique and invaluable. It won't be long before they are recognized by the medical profession.' But Mike Scott, a television producer friend of Dad's, dismissed the statements as nonsense.

'It's just one trick, endlessly, heartbreakingly and profitably used over and over again,' he said. 'People really brainwash themselves into believing these things.'

Mike Scott cited cases where the most humble of patients paid over fees to surgeons of not less than £50.

Dad tactfully didn't mention how much he had paid the Filipinos, but told the *News of the World* that 'no fee was asked for'.

The wording of that remark led me to believe that Dad had made a sizeable donation to the Filipinos, no doubt 'for the furtherance of their work'. In any event the psychic surgeons were pretty astute and with a patient as famous as my father they were certain to obtain maximum publicity.

No one in the family wanted to demoralize Dad. What galled us most was that he had been deceived and was foolish enough to go along with it. Mum took him quietly aside and urged him to go back to his own qualified doctor to establish whether the Filipinos' claims of his cure could possibly be true.

In time, with the loss of medication, Dad began to experience mild flutters of his heart once more and the truth sadly dawned on him. But again the thought of submitting to open heart surgery was distasteful to him.

After collapsing on a flight into London from Paris, my father was rushed to the Charing Cross Hospital where he had to rest.

It was essential now to have the recommended surgery. But the one alternative was to have a pacemaker fitted, which with the help of a micro-chip, would cut in at any time the heart-beat faltered. Lynne, rather than attempt to convince Dad he should have an artery by-pass, thought that the pacemaker was the solution to his problems.

In the short-term it was fine; but the one flaw of the pacemaker as far as I could gather, was that it disguised the exact condition of a patient's heart, a factor that clearly emerged at Dad's death.

But now, with the pacemaker installed, Dad took on a fresh lease of life. To friends he would joke that he was 'one third bionic' and show them the pacemaker – his latest gadget! It was just possible to detect the pacemaker – the size of a cigarette packet. At first it was inserted beneath his collar bone but his arm movements kept dislodging it, so it was conveniently slotted below his rib cage.

Dad also had to face the fact that he would have to resume medication and the pills he thought he could do without were now to become a part of his daily life. But at least, with the pacemaker he was a lot happier.

United Artists were anxious to get back into Dad's good favours after the royal premiere incident.

Their launch of any *Pink Panther* movie was always cause for a gala extravaganza, but now UA were to exceed themselves.

For their first public screening of *The Revenge of the Pink Panther* they decided to throw a party in surroundings of sheer paradise. The place was Hawaii and chartered jets were laid on from London, Los Angeles and Paris to fly in the world's most distinguished columnists and critics. Every hotel room in Hawaii was taken and flowers, fruit and gifts awaited each guest.

Dad came into Hawaii as though it was his own kingdom. He and Lynne were greeted by beautiful Hawaiian girls with orchids in their hair who placed garlands around their necks. A huge car took them to their hotel where the presidential suite had been reserved for them.

United Artists invited Sarah and myself, as well as my girl-friend Kathy. Three first-class tickets were provided for us from London to Hawaii and we were given beach cabanas, equipped with bars and colour television sets and were told we could order anything we liked and to put it on the bill.

United Artists asked Dad to choose a present and he decided on the latest Polaroid outfit which he told them to give to me. Sarah, who had borrowed some of Mum's clothes so that she could go to all of the parties, also received a lot of presents. Many sponsors liked to publicize their wares in the *Pink Panther* movies – Seiko would plug their watches, Sony their recording equipment and Dewars their fine Scotch whisky. This meant we came by a lot of free samples.

All this luxury went to our heads and we behaved like lunatics. For instance, we took in a stray cat and her five kittens in our cabana and fed them steak for breakfast which we put on the bill! We spent blissful days, swimming, surfing and motorbiking over the sand dunes and drinking Pina Coladas like pints of milk. The fruit and the food were equally exotic. All in all, we found life highly intoxicating but no doubt United Artists thought that once their guests were in a happy, relaxed frame of mind they would get even more enjoyment from *The Revenge of the Pink Panther* when it came to be screened.

Dad wasn't so sure. He was always sceptical about critics. One or two were inevitably scathing of him and were permanently on his black list; but others who recognized his talents were usually loyal to him. Lynne told Dad not to worry. 'You're going to be wonderful in it, I'm sure,' she said. She was in her element. She had only seen the film industry at a more basic level. She had never seen anything as glossy as this before where a superstar and his entourage were pampered to such extreme degrees. She babbled away from night until morning. She would talk about people as though she had known them as life-long friends – like Cary Grant. After Dad introduced her to him, he became 'CG' in every conversation thereafter.

She had plenty of opportunity to keep all this up in Hawaii, but at dinner parties I wondered what such professionals as Blake Edwards and Julie Andrews thought about Lynne's conversational habits.

Herbert Lom, who played Clouseau's paranoid superior 'Dreyfus' in the French Sûreté was also with us in Hawaii. The hedonistic life-style didn't affect the more staid Herbert, whose way of life was very different from Dad's. He was a more reserved and much quieter man, whose attitudes to life were solid and mature.

Yet he possessed a wonderful sense of humour as was vouched by his performance as the eye-twitching Dreyfus; Dad admired him as an actor, having first worked with him on *The Lady Killers*. But while valuing their friendship, he never saw Herbert as a real friend in the way he did Graham and David, both of whom occasionally played supporting roles in the *Panthers*.

Dad didn't ever forget his chums whenever he made a film. If there was a part he knew would suit a friend he would suggest their name for it. There was an actor and family friend named

Mario Fabrizzo who hit hard times and came to Dad for help. Dad got him parts in two or three movies and in other periods would employ Mario to do odd jobs around the house. Sadly, Mario died before Dad reached superstar status, for his own career might also have benefited.

From Hawaii Dad telephoned my mother in London. He wanted to show that his family still meant something to him and Mum, hearing our excited voices in the background, was pleased to know we were having a good time.

But there was not complete family harmony.

Dad, after another row with Britt, took his revenge by refusing to invite Victoria to stay. She said she thought that Dad would have been nicer to her if it had not been for the fact that he was always trying to torment Britt. He would scare her by threatening to have Britt arrested and thrown into jail, and that he would seek custody of her; then she would live with him permanently because her mother was a bad influence over her.

'Victoria is in the pop world now. She's getting more like her mother every day,' Dad would grumble.

Until then he had always taken the trouble to ask Victoria about her half-brother Nicholai and said nice things about him. But when Britt became involved with pop star Rod Stewart after she had broken with Lou Adler, caring for Victoria's welfare seemed to bother him a good deal more. Victoria unwittingly gave the impression that Rod Stewart was more famous than Dad and would tell him about all the pop concerts she was going to.

She often asked Dad for pocket money. In the past, knowing she would report back to Britt, he had brushed her aside with the remark, 'Why not go and ask Uncle Lou?' Dad's attitude stemmed from the fact that he always seemed anxious that his role as a father might be usurped. Victoria, as young as she was, cleverly turned this vulnerability to her own advantage. If he failed to give her the little things she asked for, she would deliberately say, 'Okay I'll go to Uncle Lou.' Later she began using Rod's name in the same way.

Feelings were tense. Behind the scenes both Dad and Britt
were paying out thousands of pounds to lawyers in disagree-
ments about Victoria's schooling and holiday periods.

The crisis came to a head when Dad cancelled a holiday at
the last minute which Victoria was to have spent with him and
Lynne in the South of France. The air ticket in her hand, she
was leaving Britt's house in Los Angeles when she got the
message. Britt naturally gave vent to her feelings and after bitter
words were exchanged, Dad sent a letter to Victoria saying that
she should no longer regard him as her father. It was signed by
his secretary Sue Evans, a procedure that Dad always employed
when he had something unpleasant to say. In such cases he
rarely signed anything himself. When there was 'dirty' work to
be done it was poor Sue or Bert who had to execute the deed.

Rod Stewart told Victoria, who was at a loss to understand
why Dad should write such a letter to her, not to worry about
it. 'I'll adopt you,' said Rod; later he gave Victoria a horse
together with all the riding equipment. He also bought her a
stereo and a whole collection of games.

When Victoria's relations with Dad were once more restored
she wisely decided not to tell him of Rod's adoption offer. She
was already running great risks in passing on a message from her
mother that Dad had fallen behind with her maintenance
money. Hearing this Dad nearly choked with anger, 'Will she
never give up? That stupid blonde actress.'

15

The Wounded Soldier

Lynne's influence on my father insinuated itself over the entire household in the South of France. Dad chose not to recognize the signs outwardly of course but saw their impact. Our new stepmother was now issuing most of the orders. It seemed that she wanted to take over all his affairs and to dispense with the services of those servants and advisers she saw as a threat to her.

Bert Mortimer went. Poor Bert, the most loyal and trusted of Dad's associates. Through good days and bad, Bert had always been in the thick of the action as Dad's lieutenant. He had rescued Dad from many tight corners, dragging him clear from squabbles, putting him to bed when he was drunk, listening to endless tales of agony and marital strife. Bert had started sixteen years before as a chauffeur. One of Dad's first cars when he acquired Bert was a Volvo sports model, but it had to be sent back on the ferry to Sweden because Bert was so tall he couldn't fit into it without grazing his head on the roof! Since then he had been at the wheel of practically every classic car known to the automobile world. Dad bought more than 200 cars during Bert's days of service.

They had become friends more than employee and employer. They shared family secrets. Bert's wife would often joke: 'If ever I divorce my husband, I'll cite Peter Sellers.' Bert lived in, except for weekends when he would go home to see his wife and family. Dad would call Bert at any hour, if only to chat on mundane matters that could in fact have waited until the following morning. They had established a rapport more characteristic of brothers. Whenever Dad wanted to get rid of callers on the phone he would impersonate Bert's voice and say, 'I'm sorry. Mr Sellers is not at home. Is there a message?'

Bert's first loyalty was always to Dad but he had looked after our needs too: delivering and collecting us from school and making sure that we kept out of trouble. We were stunned by his sacking, but no more than Bert himself because he could find no valid reason for his dismissal other than having earned Lynne's dislike. What upset Bert greatly was the fact that after all those years, Dad didn't have the courage to tell him face to face. His dismissal came in a letter, couched in cold terms, and delivered by a hotel chambermaid when Bert was preparing to join Dad and Lynne on a yacht at Port Grimaud for cocktails. Bert, deeply wounded, threatened to go to the Industrial Tribunal for unfair dismissal. As a result, Dad came to delete Bert's name from his final will.

In time, other key people around Dad were also to be replaced. His business manager Dennis O'Brien saw the imminent danger, with Lynne gaining more control over my father's affairs by the day.

Dennis questioned Dad's wisdom. 'Of course you love your wife,' he said, 'but isn't it wise to keep your business enterprises separate as you have done in the past? With respect, what does Lynne know about business matters?' But his argument was to no avail. Dennis's services were dispensed with.

John Humphries, the family lawyer, was also dismissed. After each of Dad's marriages, he had consulted John in matters relating to his will and estate. But the lawyer had not recently heard from Dad. When he discovered that a new set of lawyers had been appointed he drew his own conclusions; but he managed to take it philosophically as solicitors are wont to do.

Later, Theo Cowan too, the longest serving of Dad's entourage, was also dismissed. He didn't worry too much, because he had been sacked before – only to be taken back on.

Lynne wanted to run the whole show and we had to admit that she was making a good job of it. She ran around after Dad, pampering him in every conceivable way. If he was quiet, she would ask him: 'Is there anything the matter, darling? Is there anything I can do?' She wanted Dad to become totally dependent on her and indeed the power was steadily passing out of his hands. Dad's secretary Sue Evans and his personal assistant Michael Jeffery survived the purge; they remained loyal to Lynne. In earlier days Sue had been dismissed on many occasions by Dad, but she had always arrived at her desk the following morning. Dad took Sue's wedding-day pictures but then sacked her, saying she couldn't give enough time to him when she now had a husband to think about!

Sue married film director Frank Evans and later ran Dad's office from her home after he sold his Roebuck House apartment. She always referred to him as 'PS' in conversations with us when we rang through to talk to him, or purely to check on the state of his health.

Michael Jeffery had been Dad's dresser on the *Pink Panther*. Now as his personal assistant he had more opportunity to further his career and Dad appointed him as the designer for the costumes of one of his last movies, *The Fiendish Plot of Dr Fu Manchu*.

At Easter I went with my girl-friend Kathy to see Dad and Lynne in St Tropez, the house in Port Grimaud not yet being completed.

The marriage appeared to be happy with Dad still spoiling Lynne. He bought her a diamond bracelet but thought that the stones weren't big enough for her and sent it back to the shop to be changed.

It was almost sycophantic the way Lynne got round Dad. If she expressed a view that was contrary to his, she would immediately alter her opinions to coincide with his.

Only occasionally did we see flashes of Dad's old self. Like the night he got ruffled by a French driver when leaving a restaurant along the coastline. Driving Lynne's new car, Dad gave chase to the Frenchman at high speed. Lynne got worried. 'Peter, don't drive like this,' she exclaimed, 'this is my car and it's not run in yet. What are you doing?'

'Damn your car! That froggie needs carving up,' he snapped.

The chase went on for three miles, but finally the Frenchman abandoned his car and disappeared into a block of flats. After flashing his lights all over the building and getting out of his car to brandish his fist and echo a few well-chosen insults Dad retired from the pursuit.

When the house at Port Grimaud was ready, Victoria was invited once more for a holiday and this time it actually did materialize.

Dad bought her water skis, a wetsuit, bicycle, skateboard and clothes, all of which was the measure of his remorse at having earlier disowned her.

A fun fair was meant to be one of the highlights of Victoria's stay but Dad got into a row with a stallholder who tried to instruct him on the rudiments of re-loading his gun on the rifle range. Dad left the fairground in a huff and went back to the car to sulk. When he got home, one of his familiar black moods descended. He threatened to kill Lynne's dog because it had scraped the walls in their absence. Stalking about the house in his rage, he tossed out of the window a porcelain Gucci ashtray he considered unlucky because it was embossed with a white elephant.

During the early part of the summer I received the final £2000 instalment of my trust fund and Sarah got a £2000 advance on hers. We both called Dad and thanked him on a number of occasions. We should have written formal notes. But in any case he was about to set off more torpedoes – and I took the first blast. 'Michael, it's not good enough,' screamed Dad, 'I've set you up for life and you're ungrateful. You've never even bothered to thank me. I've worked myself to death to earn that kind of money and now what do you say? Nothing. I may as well not have bothered. What kind of son are you?'

I took a deep breath and kept silent. I would have liked to have given him the whole of the £20,000 back but he knew that I was in an impossible situation as I'd already committed myself to buying a flat. Eventually I answered him, 'Dad, I'm not wasting the money.' I felt by then it was necessary to defend my position. 'I'm getting my own flat and I'm buying a car. I'm grateful but how can I say "thank you" in a way that you will accept?'

Sarah didn't escape reproach either. She too was buying a car with her money and preparing to invest the rest of it – when it arrived – into a Victorian antique dolls shop in Camden Passage in London's Islington.

'You could have called, Sarah,' moaned Dad. 'It's a fortune you're getting and I want to know what you're going to do with it.' Sarah had called the day before but Dad, too busy with other matters, hadn't bothered to listen to what she was saying.

Retribution came swiftly. We both got letters from Dad disowning us. They were identically worded. The one addressed to me read:

'Dear Michael – This is to tell you how extremely upset I am by your behaviour toward me. You must, by now, have received the extra money from John Humphries, and your flat has been financed by the Trust I set up for you; yet you could not find the time to telephone or write a letter to thank me. I'm tired of being used as a source of finance, and contacted *only* when you need something. Whatever relationship we might have had is finished, the time has come for you to continue your own way. I no longer wish to be thought of as your father. Good luck with your career, if you ever choose one. Best Wishes, Sue Evans (Peter Sellers, dictated by telephone from the South of France).

Even with letters and notes within the family, Dad would always rely on Sue to carry through his less pleasant demands – we certainly weren't exempt from this practice.

I got together with Sarah and we decided to retaliate. We dictated our reply through Sue. We wrote, 'Dear Dad, It comes as no surprise to us that your feelings towards us are measured in terms of money.' We asked Sue to sign the letter, with the appendage 'dictated by Michael and Sarah by telephone from Hampstead'. We toyed with the idea of addressing Dad in our letter as 'Dear Ex-father. . . .' but resisted the temptation!

Another letter arrived next day. It was terse and to the point.
'Dear Michael and Sarah,
    Further to your note, my final suggestion is that you have
    your name changed by deed poll to Levy.'

PETER SELLERS

As From: 64 Ile des Pins,
83360 Port Grimaud,
Var,
France.

Mr. Michael Sellers,
The Chantry,
Spaniards End,
Hampstead, London N.W.3.   13th June, 1977

Dear Michael,

This letter is to tell you how extremely upset I am by your
behaviour toward me. You must, by now, have received the
extra money from John Humphries, and your flat has been financed
by the Trust I set up for you; yet you could not find the time
to telephone or write a letter to thank me.

I'm tired of being used as a source of finance, and contacted
only when you need something. Whatever relationship we might have
had is finished, the time has come for you to continue your
own way. I no longer wish to be thought of as your father.

Good luck with your career, if you ever choose one.

Best wishes,

Sue Evans

Peter Sellers
PS/se

Dictated by telephone from the South of France

Again it was dictated to Sue who signed it in Dad's absence.

Not once had we ever thought about taking our stepfather's name. We wondered what had triggered off this idea in Dad's mind. But within a few weeks, the whole affair blew over and was not mentioned again.

Dad's attentions were diverted by the start of the re-make of a Hollywood classic *The Prisoner of Zenda*. With all his old zeal, Dad was playing three roles: the eighty-year-old King Rudolph, the playboy Prince Rudolph and the London cabbie who stands in as his double to save the throne.

Dad's bride was to be played by Lynne, making her first appearance with him in a film. Lynne's acting background was impressive for her age. She appeared as the child actress in *The Amazing Mr Blunden* and her first major film was *No Blade of Grass*. She also took the role of Catherine Howard in *Henry VIII and his Six Wives* and she starred in the British television series *The Pallisers*.

As the film was being shot on location in Vienna, he felt more secure in Lynne's presence. Besides, he had generously given two roles to Britt during their marriage, so how could he ignore the career of his new wife? He started the film with his usual enthusiasm, but the whole schedule soon turned awry.

Vienna, which had seemed in his eyes the most beautiful city in the world, suddenly became a dump; the food like the weather had turned decidedly lousy and the film, with all its initial momentum, was going from bad to worse. It was to be the same familiar story; only the dateline and titles were different. But this time there was evidence that the pressures had taken their toll on him. Within days of the film wrapping up, Dad collapsed and spent a month in Geneva recovering from what was diagnosed as a chronic angina attack.

By now it was Christmas and as always we were faced with the problem of finding something suitable to give Dad. He loved presents but was truly a man who had everything. Clothes, gadgets, cigarette lighters ... we had little choice left. As a rule we searched for the novelty present that might appeal to his sense of humour. This particular Christmas there was very little

PETER SELLERS

14th June, 1977

Dear Michael and Sarah,

Further to your note, my final suggestion
is that you have your name changed
by deed poll to Levy.

Sue Evans.

Peter Sellers
PS/se

Dictated by telephone from the South of France

of ingenuity on the market and I settled for a book on photography, illustrated with beautiful colour pictures of trees and landscapes. It won Dad's approval and I got a message back that he liked it.

Sarah wasn't so fortunate. She bought Dad an old 'Vanity Fayre' cover print, featuring a collection of caricatures and sent Lynne a set of hand-made Victorian table mats. Sarah, opening a letter after Christmas from Dad, assumed it was a 'thank you' note. She was unprepared for the contents. It read:

'Dear Sarah,
   I have just been given what I believe
   to be your Christmas presents ... I know
   it is the thought that counts and not
   the money. But what a thought. Yours,
   Dad'.

She was very hurt. More so, when she reflected on the fact that Dad hadn't bothered to send her, or any of us for that matter, presents that year, only cards. Later, he told me that he considered Sarah's presents to be 'an insult' and that she had not cared about his feelings.

His attitude to presents was always odd. Sarah once gave him some beads for his birthday during his yoga days. Later, when clearing out a drawer, he found them and turning to my sister said: 'Oh Sarah, would you like these? I'm about to throw them out.' He had quite forgotten that it was Sarah who had given them to him. Yet when she had a Rolex watch stolen from her hotel room he accused her of being negligent and didn't speak to her for several weeks.

He inclined to be hard on Sarah and Victoria, finding it much more difficult to communicate with them. He could talk with me about videos, stereo equipment, cars and gadgets, but failed to realize that my sisters didn't have any interest in such matters.

We also earned Dad's anger when we forgot to send Lynne a birthday card, although we remembered her at Christmas. As a result Sarah didn't get a card or call when her birthday came round.

When Sarah was at college she was constantly maligned by Dad for not telephoning him. She could not use the line out of the college because of the house rules and she didn't have a phone at home. She once tried to call Dad from a booth and left a message for him at his hotel in Los Angeles. Later he complained she was too mean to make a second call and had deliberately left a message so that he would have to bear the expense of phoning her back!

At this stage Dad felt that Sarah owed him some consideration, as he had bought her a small car to run around in. For her student days at college it was perfect and she was very grateful for it. But Dad had forgotten to insure it. She telephoned about it, but was rebuffed by Lynne, who refused to put Dad on the line and told her that he was busy.

'Your father feels that now you've got a car you ought to put aside some money to run it. After all, he does give you an allowance. Where does it all go?' she said. Sarah's allowance was £20 a week. This nowhere covered her rent, food and clothes which meant that Mum had to assist her too. Lynne demanded to know how much Mum actually contributed.

My mother was sitting in the same room at the time of this conversation and clearly gathered the drift of what was said. 'Tell Lynne to mind her own business,' said my mother, now getting annoyed, 'it has nothing to do with her whatsoever as to how much I contribute.'

Family relations were rapidly deteriorating once more. In the beginning Sarah liked Lynne, though she felt her taste in clothes was a bit drab and dull. Of course, it was possible that Lynne deliberately dressed 'older' so that she could play her role as our stepmother more convincingly, and would not look so much out of place at Dad's side.

Sarah then found she had put herself in a compromising position by indiscreetly confiding to Lynne various details about her boy-friends. She could only hope that Lynne would not betray her trust.

Lynne left for America with Dad who had signed for *Being There* which was adapted from Jerzy Kosinski's novel about the simple life of a middle-aged gardener named Chance whose only experiences come from watching television. A friend, Victoria Lindsay Hogg – who often provided a shoulder to cry on in Dad's depressed moods – had given my father the book to read several years before. Now that Dad had actually persuaded Hollywood to make the film he sent Victoria £500 for suggesting the novel to him.

The film made more than £5,000,000 at the box office and Dad gave what he considered to be his finest performance.

Scheduled to start shooting soon in North Carolina, Dad and Lynne went first to California and spent some time with my step-sister and invited her to stay in their house.

Victoria, my sister rejoiced at their coming. Away from her mother's disciplined routines she was able to stay up as long as she wanted, choose her own hours to go to bed, and was allowed out to all her friends' parties.

'Dad seemed to let me do anything I wanted, because that was his way of getting back at Mum,' recalls Victoria. She would smuggle out bottles of champagne from Dad's wine racks by hiding them in the sleeves of her dresses. She also discovered Dad's hidden supplies of dope, much to the delight of Victoria's friends.

She might not have known he smoked dope had he not openly lit joints one day on the beach at Malibu. One or two were left over and Victoria buried them in the sands to ensure that supplies to her friends could continue. Eventually, Britt got suspicious of what was happening and threatened to have Victoria arrested if she was ever caught smoking pot at home.

This was a difficult period for Victoria, already going through the changes of adolescence. She wanted to form a closer relationship with Dad, hoping that he would be a father to her in the way that Lou Adler was to her half-brother Nicholai. But often when she rang Dad, he wouldn't take her calls and it was left to Lynne to explain to her that she should not worry for he did it with everyone.

Lynne would entrance Victoria by buying her clothes and make up. She also threw a party for her at a time when Dad had gone back to Europe for a few days on business talks.

She threw open the house and told Victoria she could invite along anyone she wanted. The word went out all over Beverly Hills among the teenage set and more than two hundred youngsters, many dressed in ghoulish vampire costumes, appeared on the doorstep. Victoria charged them two dollars each for admission so that she could pay for the 'extras' that Lynne had not envisaged – a band, bouncers and beer.

Lynne shivered at the sight of the teenagers in their weird hair styles and costumes and afterwards spoke to Victoria about her choice of friends and inferred that it was under the influence of Britt that she associated with such people. But she promised not to tell Dad on his return and that it would remain a secret between them.

Filming began on *Being There* and Dad grappled with the problem of finding the right interpretation, suffering all the familiar tensions and pressures. Life was always a nightmare for those around him in periods like this and although Lynne had already seen Dad in many of his black moods she had not seen him so isolated. Quarrels developed and Dad, in calls to home, began to ask us what we thought of Lynne. It was a question I recognized as one that had anticipated all his marital problems. If he asked for an opinion of someone then it was a clear indication of the anxieties he was feeling.

In North Carolina, where Dad had taken a hotel suite, he became a real recluse. Lynne could not break down the barriers he was hiding behind.

Spring came and Dad flew into London alone. He was looking thin and his face was darkly gaunt. He was fretful and depressed. I dined with him at the Dorchester and the subject of his marriage outweighed all other thoughts.

'I'm going to have to tell Lynne that I can't go on with it. It's just not worked out,' he said. 'She doesn't understand my way of life. I shouldn't have married her. I should have listened to what you said. She was far too young.'

Dad's eyes were sullen. His manner lethargic, as though he had lost all interest in the world as a whole. The morning's newspapers were spread out on a table untouched.

'I don't know when I last made love with Lynne,' said Dad suddenly, as though it was something he was secretly fretting over but could no longer keep to himself, 'we haven't made it for months ...'

He looked at me for my reaction.

'I can't find any reason for it,' he gesticulated. 'It's not her fault. It's mine. I can't get it together.'

'Maybe it's psychological,' I volunteered, 'you've got a lot of pressure on.'

'I daresay,' nodded Dad, 'but I've been thinking about going for another check. Can you imagine facing life without sex? ...'

Most doctors, I am sure, would have decided that Dad's impotence was due to the agitation he was suffering in his marriage. Only later was it discovered that his virility was being affected by a worsening of his blood condition.

Dad had not given any indication that he wanted children. Now he said, 'Lynne would have been happy if we'd have had a child.'

He shrugged. 'I imagine it's just as well that we didn't, considering the way things have worked out.' He seemed ready to absorb the failure of the marriage.

'Four wives. What is wrong with me, Mike? Can't anyone understand me? Am I that difficult to live with?' he asked forlornly. 'I thought I'd got it right with Lynne. I really thought she was the right woman ...'

Dad sat silently now on the sofa though his thoughts were clearly ones of extreme frustration. I tried to switch the conversation to other things, but it always came back to Lynne and their marital problems. I knew that trouble loomed nearer – indeed it came only a day or two later.

Dad, still in a state of depression, unburdened his troubled soul to David Lewin of the London *Daily Mail*.

'My marriage,' he said, 'is over. We thought it would last forever. But few things do.'

Lewin didn't consider Dad's meanderings as classified: he applied the journalist's rules as he would to any official interview. Dad said afterwards that he thought he was speaking aloud to an old chum. If that was so, then the next morning he knew he had made a bad error of judgement. The story appeared on the *Mail*'s front page; the first Lynne heard of this formal announcement of their marriage split was when rival newspapers rang her seeking comment.

Dad was filled with contrition but the damage was done. Lynne refused to answer his phone calls so he despatched Michael Jeffery to California to mollify her, and persuade her to talk to him.

Lynne showed little sign of putting out the olive branch, so Dad took a harder, if reluctant course – to press for a divorce. Once more in Dad's life there was a sudden flurry of lawyers. Lynne agreed to the divorce but demanded a hefty settlement.

Dad grimaced. 'It's like paying a ransom,' he said, 'but I've got to get out of this mess whatever the cost.'

Lynne had found a beautiful house on Beverly Hills. It cost Dad more than a million dollars, but under the settlement thrashed out by the lawyers, it was to become hers. Dad also agreed to pay Lynne a sum of 50,000 dollars a year alimony.

'She's taken me to the cleaners, Mike, but what can I do?' said Dad. 'She's had more out of me than anyone else. I've never had to pay a divorce settlement like this before. Your mother didn't take a penny. I paid Britt £30,000 and about the same to Miranda. But Lynne ...'

I felt sorry for Dad but there was nothing I could say nor could I find any comforting words to offer.

Distraught, he returned to the chalet in Gstaad that he and Lynne had chosen just before their separation. The chalet, long roofed in typical Swiss style, was named La Haute Grange and it commanded one of the most exhilarating views of the towering Alps.

But Dad could find no solace there. Angry with Lynne, he struck her name from his will, leaving his entire estate to the British Heart Foundation. Under this will, when he felt he was deserted by everyone, we fared only fractionally better than Lynne. Dad said that the £20,000 he had given us each under the trust fund was 'adequate provision' and he only made token bequests to us of £40.

Dad was alone and suspicious of everyone. He sacked Sue, accusing her of siding with Lynne, though he later apologized to her.

After another broken marriage Dad must have wondered whether there was anyone left he could turn to. Then, as always in periods of depression and distress, his thoughts returned to his family. We all started getting calls from him.

In the summer I married my girl-friend Kathy and Dad journeyed to London for the wedding. At one point he whispered to Mum: 'Fancy our Pooh getting married. It doesn't seem possible does it?' For our wedding present he gave us an expensive three-piece lounge suite. Dad winked at Mum: 'In our day, Annie, that would have only cost 135 quid!'

He was now very friendly with Mum and Ted. Whenever he was in London he called at the house and one night actually put Mum on the extension so that she could listen to the voice of Prince Charles having a conversation with him!

At the wedding reception Dad quietly despatched his driver on a mission to buy Ted a wide-angle lens for his new camera, though Ted had merely sought his advice because he was now using a camera for his architectural work.

My father didn't mention Lynne and neither did we. We all thought how ill he looked and he expressed the most alarming fear to Mum that he might have suffered brain damage on the first series of his heart attacks. Now a sad figure, it was as though he had nothing in life at all. A millionaire with nothing. And no one. Even the clown within him had gone. There was not one of us who didn't feel moved by the state he was in when he left to go back to Switzerland that day.

Kathy and I set up home in Hampstead and Dad would call us at all hours. Kathy, as any new wife might have done, got irritated sometimes because Dad didn't ever seem to consider the time. It could be three or four in the morning, but this didn't deter him from engaging me in a long conversation which I would listen to patiently. Kathy didn't understand Dad. Unfortunately, our marriage was painfully brief. Kathy fell in love with someone else and we parted exactly six weeks after the ceremony.

I didn't tell Dad, as I preferred not to burden him with my problems when he was still shouldering his own.

I was also scared that Dad might send over 'one of the boys' to 'fix' Kathy's new boy-friend. Dad, in circumstances like these, was always talking about sending over the 'boys', but the only evidence I found of their existence was when he despatched a film 'heavy' to give someone a gentle squeeze of the hand when settling an overdue bill.

Nevertheless, I couldn't be sure. He was very protective towards us; he could malign us in any way he saw fit, but others did so at their peril. When he finally learned of our break up he said: 'That's sad, Mike, but I had a feeling that something like this would happen.'

Dad went to Barbados for a few days' rest with Michael Jeffery. Their plane into the West Indies hit an air pocket and dived towards the ocean. At the time it was cruising though the mysterious Bermuda Triangle, where many planes and ships have disappeared without explanation. Dad said he chanted a Hindu Mantra and the plane managed to pull out of its dive. When they got into Barbados, fresh trouble awaited Dad. The customs stripped him down from tip to toe. They were not happy about all the camera equipment he was carrying. He lost his cool and caught the next plane out to New York.

Customs barriers were always his *bête noir*. If he was stopped at any airport in any part of the world and asked if he had anything to declare, he would immediately go off the deep end. His antics were well known at Heathrow and I would be asked quietly by officials to calm him down. Sometimes, if customs men dared search his suitcases, Dad would storm away in disgust and an officer once told me that under such circumstances they were quite entitled to arrest him.

In the autumn Dad, frustrated by reports he was hearing about Victoria, sent Sarah to Palm Springs to see how she was getting on in her new boarding school. He said he had not heard from Britt for a while; she had recently broken from Rod Stewart whom she was now suing for 12,000,000 dollars.

'That's typical of Ekland. She's a gold digger,' said Dad, finding a certain pleasure in news of their split. Lynne, on the other hand, apparently telephoned Britt and offered her condolences. The two had never met.

But now with Britt making a film somewhere, Sarah set out on her mission in Palm Springs. Dad laid on a chauffeur-driven car, booked her into a suite in a five-star hotel and gave her £500 spending money. He said he wanted a full report on Victoria, having heard from various sources that she was getting very involved with pop stars.

'We've only got to remedy the Ekland influence,' Dad told me.

Sarah talked with Victoria's teachers and found that she was doing well in some subjects, but lagging behind in others.

We only saw Victoria once or twice a year and sometimes she was more of a stranger to us than a sister. But she was pleased to see Sarah, who threw a small party in her suite for Victoria and took her to Disneyland. Dad was pleased with Sarah's report and later dropped a note congratulating her on her progress, which had pleasantly surprised him.

Dad had now got the Swiss chalet furnished, curtained and redecorated. His beloved records and books – mainly glossy biographies like the one he treasured of Marilyn Monroe – had all been shipped from England. So, too, was the solarium he had once had installed at his own expense at the Dorchester Hotel. It had originally been carried up seven flights of stairs, being too cumbersome to get into the lift at the Dorchester; now it was carried reverently down for its despatch to Gstaad.

Dad's personal bathroom was equipped like no other man's. He named it, with some justification, 'Boots'. If I wanted a toothbrush or an aspirin he would say 'Go to Boots, Mike'. Opening the door into the ante-room of his bathroom was like walking into an Aladdin's Cave of medicine and accessories, still wrapped in their cellophane. Sleeping pills, stay-awake pills, indigestion tablets, aspirin, vitamins, sore throat lozenges, gargles ... hair creams, sprays, soaps, shampoos, nail clippers, hair brushes and combs.

Hygiene was always a priority in Dad's daily routine – sometimes he would shower or bath two or three times a day. Around the house he would happily wear a track suit but his wardrobes were full of highly expensive clothes. Once he flew to London to attend a premiere and forgot to pack his evening dress. Rather than buy a new suit he sent Michael Jeffery back to Switzerland to collect the one he thought he looked best in.

Old superstitions still pursued him in Switzerland. Some saplings that had been grown from a tree that once stood in Peg's garden were planted out at the chalet. But the next morning Dad saw a blackbird flying around them. Feeling this was a bad omen he went out into the garden and pulled the young trees out by their roots. He put them into a heap, poured petrol over them and set them on fire.

He was now ready to sign the final divorce papers but he kept pushing them aside as if putting off the fateful hour and the holocaust it would cause. For weeks now, in his solitude, he had been gradually wilting and the thought of phoning Lynne to find means of a possible reconciliation played on his mind. Finally, succumbing to the idea, he picked up the telephone.

I am certain that Lynne had been waiting for it. Dad was both pleading and acquiescent: ready to promise her anything if she was prepared to make a fresh start with him.

Lynne could practically name her own terms – and she did not hesitate to do so. The divorce settlement, she ruled, would have to stand as a surety against a repetition of the unbearable experience she had been going through.

Wary of Dad's mercurial temperament, she knew he was quite capable of going back on his word. Dad also changed his will back in Lynne's favour.

The British Heart Foundation was written out and could only hope to press a claim on the estate if Lynne did not survive Dad for less than thirty days.

These changes were effectively made in a codicil signed by Dad in Paris on 29 October 1979.

Under the codicil we also fared a little better. Instead of £40 we would each receive £800. Dad referred to the amendments as the '*First* Codicil'. We never learned whether he signed any others. Dad sent red roses and a telegram signed 'Your nearly Ex-Husband' to Lynne who now flew to Paris to be reconciled with him once she was assured by the lawyers that all the documentation had been cleared legally.

Dad was very loving and attentive towards her and put her on the payroll of *The Fiendish Plot of Dr Fu Manchu* which he had just begun in Paris. Lynne was appointed as a production executive.

People on the set who had worked with Dad before said he didn't look at all well. Pallid and grey in colour he had the appearance of a haunted, sick man. I knew that he was fighting increasing sickness, but I wondered if Lynne realized just how ill he was. She said he was making a fuss over headaches – and that most people got headaches.

We were supposed to be spending that Christmas with Dad in the chalet in Gstaad but he cancelled the plans. He wrote to all three of us: 'As Lynne and I have seen so very little of each other this year, we have decided that we really need to spend Christmas alone. I'm sorry to have to do this to you.'

Early in December he was alone once more since Lynne had gone for a visit to California. Suddenly he felt unwell, and believing that another attack was imminent he got into his car and drove himself to a Geneva clinic. He was ordered to rest for a month and his film in Paris had to be delayed. When he got back on the set, neither the rest nor Christmas seemed to have improved his health greatly. He insisted on re-shooting some of the scenes he was dissatisfied with and despite the grievances aired by the director, Piers Haggard, he was given permission to go ahead.

Most weekends he would travel home to Gstaad in a private jet he liked to hire. Dad had tired of airport queues and barriers. The jet Falcon which he chartered from a Swiss company was even flown to London to pick up his secretary Sue Evans. Three or four local secretaries in Gstaad had either been sacked or had left him. On a couple of occasions I had also travelled in the eight-seater jet, whose crew included a stewardess to serve our drinks and meals aboard.

In the previous eighteen months Dad had spent £300,000 on keeping the Falcon jet on hire for his world-wide travels.

'You can go through airports without any of the usual hassles,' said Dad, 'you don't get molested.'

Lynne profited from the convenience and comfort of the Falcon too, and insisted on travelling in it. She stepped in and out of the plane like a princess.

At one point Dad was in Switzerland while Lynne remained in Paris. They spoke to each other every day, but one night Lynne went missing. Dad rang every friend in Paris to see if he could locate her. He also rang through to various restaurants where he thought she might have gone.

Finally he got the manager of her hotel to go up to Lynne's room and unlock it, persuading him that she may have fallen sick or taken sleeping pills. The manager, recognizing Dad's voice, obediently did as he was told. The bed had not been slept in.

Dad was stunned.

'Then where the hell is she?' he cried, suspecting that Lynne had gone out with another man. But when Lynne surfaced he learnt that she had only been with Sue Evans. A furious row broke out between them and Lynne accused Dad of not trusting and severely embarrassing her.

Dad still wanted to bridge his troubles with Lynne. But his impotence worried him and he now felt that this condition had caused the original rift between them. When Lynne spoke to Dad after the Paris hotel incident, he taped the conversation between them and played it back to me.

The conversation was pretty revealing. It began with Dad explaining to Lynne why he asked the hotel manager to check her room. 'Oh, my God, you sounded so down on yesterday's call that I didn't know what to expect. I didn't know whether you'd done something silly or whether you decided to sleep out or something. I got myself in such a state ... well never mind.'

Then Lynne spoke. 'No,' she said, 'but you thought I was staying with a man didn't you?'

'Well that occurred to me, I must say.'

'Yes that occurred to you before you thought about phoning Sue [Sue Evans]. It was highly embarrassing for the hotel manager to have to do this . . . it was all kind of tacky, you know.'

'Well you were having a bit of a thing with our friend the newspaper man weren't you?'

'With who?'

'The newspaper man,' said Dad, referring to a celebrated show business columnist.

'How do you mean? I was with Sue last night.'

'No, I know that.'

'Well, why come and ask the manager to look in my bed? That's sort of silly isn't it?'

Later in the conversation Dad pledged his love to Lynne. He told her that he didn't want to divorce her. That the marriage could still work a second time around.

Lynne wasn't so sure. 'So much water has gone under the bridge,' she said, 'it's a case of trying to live together again. It will be a bit funny you know . . .'

Dad talked about his impotence to her.

'If you want to sleep in another room you can, Lynne,' he said. 'Well maybe in the beginning, you know,' she replied, 'and then we'll sort of take it from there. It's funny, when you've been on your own for a while.'

Dad cut in: 'But anyway it's a very large bed and you know me well enough. I wouldn't bother you with anything until I knew that you wanted to be . . . I got a bit low because things weren't functioning sexually between us. I got so desperate about this. I want to lead a normal married life again. But I'll get over this sexual problem, darling. There's got to be a reason for it.'

Dad expounded the practices of an American doctor who claimed cures for the problem of impotence by utilizing video slides. He also said he had arranged tests with his own physician, Dr Brock. Then he said to Lynne: 'I told him that the problem resulted in a rift between my wife and me and was causing an awful lot of pain and depression and that one of the reasons we'd split up was because I was unable to perform as a normal husband and I've never been like this before in my life. Just the opposite in fact. The suggestion is my body is not getting enough blood and therefore I might have to have an artery by-pass and the doctor says that this is a possibility. He's going to do tests on me.'

Dad paused and said, 'I can tell you one thing. I've been completely and totally faithful to you since I last saw you.'

'Oh, that's good,' said Lynne.

'Have you?'

'Yes, darling,' said Lynne.

The tape lasted for more than an hour and after it was over I found that Dad was gently weeping. 'I still love her,' he said.

In time Lynne suggested that Dad should also see a psychiatrist, but he wasn't disposed to. Again, he talked his troubles over with me.

'What's the point of going to a shrink, Mike?' he despaired.

'Well, there isn't any point unless you actually believe the psychiatrist can do you some good,' I told him.

Dad frowned. 'I once went to the best shrink in California and spent a fortune with him. He didn't do me a damn bit of good.'

Dad was deeply divided about Lynne at this time. His mood of suspicion returned and he told me he was hiring a private detective to check on her. 'Is that wise?' I asked him. 'Do you really need to do that?'

'Mike, I've got to know the truth,' he said. He did hire a private eye, but then felt guilty about it and pulled him off the case. For Dad thought he'd now got to the heart of the matter. 'Mike, I can't take it any more. She's messing me about. She's got the hottest pants in Hollywood. No wonder she doesn't want to come back here ...'

I told him I thought he was imagining things.

He shook his head sadly.

'I wish I was,' he said slowly.

16

Being There

Dad always wanted to win a Hollywood Oscar.

When *Being There* opened in America to rave reviews he almost convinced himself that he might at last achieve his life's dream. But then he thought about all the derogatory remarks he had passed about Hollywood in his time and knew that he didn't have a dog's chance. He was right. Passed over once more, he threw the Academy's nomination certificate into the rubbish bin as a worthless piece of paper.

Earlier his CBE medal had also been tossed into the dustbin. The actual scroll signed by the Queen was safely framed and hung in the loo. But when Dad did not get a title like Sir John Mills or Sir Richard Attenborough, he dismissed the CBE as such an insignificant honour that there was no room for it in the house any longer.

'I guess I blew it because I became a tax exile,' he once said. 'John and Dickie played it by the letter. Trust them to do the right thing. Do you think I live out of England by choice?'

We didn't ever find the CBE, but Sue Evans salvaged the Oscar nomination. She had it mounted and put on Dad's office wall in London.

To get early warning of Dad's moods, one only had to inspect the dustbins before going into the house. If the lids were spilling over with all sorts of clutter then one could assume there had been trouble.

Lynne's photographs, a whole pile of them, also found their way into the dustbin and Michael Jeffery was stealthily restoring them to the house, one by one, so as not to irritate Dad's feelings.

As with all his previous marriages, Dad desperately wanted to save this one. But Lynne's sympathies didn't seem to be with him when he most needed them.

When he was in Dublin cutting a television commercial for Barclays Bank, he was again stricken by a heart attack. Lynne didn't appear and the first we heard of Dad's illness was on the radio.

Sarah remonstrated with Sue Evans. She asked her to make sure that we knew when Dad was sick. We were his family. We were entitled to know. Why should we have to listen to the radio to have news of him?

Victoria tried reaching Dad by telephone from Los Angeles but the doctors in Dublin said that he was resting and could not take calls.

When Easter came round, Dad and Lynne were uneasily back together and they checked into the Dorchester Hotel in London. I could see that Dad was doing his best to hang on to the last shreds of the marriage. He had bought Lynne a new fur coat in Paris and he acquired a specially equipped Range Rover they were to share in Switzerland.

Dad saw the holiday as an opportunity for a family reunion and Victoria flew in from Los Angeles. She was excited at seeing Dad and was very proud of him. But after a thirteen hour flight she was tired and all she wanted to do was to crash out in a chair in the suite and listen to music on a pair of headphones. Lynne was in a blatantly difficult mood. The presence of Sarah and Victoria must have irritated her. First she criticized Victoria.

'Well darling,' said Lynne to Dad, 'if Victoria is going to listen to cassettes throughout the holiday, at least you won't have to talk to her. That's your problem solved.'

Dad, shrugging off the remark, put on a video clip from *Being There*.

'Have you seen the movie, Victoria?' asked Dad.

Victoria, removing her headphones, nodded.

'I thought it was great, Dad,' she said and in her innocence added, 'You looked like a little, fat, old man in the part.'

Lynne was startled.

'Did you hear that, darling? Victoria thought you were a little fat old man . . .'

Sarah shuddered as she saw Dad's face turn to thunder. Spinning round he threw his drink all over Victoria. Her lips trembled but she didn't cry, she was too bewildered to grasp what had happened. Sarah helped her dry her face with a towel from the bathroom. Lynne frolicked around as though the incident had been funny, but Dad scowled and went into the bedroom, remaining there until dinner.

Feelings were still upset over the meal. Lynne was now reminding Victoria about the 'terrible party' that she had thrown for her in Los Angeles, telling her that the neighbours were still talking about it. She said to Victoria: 'All those ghastly friends of yours in their vampire outfits. Do you still see them?' Britt's name was also dropped into the conversation and next Lynne was making a remark about Victoria's clothes.

Sarah hadn't noticed, but our young sister was sitting at the dinner table clad in purple from head to foot. She was wearing a purple shirt, jacket, pants and shoes. Purple was apparently her favourite colour and no one had told her that Dad had any form of allergy towards it.

Abruptly, Dad got up from the table saying he was going to bed and turning to Victoria he said; 'Never let me see you wearing purple again. Never . . . do you hear?'

Victoria went to bed that night in a state of confusion wondering what she had done wrong. Lynne had clearly turned against her. But more was to come. The next morning Victoria asked Dad for some money to buy new clothes with. She had only brought purple outfits with her.

Lynne came out of the bedroom and told Victoria that her father declined to give her any money. 'I'm afraid he is not going to do it. Your mother must give you plenty of money for your clothes,' she said.

Victoria hung on until Dad appeared, his face contorted with rage. 'As far as I'm concerned you can get the next plane and go home – I never want to see you again!' he yelled. 'Your behaviour's disgusting. I give your mother enough money for clothes. What does she do with it? You've got no right to ask me for any more. You're going back on the next plane.'

Sarah stepped in to help Victoria, having heard enough of the conversation. 'Look, Dad, it's nothing to do with Victoria what goes on between you and Britt. You're making Victoria the scapegoat and that's not fair,' she said. Dad glared at her.

Sarah turned heel and went down with Victoria to her room. They were both crying when Lynne came into the room. She patted Victoria's head.

'There, there,' she said, 'you know what your Dad's like!'

But Victoria edged out of Lynne's reach. After lunch she rang Britt in Los Angeles. Britt was furious and told Victoria to tell her father that he was a liar and that he had never sent any money through for her.

Sarah recommended a bit more tact and said it was possible that Dad might react more sympathetically if Victoria offered an apology for the remark she had made about the film. Dad didn't find it in his heart to refuse Victoria's request after she had apologized. He gave her £200 so that she could buy what she needed.

Sarah was the next to land in trouble. Five months earlier, after opening her Victorian dolls' shop, she had given an interview with a freelance reporter. The interview was slanted in such a way that it appeared to be critical of Dad, saying how much he liked to talk about himself and how his wife was younger than one of Sarah's boy-friends.

Sarah was very upset about it. Especially when the interview did not appear in a woman's magazine as she had expected but in the *News of the World*.

Lynne suddenly chose to raise the topic with Sarah that same day, saying that it was just as well her father hadn't read it.

'But Dad did know about it,' argued Sarah, 'because I telephoned him and warned him about it.'

In fact Sarah apologized for the misrepresentation of the article and Dad said at the time, 'Well, don't worry, darling. I've had plenty of experience with the press. I know what they get up to. This is your first newspaper interview. I understand.'

Dad must have forgotten about the conversation entirely, for in the Dorchester that afternoon he sent a telegram to Sarah. It read:

'Dear Sarah, After what happened this morning with Victoria I shall be happy if I never hear from you again. I won't tell you what I think of you. It must be obvious. Especially after the *News of the World* article – Goodbye, Your Father.'

Sarah was very distressed. She phoned through to the suite and got Lynne, who denied having shown the *News of the World* article to Dad, and said he had got the text from his press agent, Theo Cowan.

'It had nothing to do with me,' said Lynne, 'but I think he's very cross with you.'

Later Sarah phoned again and asked to speak to Dad. But Lynne refused to put him on the line. 'I don't think your father wants to talk to you,' she said.

'Please, he must,' said Sarah, 'we've got to sort this whole thing out.'

'Well, your dad's here and he doesn't seem to want to talk to you ... I'll ask him ... but he doesn't appear to want to ... He's standing right next to me and I'm putting the phone by his ear now and he doesn't seem to want to speak to you, does he?'

Sarah screamed into the phone, not being able to contain herself any longer. Dad then came on the line.

'I'm sorry, Sarah,' he said, 'yes, we did have a discussion about the article but you didn't tell me everything you said about me in it. Now that's not good enough and I'm not going to forgive you for it.' Sarah tried to reason with him, but he hung up on her.

Lynne phoned back and suggested that they should all have dinner together and let bygones be bygones. But Sarah felt that Dad owed her an apology.

'I'm very upset by what Dad said. Why can't he say sorry when he must know he's wrong?' Sarah said to me.

BHB027(1107)(1-009358C283)PD 10/10/77 1107
ICS IPMLYLA LSA
01040 (2-052895G283 0539) 10-10
PMS
UWE3747 GLD560 FM WUI
UWNX CO GWLG 044
LONDON 44/43 10 1049
MISS VICTORIA SELLERS
391 NORTH CAROLWOOD DRIVE LOSANGELES?ALIFORNIA NFL RTE BEVERLY HILLS
CA
DEAR VICTORIA
YOU PROMISED YOU WOULD TELEPHONE ME AND I WAITED FOR YOUR
CALL BUT YOU NEVER DID STOP ALSO I HAVE STILL NOT RECEIVED
YOUR BIRTHDAY PRESENT I AM VERY UPSET WITH YOU
    DADDY

SF-1201 (R5-69)

8890 12 PO HE G
299992 PO TS G
FB71 1438 LONDON T 53

MISS SARAH SELLERS FLAT 3C GREVILE RD
NW6

DEAR SARAH AFTER WHAT HAPPENED THIS MORNING I SHOULD BE VERY
HAPPY I NEVER HEAR FROM YOU AGAIN STOP I WONT TELL YOU I THINK
OF YOU IT MUST BE OBVIOUS ESPECIALLY AFTER THE NEWS OF THE WORLD
ARTICLE GOOD BYE
    YOUR FATHER

31 MAR 30

It was the last conversation that Sarah was to have with her father; it still clouds her memory now like a bad dream.

Mum later told our stepmother it was very sad that Sarah never spoke to her father again after receiving the telegram. Lynne argued that it was Sarah who chose not to speak to Dad again, so she only had herself to blame.

When I was alone with Dad later I told him exactly how I felt about his attitude to both Sarah and Victoria. I think he was genuinely saddened by the incidents and thought he may have acted too hastily.

Dad and Lynne journeyed on to Cannes for the film festival still trying to patch up their own differences. Dad hoped that the jury panel, presided over by Kirk Douglas, might give him the Best Actor award for *Being There*. But again he failed by a narrow margin.

Though Dad's health was declining fast, Lynne, as she had done in Paris and elsewhere, liked to go out to discotheques and Dad reluctantly went with her. He rarely danced, but he encouraged Michael Jeffery to go on the floor with her. Often rows would flare up when Dad would suggest leaving a disco earlier than Lynne wanted to.

From Cannes they went on together to Gstaad but Lynne didn't dally too long. She was itching to get back to California. Since the turn of the year she had chosen to spend more time in America than with him. She advanced the explanation that someone had to look after the Los Angeles house.

In her absence Dad tried to have some fun. He phoned Spike in London and said: 'Let's write another Goon show. I want to laugh again.'

To the chalet came Helen Mirren and David Tomlinson who starred with him in *Dr Fu Manchu*. Dad threw a party and organized some parlour games and impersonated Toulouse Lautrec.

When they were gone the house seemed empty once more. Every morning Dad read the English papers that came into the station and he punched messages out on his telex machine to Sue in London. Or he telephoned friends, spending hours on the line regardless of the cost. He was very, very lonely. I saw the desperation that imprisoned him.

More and more he became introspective.

'I don't mind if I die,' he said to me, 'in some ways I might be glad if it happened.'

I told him to stop talking in that way.

I urged him to phone Liv Ullman the Swedish actress he met at the premiere of *Kramer v Kramer* in London. They seemed to have got along well and Dad described her as a very beautiful and arresting woman.

'Mike, I'd like to ring her and I daresay she'd come out to dinner,' he replied, 'but I haven't got the energy.'

My own relations with Dad were now closer than at any other period throughout my life. I think Dad had recognized that I was not only his son but his best friend too. We could talk as man to man, knowing that there could be no breach of trust between us. The blood ties ran strangely deep.

When I went to Switzerland in the early part of the year Dad arranged for me to go up in a hot air balloon. I was 13,000 feet up when Dad, sitting in the lounge at home, decided to telephone Mum in London.

'He's perfectly safe, Annie,' said Dad, 'I've got someone following him in a car.'

Mum laughed. 'That's all very well, Peter,' she said, 'but they haven't actually got him on a piece of string . . .'

In the summer I went back to see him. Dad allowed me to drive his Porsche car in Gstaad and one afternoon on our way to Geneva, seeing the excitement it gave me to be at the steering wheel, he said: 'You know if you want one – I'll get you one.'

I shook my head and smiled.

'No, Dad. I don't want you to buy me one. I'll get one of my own when I save enough money myself.'

Dad nodded with appreciation for what I was telling him: I didn't say it for effect. I meant it. Dad always assumed that the only reason we wanted him was for what we could get out of him.

As a boy and in my early youth, I had a yearning to persuade Dad to come out with me to a cricket match, or into a pub for a pint of beer or into a snooker hall. I would have also liked to have got him into a transport cafe that I knew where the food was superb, instead of all the smart restaurants he ended up in. But Dad couldn't ever do these simple things for fear of being recognized and having to put on 'a Peter Sellers performance' that the public always demanded from him. Out among their public, funny men are at ransom. The trouble is, they always feel they have to be funny. They have to clown and tell a joke, otherwise the public might get disillusioned with them. 'In real life,' they would snigger, 'he's a terrible letdown. He's got nothing to say.'

Dad, like all other artists, had heard that comment about himself. It didn't hurt particularly but he didn't want to run into it deliberately.

'Mike, I would have loved to have gone out with you like that when you were a boy,' he said, 'but don't you understand why I couldn't?'

I was glad that I did most of the driving on that trip because Dad, once the proudest of motorists, had become a menace behind the wheel. He had lost his concentration and discipline. He would climb into a car, push the starter button and accelerate away without checking the rear mirror or whether anyone was ahead. Motor cyclists and pedestrians would be in real peril; it was a nightmare to be with him.

He had become absent minded. He fumbled with everything. Once he was an expert on every single gadget in the household: now he did not know how to turn on the video machines without being reminded of the correct procedures.

He would indulge in sentimental recollection, recounting stories of his early family life and of his childhood. I had heard them all before but I listened again knowing how much it all meant to him. Dad said that Mum was the best of his four wives and regretted his infatuation with Sophia Loren, agreeing that it had destroyed his marriage.

'Otherwise, Mike, we might still have all been together as a family ...' Then he grunted. 'What do you think of Sophia Loren? She didn't even mention me in her book ...'

Dad's remark was funny. Only a few days before he had been growling about Britt's book and the way she had made use of his name in the manuscript! He wished she had omitted reference to him altogether.

Dad's physical appearance was frightening. He looked hollow faced and emaciated. He said he could not sleep without pills. Sometimes he forgot whether he had taken them or not and he would swallow a second dose. Whenever he had palpitations he would take a 'red bomber' that would totally wipe him out the following day.

Dad saw the peril he was in when he caught sight of himself in the mirror.

'I've got to have that operation, Mike,' he said. 'I've got to ...' I kept silent.

At last, Dad had been forced to make the decision on his own account. There were no other alternatives left open to him. Dad would have wanted to seek the advice of Dr Barnard, but the South African surgeon had now developed arthritis and could not operate.

So Dad made contact in Los Angeles with Dr Gary Sugarman who had been a member of the team which had brought him through his first crisis in 1964. 'It's going to be a gamble, but don't you think it is going to be worth it, Mike?' he said, when making the final arrangements, when we were together in Gstaad. I tried to boost his morale. 'Of course it is, Dad,' I said, 'you'll feel a different man.'

Secretly, I feared it was going to be a much bigger gamble than Dad imagined. His condition worried me greatly.

He was only 54, but he now looked much older. A frail, ailing figure, he was left panting for breath if he walked further than 50 yards, his exhaustion being more pronounced than that of a man at the end of a marathon. His face was strangely hollow, the ebony eyes, once so alert and inquisitive, were now sad and desultory.

He was listed to report to Los Angeles by the end of July where he would have tests and an angiogram before the major surgery was proceeded with.

In the meantime he had other matters more pressing in his mind, having signed for yet another *Pink Panther* movie. From Gstaad he had to go to Geneva for talks with script writer Jim Maloney and Clive Donner, who was to direct the movie.

All the earlier *Pink Panther* films had been produced, directed and co-written by Blake Edwards, but Dad's quarrels with Blake were legendary: few *Panther* films were completed without a fearsome clash of their opposing temperaments. That they were able to speak to one another afterwards was a remarkable tribute to their respect for one another. Both vowed on frequent occasions that they would never collaborate with one another again. This time they were determined to carry it through and when United Artists made the casting announcements Blake's name was noticeably absent. Blake, it was learned, got a million dollars compensation and so anxious was the film company for Dad to continue his role as Inspector Clouseau that they would have met any conditions he demanded. He, too, was getting a million dollars – but that was by way of an advance for his signature on the contract. The money was to be paid into a bank account and transferred to him on the first day of shooting which was to start in August.

On completion of the movie he was to receive a further million dollars as well as a large percentage of the box office profits.

Dad was elated by the deal, although privately he felt that the *Pink Panther* movies had come to the end of their natural life span and that every feasible comedy situation involving Clouseau had been exploited. He worried about artistic prostitution, but even he had a price, for as he remarked to me: 'I would have been crazy to turn down that kind of deal. It's going to set me up for the rest of my days.'

Dad, who had known hard times in his youth, didn't think he was a rich man. He complained that he couldn't ever get access to his £4,000,000 worth of assets because they had been tied up in stock and property by his lawyers and accountants. He needed, he said seriously, some 'spending money'.

He flew from Geneva to London on the morning of Thursday 19 July, a day or two earlier than I expected. He was to spend three or four days in London before going on to Los Angeles for the operation.

I was going to the airport to pick him up, but Sue Evans volunteered. She had booked Dad into Suites 610 and 611 at the Dorchester Hotel, where many of the more traumatic moments in his life had occurred.

He phoned me shortly after he got in and I lunched with him on Sunday. But when I got to the hotel he wasn't feeling well and said he didn't feel like eating. I quickly got to the cause of the trouble. He had spoken to Lynne on the telephone and they had been rowing once more.

'She annoys me,' said Dad, 'I just wish the divorce was over and done with.' His expression conveyed the emotional anguish he was enduring. Impatient and restless, he was pacing the suite, wearing the dark blue track suit which he always wore when languishing in a hotel. Suddenly he said, 'I'm feeling awful. I must get some sleep. Mike, why don't you watch one of the movies on television?'

I agreed, knowing that he would rely on me to stay with him for dinner.

I watched television with Michael Jeffery who had drifted along to the suite from his own room.

Dad woke and reappeared from the bedroom about six o'clock but he was still feeling depressed and we abandoned plans to go out to a restaurant for dinner.

We ordered steak and spinach from the Dorchester's kitchens, and the dinner was brought up on a trolley with three bottles of wine. Somewhere during the proceedings Dad produced a joint and lit it, was about to hand it on to me but then remembered I'd given up smoking. It worried me that he was still drinking and taking drugs when it was clear that his health was in a bad state. When a waiter knocked on the door to clear the dishes, Michael sprang from his seat and sprayed some cologne to camouflage the unmistakable aroma of marijuana wafting around the room.

We settled down to watch another television movie, the classic John Wayne thriller *Brannigan*, and Father identified many of the stuntmen appearing in it as those he had worked with at some stage in his career. His mood brightened, and the conversation turned to the new *Pink Panther* film and his more immediate task of selecting his leading lady.

It was my father's boast that he had slept with practically all his leading ladies. But there were some rejections, and much to his chagrin the Swedish beauty Maud Adams was one of them.

She had apparently resisted his charms on the set of *Return of the Pink Panther* and as a result made a rather premature exit.

Dad, who naturally retained the right of approval over the selection of his leading ladies, had already been handed a 'short list' of possible candidates. In his own mind he had already settled for a virtually unknown actress – a young comedienne named Pamela Stephenson, who appeared on the satirical revue 'Not the Nine O'Clock News' on BBC television.

He considered Miss Stephenson exceptionally talented, and was convinced she would be ideally suited for the part.

'We hope to sign her on Tuesday,' he enthused.

But more disquieting thoughts descended on him as he retired for the night. Ahead loomed the Los Angeles heart surgery and now Dad was counting the days before he was likely to have the operation.

'I'm worried about it, Mike,' he said.

It was a family custom for Dad to engage us in conversation before going to sleep, and I sat on the end of his bed and chatted with him. I tried to reassure him that the doctors would hardly go ahead with the surgery unless they were first satisfied that there were strong chances of success.

'Otherwise, Dad, they won't get into it,' I said. 'Don't worry, they know what they are doing.'

But he was still uneasy.

'It's not only the operation, Mike. It's Lynne. What if she shows up at the hospital? I don't want her there.'

I shrugged. 'Okay. But you don't have to tell her where you choose to convalesce,' I said.

'She's bound to catch up with me,' said Dad, still looking vexed.

'Not if you use another name. You'll be out of the hospital and away before she discovers you're gone.'

Dad nodded.

'I guess you're right,' he said, lying back on his pillow.

He paused.

'It's a big operation, Mike. If only I'd gone through with it when I had the chance with Christiaan Barnard. I'm not as fit now ...'

'Don't think like that,' I said. 'Once you've had the operation you won't have to take all the hundreds of pills you do now. You're going to feel 100% fitter. You'll be a new man. After the operation you can go to that health resort in San Diego and convalesce there and have all the saunas and massages you want. You can start to enjoy life again ... and we can take off wherever you want to go.'

He nodded, and a faint smile broke his frown. 'I know you're right,' he said, 'but I can't always think about it that way.'

He reached for a sleeping pill and his glass of water which were always at his bedside: it was the signal for me to leave. I said good night and gripped his hand.

I didn't know it then, but I was saying goodnight to him for the last time.

17

The Last Will and Testament

News of Dad's death was already spreading around the world. Outside the Middlesex Hospital hundreds of press men and television crews were now assembled.

It was 1.30 a.m.

Flashbulbs lit the precincts as we emerged from the hospital doors. Someone ran forward and grabbed my jacket and Sue Evans was almost trampled down. Michael Jeffery and Dad's lawyer Elwood Rickless managed to get Lynne into one of the two cars at our disposal. We headed back to the Dorchester.

In the suite a heavy atmosphere hung over us all.

Lynne was quiet now. She had exhausted her tears. The funeral had to be arranged and I accompanied Elwood and Lynne to the undertaker's parlour the next morning. Lynne put on a black suit but forgot to put on dark glasses. She went back for them, saying she couldn't face the press otherwise. She slid her hand into mine as we got into the foyer and the photographers pictured us leaving in the morning sunshine.

When we returned to the hotel Lynne was conducting a press interview. It seemed inconceivable that she could gather her thoughts so quickly. I asked Theo Cowan who was responsible for arranging the interview, but he shrugged his shoulders.

No one wanted to avoid the press: Dad always enjoyed good relations with them. His public image had been precious to him. But how Lynne, having lost her husband only a few hours earlier, could be so composed as to consider meeting a representative of the press, astonished me.

Some time during the afternoon I overheard Lynne talking with Elwood on the telephone arranging for Fred Sicking, who was Dad's business manager, to be contacted. She was reviewing the order of a new Porsche car she said Dad had ordered for their use at Gstaad.

Again, I could not help but conclude that the conversation was an extraordinary one to have when so recently bereaved. Besides, what she was telling Elwood was not my understanding. I had been present in Gstaad when Dad refused point blank to buy her another car – she already had a Lancia – saying that he had given her 'quite enough' since their marriage.

A strange impatience now gripped Lynne. When she finished one telephone call, she would instantly make another. She also kept ordering drinks and food from room service, as though she had to create activity.

She complained about the heat, and said there was no air conditioning in the suite; she rang through to the manager's office to see whether she could move up to the next floor. There was the £500 a day Harlequin suite which had french windows leading on to its own terraced balcony. Dad had often stayed in this suite when a film studio was prepared to foot the bill.

Television and radio programmes were now carrying tributes to Dad virtually non-stop. Clippings of many of his films were being screened and in between people like Spike Milligan, Harry Secombe and David Niven talked of their friendship and association with him. I felt proud of Dad; just why had he always thought he was so alone?

That afternoon Tony Snowdon called at the hotel to offer his condolences in person. He invited me to stay at his country home whenever I wanted. Lynne dabbed away tears with her handkerchief and adjusted her dark glasses once more. But when Tony had gone she was busily directing operations for her move up to the Harlequin suite.

She promised to dine that night with her mother and grandmother, who had now booked into the hotel, but she kept them waiting in the restaurant until 10.30 p.m. This was because she was now ensconced in the Harlequin suite, talking to Elwood about legal matters.

I was getting more suspicious of Lynne's motives by the hour. I later phoned Elwood expressing my concern that Lynne had assumed total control of all arrangements and pointedly asked him to reveal Dad's instructions from his will.

Elwood said: 'I think it is better, Michael, that we leave these matters until after the funeral. Why don't you come and see me on Sunday at midday?'

I kept wondering about it. I was sure that something was happening behind the scene we didn't know about. Was it possible that Dad had cut us out of the will? He had always used it as an instrument of blackmail against us. But for that matter it had always been a weapon in his arguments with Lynne.

Unless Dad was seething with rage, and determined to administer vengeance, he usually had to be humoured before he would rouse himself to sign legal papers and documents. Could it be that his heart attack precluded him from making any of the final changes he might have planned in his will? Who could really say?

Sunshine poured in through the hotel windows as I pulled back the curtains the next morning. Across Hyde Park I could see a bunch of kids chasing one another. In Park Lane there was a traffic jam. The world didn't stop because of Dad's death, it just went on.

It was Friday. It also happened to be Lynne's twenty-sixth birthday. It was suggested we all went out to dinner at San Lorenzo's, a fashionable restaurant in Knightsbridge, but, in the circumstances it was considered inappropriate.

I didn't see Lynne until 5 p.m., but I learned it had been a bad day for her. She had gone out to Bond Street with Sue Evans to buy a black costume for Dad's funeral when her handbag had been stolen in one of the shops. She lost her credit cards, about £200 in cash and a picture of Dad he had apparently given to her and which was of sentimental value to her.

Lynne had promised to give Sarah some money to buy a

suitable dress for the funeral, but all her cash had been lost with the handbag. Sarah finally got a dress from a Hampstead boutique.

I was also experiencing problems in getting something respectable to wear for the funeral. My wardrobe was made up of jeans and casual clothes. I didn't possess a black suit, but my friends found me one, and also the shoes I needed. Dad would have wanted me looking smart. Then I went to a record shop and bought a copy of Glenn Miller's recording of 'In The Mood'. For many years Dad had joked with his fellow Goons that he wanted the song played at his funeral. I had a word with Father John Hester, the Soho priest who had been Dad's life long friend and who was conducting the funeral the next day.

'That's what your father wanted and we will play it at the funeral as he would have wished,' said Father Hester, finding nothing sacreligious in the request; another priest might have insisted on a hymn or a psalm.

Dad had left specific instructions about his internment with our family lawyer John Humphries. He wanted to be cremated at Golders Green where his parents were buried. He had even visited the crematorium on the previous weekend to see the plaque he had erected in memory of them.

When I got back to the Dorchester the phone rang in my room as I put the key in the door. There was no mistaking the voice. Britt had never lost her Swedish accent.

She had kept discreetly in the background since arriving in London, but now she wanted to check on the funeral arrangements for Victoria. 'Do you think anyone would object if I came too?' she asked me. 'I would like to pay my last respects.' I felt she had a right to be there.

I didn't hesitate: Britt had always been good to us when we were kids and I felt that Victoria would need her mother there. It would be such an ordeal for her.

Britt said she would send Victoria over to the hotel to join the main family mourners, but she would make her own way to Golders Green. I thanked her for being so discreet. 'It will probably be better that way,' I said. I was of course thinking about Lynne.

I think the strain was affecting us all, but I had to see Lynne to make the final preparations, ensuring the cars and flowers were ordered. I reminded her that Vi and Doe – Dad's aunts – had joined us and she promised she would make contact with them.

'I'm sorry,' she said, 'I've forgotten to ring through to them. Are they in the hotel?'

I nodded. 'Dad was very fond of them both.'

'Yes, Michael,' she said, 'I know ...'

Victoria booked into the hotel to share Sarah's room. The family were now all gathered and everyone was reminiscing about Dad. I thought it might relieve the tension if we dined as a family together in the restaurant.

Lynne agreed. She promised she would join us, but first she had to have talks with Elwood Rickless's partner Michael Wolfe, a moustachioed, clean-cut type who had flown in from Los Angeles.

When I woke next day, I wondered what had become of the dawn. It was 8.30 but the sky was still black. Headlights were blazing from cars in Park Lane. Rain was sweeping down like a monsoon. I doubt if London had seen a blacker mid-summer's day. Dad's mischievous sense of humour was already at work. He was pulling the plug out on us from the heavens.

We congregated in the hotel foyer as the funeral cars drew up on the forecourt. Vi and Doe were remarkably composed, but they had lost so many friends of their own age it seemed that now they were almost accustomed to attending funerals.

Lynne was the last to appear. She wore a diamond-buttoned black shiny dress and said that she had been consoled by Michael Wolfe, who had stayed up talking with her.

'I needed someone to talk to. I couldn't sleep. It was so thoughtful of him,' she remarked.

Outside the hotel the press were gathered like hornets. We walked out into a blaze of lights and climbed into the two hired limousines. I got into the first car with Lynne, Sarah and Victoria.

Vi and Doe, together with Lynne's parents, filled the second car of official family mourners and the cortege moved away, without any sign of a respite in the weather. We hardly spoke in the car. The rain ran like a torrent down the windows, hiding our own tears from anyone's stare.

We were shocked and not quite prepared for the scenes that awaited us at the cloistered yellow-bricked crematorium. Braving the weather, vast crowds had gathered and the police had to form a cordon to allow us through. We were faced with a battery of television cameras and blinded by the arc lights as we dismounted from the cars. Helpers came to guide us into the tiny chapel; the four of us occupying the front pew and others filling the row behind.

The chapel was full. I noticed Lord Snowdon, Baron Rothschild and Spike, Harry and Michael Bentine as well as Dad's cousins. These were his friends; the people who were closest to him.

Lynne also glanced round. Her almond-coloured eyes settled on Britt, standing next to Spike, and I saw a sudden flash of anger appear on her face. Then she tossed back her head as Father Hester started the service.

The service was simple and brief. I think only the Goons would have known why Dad had preferred to go to his Maker to the strains of 'In The Mood' rather than 'The Lord Is My Shepherd'.

It was still raining heavily when we emerged from the chapel. As a gesture of courtesy, I took hold of Lynne's hand to give her some protection as the crowd surged forward against the police cordon. Nervously, we paused to look at the flowers laid out in long rows beneath the cloisters. We had sent a large family wreath which had been placed on top of Dad's coffin, but it was impossible for us to stoop and read the cards. The crowds were too close upon us and we were dazzled by flashbulbs and arc lights. The funeral had already lost its solemnity. The undertaker's cars became our only means of escape.

Things were more peaceful at the Dorchester. Drinks and sandwiches had been arranged for the family mourners and the closest of Dad's friends. Naturally all the Goons and their families came, along with David Lodge, Graham Stark and others. Blake Edwards and his wife Julie Andrews also arrived later to pay their respects.

Lynne sat quietly in the main lounge. Suddenly, as the room was emptying, she burst into a fit of anguish. My first thought was that she was giving vent to another hysterical outburst in the way she had done at the hospital on the night of Dad's death. But I was wrong.

'Why did Britt come?' she cried. 'Who invited that woman to my husband's funeral? How dare she do it? Why didn't she keep away?' Sue Evans and one or two of Dad's cousins tried to placate her. But there was no stopping her.

Those of the family who remained in the room were filled with acute embarrassment, for Victoria was listening intently to every remark that Lynne uttered about Britt.

Poor Victoria. Her lips began to tremble and then she started weeping. Sarah comforted her and hastened her through to the next room where Michael Jeffery also tried to calm her down.

'Please don't cry, Victoria,' he said, 'we all knew your father once loved your mother, so please don't pay too much attention to what Lynne is saying. She's too upset to know what she means . . .'

I doubted that myself. I could find no excuse for her tactless, hurtful outburst, and I left in disgust. The next morning the newspapers upset Victoria by describing Britt as the 'unwanted mourner': Lynne had apparently conveyed this to the press.

Foremost in my thoughts now was the daunting task of attending to Dad's estate. I imagined that his will would contain a lot of complex clauses and bequests. I also imagined that I would be spending the next few weeks signing papers and documents and closing down his business affairs.

When I left for the noon meeting with Elwood Rickless on Sunday, I was already working out the order in which I would tackle Dad's affairs. It was a short drive. Elwood's office was only a couple of miles south of the hotel, a large, elegant Georgian house. Elwood greeted me at the door as I rang the bell. He led me through into the lounge where Michael Wolfe pored over a pile of legal papers. Other documents were strewn over a coffee table. From the strained conversation I thought I could detect that the two lawyers had something rather unpleasant to unfold to me.

At first they began to hedge but then Elwood drew a long breath and came to the crux of things. 'I don't quite know how to tell you this, Michael,' he said, 'but I'm afraid your father has made no provision for the children in his will ...'

Even allowing for Dad's inconsistent nature, the news was shattering.

'We've been left with nothing?' I asked, unable to contain my disbelief.

'Dad has actually left you with 2000 US dollars each,' said Elwood apologetically.

He continued: 'It was necessary he should leave you something. Legally, he had to indicate he had not accidentally omitted you from the will ... in the event of you contesting it. As solicitors acting for your father, you will appreciate we had to make things as watertight as possible.'

I remained silent as Elwood went on: 'You may wish to get legal advice from another lawyer about this, and if you decide to do that then of course we will assist you with any documents you may want to see.'

Michael Wolfe passed a copy of Dad's will to Elwood who offered to read it to me paragraph by paragraph. But I indicated that the exercise would be wasted on me.

'It's probably all in legal jargon and I won't understand a bit of it,' I smiled, accepting their summary of the contents of the will.

The two lawyers looked at me, hard pressed now to find adequate words to express their thoughts: they must have wondered how a man could deny his children in the way Dad had done.

I learned that the entire estate, apart from one or two minor bequests, was going to Lynne. Even Vi and Doe, whom Dad had financially supported with a monthly allowance as well as paying for their yearly holiday, had been left out of the will.

I resigned myself to the situation. 'Well, if that's the way Dad wrote it down, then that's the way he must have wanted it,' I said.

But my next question to Elwood caused him to exchange an uneasy glance with his partner. 'What is the date of the will?' I said, out of curiosity. Elwood flicked over the pages. 'Your father made his last will, revoking all others on 27 July 1979, but he added a codicil on 29 October 1979,' said Elwood.

'Did he?' I said quietly, knowing well that Dad had once stripped Lynne from the will after making the divorce settlement on her.

The effect of Dad's brief reconciliation with Lynne was to reinstate her name in the will, as the main beneficiary. I remembered Dad saying: 'I was soft with her, Mike, but that's the only way she would come back. At the time I thought it would work out. But I was wrong. So wrong.'

Nevertheless, in view of the circumstances in which we found ourselves, I felt there was no harm in having a word with Lynne about the will. I presumed she was already aware of its contents.

When we met I had to keep the conversation going; then I told her that we had been cut out of the will and she reacted with apparently heartfelt concern at our plight.

She burst into tears and said: 'Oh Michael, if only I had known. I would have got your father to change it, but he didn't consult me. I can't understand it. What was Peter thinking of at the time? Oh dear ... I know how you must feel. It is dreadful ...'

I might have assumed that Lynne, in displaying such sympathy, was ready to amend things, and waited for her to suggest some kind of solution. She now had the power to put right what she apparently saw as an injustice. But other than repeat sympathetically, 'Oh dear ... you poor things,' she did not even hint at apportioning reasonable settlement on us. She left our meeting saying: 'I'm sorry, Michael. I know how you must feel.'

Lynne was not going to commit herself in any way. In time, her attitude would harden against us. Of course she had the perfect defence in remaining resolute about the will.

She would always be able to say that we never cared for Dad as a father. That as kids we had let him down. That we had only used him and that, from time to time, he had disowned us. We would not be able to dispute any of those facts. We could of course have been equally critical of Lynne's relationship with Dad, but legally she was his wife at the time of his death.

Britt, summoned to meet Elwood, then broke the news to Victoria. She was stunned since Dad's will was particularly insensitive to her needs and had not even made provision for her to finish her education. Sarah spoke to Victoria that night on the telephone; they were both feeling dazed that Dad could have done such a thing to his own daughters. Sarah also went to see Elwood and got copies of Dad's previous will. In this, we were only left one hundred dollars each, but Lynne had been totally eliminated from any bequest whatsoever. All of Dad's estate would have gone to the British Heart Foundation.

Sarah decided to make further representations to Lynne about our position. It was a pretty futile exercise, although Lynne did concede one or two minor points. She said she would consider paying for Victoria to finish her education and also said she would make over two legacies to Michael Jeffery and Sue Evans that Dad had forgotten to sign before his death. Michael was getting £10,000 and Sue a sum of £20,000.

Lynne soothed Sarah: 'I want you to think of me as a sister. My greatest wish is that the family should stay together. There is no reason for us to drift apart or to be distant to one another. If you want something you have only got to ask, you know that.' Over the next few days, there were some indications that Lynne wanted to pursue that policy. She then returned to Switzerland for ten days before next coming to London.

There was one family reunion, but it was arranged by Spike Milligan who invited us all to dinner at his home. Unfortunately, the atmosphere was strained. Lynne played the role of the distressed widow and tried to be aloof, but it wasn't accepted by any of us. Least of all Spike, who, now in his sixties, couldn't really relate to Lynne in the way she hoped. When, a few days later, Spike learned how Dad had treated us in the will he was appalled and said he would write to Lynne to tell her how unjust it was. 'Pete must have made the will in one of his fits of insanity,' declared Spike.

It was my mother who finally took it upon herself to see Lynne at the Dorchester Hotel to resolve our situation, feeling that we were in an invidious position. Lynne told her that she could not make any settlement on us, unfair as the will might appear.

'I must follow Peter's last wishes,' she said. 'He would not have wanted me to alter the things he set down and expected to be carried through. Don't you really think the children should respect his last wishes?' My mother was astounded by her detachment. 'But Lynne,' she asked, 'do you really think you are being fair? In a couple of years' time it is possible that you will marry again and have kids. Then all of Peter's money will go to your children and Michael, Sarah and Victoria will have nothing.'

Lynne stayed silent but Mum said that her cheeks flushed considerably. Then she tried to justify the will by saying that we did not care about Dad and never bothered to get in touch with him, except when we wanted something. 'Peter knew his children didn't love him and that they were ashamed of him,' she said, 'they didn't want his name.'

'That's rubbish,' said Mum. 'It simply isn't true and you must know it isn't.' Lynne spoke of the Porsche car I turned down and implied this was a deliberate rejection of my father.

'Do you mean to say Peter wouldn't understand why Michael wanted to save for his own car? He was showing his father that he was his own person,' Mum said.

'If you had a rich father and all you wanted was his money

how would you go about getting it?' Mum asked our step-mother.

'I would spend all my time with him,' Lynne answered her.

'Yes exactly,' said Mum, 'so isn't it clear to you now that the children weren't after his money?'

Lynne, as if to show she wasn't devoid of compassion, related to Mum how Dad had forgotten to sign the legacies he had left to Sue and Michael Jeffery.

'I am going to make them over to both Sue and Michael,' said Lynne, 'even though I'm not obliged to. I'm making a gift of the money to them ...'

Mum took her leave knowing that it was impossible to carry the conversation any further. Lynne was not going to be moved to make any gesture on our behalf.

Our position was unimproved and we also had very few of Dad's possessions. So I was surprised when Lynne arrived one day to give me Dad's watch – the one he was wearing when he died. It was a steel and gold watch inscribed on the back: 'For Peter – I Love You Very Much You Know – Lynne, Christmas, 1978.'

'I know your dad would have wanted you to have it,' she said. Later she suggested I might give it back so that she could get the strap altered for me. I told her that I would get it done in London. I knew she had bought the watch for Dad with his own money, so I did not have any compunction about accepting it.

All that Sarah possessed in Dad's memory were three gold bracelets that once belonged to Peg, but Victoria could find nothing. She had lost the heart-shaped locket bracelet he had once given her.

The memorial service at St Martin-in-the-Fields in London was not how we felt Dad would have wished it. His real fans weren't there. Lynne, who didn't consult us about the arrangements, had filled the pews with friends, stars and celebrities. But it was some consolation that Harry Secombe sang one of the hymns and

Tony Snowdon read from the Bible. David Niven delivered the eulogy, in which he made reference to Lynne saying how much happiness she had brought into Dad's life in the last few years by being such a devoted and loving wife. There was no gathering of friends after the service. The congregation drifted out of the church and into the congestion of Trafalgar Square.

We saw Lynne at the service. She was in the front pew, but showed no sign of looking for us. We did not speak to her that day – neither have we seen or heard from her since.

Some days later Sarah went to see *Being There* at the Odeon cinema. It was raining and there was a queue that Sarah didn't feel like standing in as she sensed that people would inevitably be talking about the tragedy of Dad's death and she would not have been able to listen. She went into the foyer and knocked on the manager's door.

'I'm Peter Sellers' daughter,' she told the astonished manager, 'do you mind if I come and see the film?'

The manager gazed at Sarah who was wearing a woollen sweater and the scruffiest of her jeans.

'You're Mr Sellers' daughter?' he questioned.

'Yes,' replied Sarah, 'I am.'

The manager seemed to understand and led Sarah up to the dress circle, where she saw the film and loved every minute of it. She thought Dad deserved to have won some kind of award for his performance.

'The manager didn't even ask me to pay for my ticket,' said Sarah, 'and when I think about it I'm glad I got in free. Why should I have been responsible for putting more royalties into Lynne's pocket?'

We instructed lawyers to contest Dad's will. We felt that one day, as my mother had argued, it was possible that Lynne might marry again and have children. Dad's money would then be diverted to them. We would have been happy if Lynne had made over the estate to the British Heart Foundation where it was originally intended. We would have been prepared to drop our claims if she had taken this step, but again she showed no sign of doing this.

On 24 January 1981, in the Suffolk village of Theberton, near Ipswich, Lynne married David Frost. It was six months to the very day that Dad died. We learned from newspaper reports that Lynne was seeing David.

We were not invited to the wedding. Indeed, the first we knew of it was when a London *Sunday Mirror* reporter telephoned Sarah. We were stunned, wondering how she could so easily forget Dad. Only a few weeks before, she told the English magazine *Woman's Own*: 'I think Peter would have been jealous at the thought of my re-marrying. I don't think he would have liked it. The big problem for any man who falls in love with me is that he won't match up to Peter. I pity the man who tries to live up to Peter.'

For his part David Frost told the newspapers: 'Knowing Peter and seeing how happy Lynne is I'm sure that Peter is happy too.'

Two weeks after the marriage Lynne was consulting Dad's medium, Doris Collins, who in a seance apparently relayed a message from Dad to Lynne saying: 'I always want you to be happy.' Lynne, as if to justify her marriage to David, interpreted this in the newspaper columns as being a token of Dad's blessing on their union. It's a pity she didn't ask Dad about the will.

The one bequest we have from Dad is shared by millions throughout the world.

Many of Dad's films are already screen classics. Our children will one day come to see them and our grandchildren too. And the generations of our family will pass down not only his films but all of Dad's stories right back to the great Mendoza.

No one can deprive us of our memories. At last we are a united and peaceful family and we bear the name of Sellers with pride.

COLLINS